I kept passing by this one but Borders is winding down, & religion is 40% off & this is the only copy I've ever seen so I fina_____it.

I had hit the bank & made a deposit this morning but it hasn't been credited so my Debby only had 14 dollars to its name. Luckily I had enough cash for this. Slaved the Adventure Bible.

Michael R. Doman

↰H↗

Aug. 18, 2011

For Steve. M.J.
For R. A.H.

Text by Mary Joslin
Illustrations copyright © 2007 Amanda Hall
This edition copyright © 2008 Lion Hudson
Digital imaging by Jacqueline Crawford

The moral rights of the author and illustrator
have been asserted

A Lion Children's Book
an imprint of
Lion Hudson plc
Wilkinson House, Jordan Hill Road,
Oxford OX2 8DR, England
www.lionhudson.com
UK ISBN 978 0 7459 6132 3
USA ISBN 978 0 8254 7803 1

First UK edition 2007
First USA edition 2008
1 3 5 7 9 10 8 6 4 2 0

Acknowledgments
Bible excerpts are taken or adapted from the *Good News Bible*,
published by The Bible Societies/HarperCollins Publishers Ltd, UK
© American Bible Society 1966, 1971, 1976, 1992.

A catalogue record for this book is available
from the British Library

Typeset in 11/16 Latin 725 BT
Printed and bound in Singapore

Distributed by:
UK: Marston Book Services Ltd, PO Box 269, Abingdon, Oxon OX14 4YN
USA: Trafalgar Square Publishing, 814 N Franklin Street, Chicago, IL 60610
USA Christian Market: Kregel Publications, PO Box 2607, Grand Rapids, Michigan 49501

THE LION
DAY-BY-DAY
BIBLE

Retold by MARY JOSLIN
Illustrated by AMANDA HALL

LION
CHILDREN'S

CONTENTS

❧

January

Creation, Adam and Eve, Cain and Abel, Noah, the tower of Babel, Abraham and the promise, wicked cities, Sarah, the birth of Isaac, Rebecca, Jacob and Esau, Joseph and his brothers

February

Joseph in Egypt, Joseph and his family reunited, the birth of Moses, Moses and the burning bush, Moses and the escape from Egypt, the journey through the wilderness, the Ten Commandments, the golden calf, the tabernacle, the covenant box

March

The land of Canaan, Joshua and the battle of Jericho, the time of the judges, Ehud, Deborah, Gideon, Samson, Naomi and Ruth, Hannah, Samuel, Saul

April

Saul's reign, David, Goliath, Jonathan, Bathsheba, Absalom, David's psalms, Solomon, Jerusalem and the Temple, the queen of Sheba, the divided kingdom, Elijah

May

The northern kingdom of Israel, Ahab and Elijah, Elisha, Naaman, Jehu, Jezebel, Amos, Jonah, Hosea

June

The southern kingdom of Judah, Isaiah, Micah, the destruction of Israel, Hezekiah and the siege of Jerusalem, Josiah and the restoration of Temple worship, Jeremiah, the destruction of Jerusalem, exile, Ezekiel, the fiery furnace, Daniel, the story of Job

Contents

July

The return to Jerusalem, the second Temple, Esther, Nehemiah, Ezra, the New Testament, the birth of Jesus, the boy Jesus, John the Baptist, Jesus' baptism and temptation, Jesus the preacher

August

The teachings of Jesus, the Our Father, parables and their meaning, miracles, friends and followers, the transfiguration

September

More teachings, parables and miracles, Jesus and the children, Jesus rides to Jerusalem, Jesus in the Temple, Judas Iscariot, the last supper

October

Jesus' betrayal and trail, the crucifixion and burial, the empty tomb, the risen Jesus, Mary Magdalene, Emmaus, Thomas, Peter, ascension, Pentecost, the apostles in Jerusalem, Stephen

November

Saul's conversion, Barnabas, Peter, the Christians in Antioch, Saul becomes Paul, Paul's missionary journeys, letter to the Philippians, letters to the Corinthians

December

Paul's words about faith, hope and love, more of Paul's travels, letter to the Romans, the journey to Rome, letter to the Ephesians, letter to the Colossians, letters of Peter, John and James, the letter to the Hebrews, Revelation, a vision of heaven

"Love the Lord your God with all your heart, with all your soul, and with all your mind." This is the greatest and the most important commandment. The second most important commandment is like it: "Love your neighbor as you love yourself." The whole Law of Moses and the teachings of the prophets depend on these two commandments.

Words of Jesus from Matthew 22:37–39

THE OLD TESTAMENT

The story of beginning

❧

*Dear God,
The world and
everything in it
belong to you.
Thank you
for all you
have made.*

I N THE BEGINNING, before this world had any shape, there was utter darkness. It was darker and wilder than the stormy nighttime ocean.

In the middle of the chaos, God spoke: "Let there be light."

At once the light shone, clear and pure and lovely.

"That is good," said God. "I shall call the light, Day and the dark, Night."

That was the first day of creation.

On the second day, God made the great sky that stretches across the whole universe; and, on the third day, God divided land from sea.

"These things are very good," said God. "And now, I want all kinds of different plants to grow in every place on earth."

Tall grasses grew and flowered and produced their seeds. Trees reached up to the sky and opened their blossoms to the light. Then the petals fell and the fruits began to swell and ripen.

"I am pleased with this day," said God.

On the fourth day, God made the bright sun for the daytime and the gleaming moon and stars for the nighttime. Then as the red-gold sun rose on the fifth day, God spoke again. "I want the seas to be filled with living creatures." At God's command they came, swimming and diving and leaping and plunging.

"Now I want creatures to fill the air," cried God. In a great whir of wings, flocks of birds came down as if from heaven. They were twittering and trilling, chattering and cawing.

Everything was very good; but God's work was not yet complete.

The making is completed

THE SIXTH DAY of the world began with a dawn chorus: all the birds sang to greet the sunlight.

God whispered to the earth. "Listen. I want you to provide food and homes for the animals I am going to make. Keep the grasslands clear for the bison; make secret places for the shrews; let tigers shelter in the shadows of the forest; and let cattle gather by the waterholes."

Then God made all the animals, each with its own shape and patterning, its own wildness and wisdom.

"Now," said God, "it is time to make human beings. They will be my children, and I will put them in charge of everything. They will have children of their own and, as time goes by, my people will make their homes all over the world. Wherever they go, the world will supply them with all they need."

When the making was done, God looked at everything together, and God was pleased.

On the seventh day God rested.
"The seventh day will be a special day," said God. "Forevermore, it must be a day of rest."

Dear God, The whole world stands in awe of the great things you have done.

9

Dear God,
To honor you
is to turn away
from evil.

The garden of Eden

HERE IS A STORY about the first man and the first woman. In the beginning, the earth was bare and no rain fell. God took the clay of the earth and shaped it into a man. God breathed into the clay, and the man began to live.

God planted a garden in Eden and took the man there. A river flowed through the garden, and its abundant water allowed the trees to grow tall and green. "You may grow crops here and gather the fruit from the trees," said God, "but you must not eat fruit from the tree that gives knowledge of good and evil. If you do, you will die."

God wanted the man to be happy. "It is not good for him to be alone," said God. "I will make all kinds of creatures out of clay and breathe life into them." In that way, God made all the animals and all the birds.

"Now I would like you to give them names," said God to the man. The man did so. "But none of these creatures is a real companion for me," he sighed.

God felt sorry for the man and made him fall into a deep sleep. Then, taking a rib from the man's side, God used the bone to make a woman.

"At last! Here is someone like me!" exclaimed the man. "Here is someone who can truly be my friend and companion."

The snake in the garden

✍

THE SNAKE WAS the most cunning creature that God had made. One day, it came sneaking along to ask the woman a question.

"Is it true that God has forbidden you to eat the fruit that grows here?"

"Oh, we can eat any fruit we like," replied the woman. "The only thing we must not touch is the fruit that grows on the tree in the middle of the garden. If we eat from that tree, we will die."

The snake narrowed its eyes. "That's not true," it whispered. "When you eat that fruit, you will be truly wise. It will make you as wise as God!"

The woman was curious about what the snake had said. She went to look at the fruit. "It IS beautiful," she murmured, "and it would be wonderful to be truly wise." Slowly she reached up, picked some fruit and ate it. Then she gave some to the man.

"Oh!" they both exclaimed. "Now we see everything differently."

They looked at one another and then lowered their eyes. "Before we ate, we were just happy to be together," mumbled the woman. "Now I'm embarrassed, and so are you. We're naked."

They felt tears welling up in their eyes. "Well, we must do what we can to put things right. We can cover ourselves up," they agreed. For the rest of the day they sat and sewed leaves together to make clothes.

That evening, as usual, God came walking in the garden and, seeing no one, called out to the man: "Where are you?"

"I was hiding," replied the man. "I was afraid, because I was naked."

God understood at once what had happened and sorrowfully asked the question for which no answer was needed. "Did you eat the fruit I told you not to eat?"

"The woman you created gave me some," replied the man angrily.

"The snake tricked me," pleaded the woman.

*Dear God,
Make me wise
enough to stay
out of trouble.*

11

Dear God,
You set the time
for sorrow and
the time for joy.

Adam and Eve

🐦

GOD TURNED TO speak to the snake. "What you have done is wicked, and you will be punished for it. From now on, you will crawl along on your belly, and the man and the woman will be your enemies!"

Then God turned to speak to the man and the woman. "Life will be hard for you now," said God. "You will have to work long and hard to make the earth produce the things you need. Weeds and thorns will choke your crops. You will wear yourselves out simply making a living. In the end, you will die and become part of the clay from which you were made."

Then God made clothes from the skins of animals and gave them to the man and the woman to hide their nakedness.

After that, God returned to heaven and addressed the creatures there. "The man and the woman know about good and evil now. They must not be allowed to eat the fruit from the tree of life, because then they would live forever. I am going to send them out of the garden of Eden. You winged creatures – I want you to stand guard at the entrance. Take with you a flaming sword and wield it forever. You must not let anyone come near the tree of life."

And that was the beginning of humankind as it has been through all the ages. The man and the woman, Adam and Eve, chose to go their own way instead of trusting God. They found themselves alone, struggling to survive in a harsh world.

Cain and Abel

❧

ADAM AND EVE had a baby boy. They called him Cain. He was their pride and joy.

Not long after, they had another baby boy. They weren't nearly as excited about the second baby. They called him Abel.

When the boys grew up, Cain became a farmer who plowed the soil and grew crops. Abel became a shepherd who led his flocks to pasture and tended the ewes when they gave birth. Each in his own way was taming the wild world.

At harvest time, Cain brought some of his crops to offer to God. He was used to being his parents' pride and joy, and he was dismayed when God seemed not to want the gift he had brought.

Abel brought a young lamb, the firstborn of one of his sheep. God seemed delighted, and Abel felt that at last he was somebody's pride and joy.

Cain was furious at this unexpected turn of events, and his face twisted into a scowl.

"Why are you so angry," asked God, "and why are you letting that anger fester and grow? Now sin is crouching at your door. It wants to rule you, but you must overcome it."

Cain did not heed the warning. Instead, he asked Abel to come for a walk with him. When they were out in the fields, he turned on his brother and killed him.

God was not long in coming to question Cain. "Where is your brother?"

"I don't know," the young man retorted. "I'm not his babysitter."

But God knew what had happened. "There is blood on the soil and it is calling out to me for revenge. Now the very stuff of the earth will be your enemy. No crops will grow for you. You must go – far away and forever."

"But that is too awful!" cried Cain. "I will be a homeless wanderer, and anyone who finds me will kill me."

"I will put a mark on you," said God, "to warn people not to hurt you. I want no more killing."

Dear God, May you never be angry with me; may you always have pity on me.

God speaks to Noah

*Dear God,
Help me to do
what is right,
even when it
seems there
are no good
people left.*

AFTER THE TIME of Adam and Eve and Cain and Abel, more children were born. Their children had children, and the generations went by. Soon the human race had spread all over the world.

But as the years went by, the wickedness grew, and God was dismayed. "I am sorry I ever made people," said God. "I shall flood the whole world and give it a new start. Only one man, Noah, lives in the way that pleases me, and he will be part of my plan."

Noah listened in astonishment as God told him what to do. "Build me a boat out of good timber. It must have three decks and a door in the side. Follow the measurements I will give you: this boat needs to carry enough from the old world to be the beginnings of a new one.

"You will need space for yourself and your wife. You will also need room for your three sons – Shem, Ham and Japheth – and their wives.

"I also want you to rescue a male and a female of every kind of creature. You will need to make space on the boat for all the animals and birds. Not one species must be lost."

The great flood

❧

NOAH SHOOK HIS head in disbelief. God continued to spell out the details.

"Remember, Noah, that this flood is going to last a long time. You are going to need all kinds of food for yourselves and the animals. Now – to work!"

Noah did exactly as God asked. He and his family cut the trees and built the boat. They covered it with tar inside and out so that not one drop of moisture could seep in.

Then they harvested fields of grain. They filled basket after basket with fruit and dried it in the sun. They heaped these provisions into the storerooms on the ark.

And then they began the most amazing task of all: they called the creatures to come to them and led them into the boat.

At last, everyone and everything were safe aboard. God shut the door behind them. Seven days went by.

Then God commanded the rain to begin: first a few heavy drops splashed on the dry earth; then Noah heard a rapid pattering sound on the roof of the boat. He looked outside: a torrent was falling from the sky.

Once the rain began, there was no way of holding back the flood. The rivers rose and spilled over their banks. Water filled the valleys and began to rise up over the hills. Noah's heavy boat began to float.

Every living thing aboard the boat was safe and dry; everything else in the world was washed away. There was rain for forty days and forty nights, and by then the world was completely drowned. There was just gray water and gray sky… and Noah's boat, and God.

*Dear God,
You keep your
people safe
through storm
and flood.*

Dear God,
Give us patience
to wait for you
to bless us.

The dove and the olive twig

DAYS AND WEEKS went by: a long, long time of waiting for God to act and seeing nothing but rain and flood. But God had not forgotten Noah and his boat. At last, a wind began to blow and the flood began to go down. Slowly, slowly, the water ebbed away.

On the seventeenth day of the seventh month, Noah's boat shuddered to a stop. It had grounded on a mountaintop. There Noah waited as, one by one, other mountaintops emerged from the flood.

Forty more days went by. Noah opened a window and sent out a raven. It flew and flew but did not come back, so Noah sent out a dove. It flew around for a while and then came back and perched on Noah's hand.

"We'll wait seven more days," said Noah; "then it can go looking again."

The next time the dove went out, it came back with a fresh green olive twig in its beak.

Noah waited another seven days before letting the dove out for a third time. It did not come back. It had found a place to roost.

16

Noah's celebration

AT LONG LAST, the land was dry. "Time for everyone to leave the boat," said God. Noah opened the door. The animals ran and leaped and hopped onto the moist brown soil. The birds flew into the clear, clean air.

"They must go out into every part of the world, make their homes and have families," said God. "Then my world will be full again."

Noah and his family held a celebration. They brought special offerings to thank God for keeping them safe.

"Never again will I flood the earth," said God. "For as long as the world exists, there will always be a time for sowing seeds and a time for gathering a harvest; there will be summer and winter, day and night.

"I make my solemn promise," said God. "Whenever you see my rainbow in the sky, you can remember my promise. It is my covenant with you and all of humankind forever."

10 January

❖

Genesis 8–9

*Dear God,
Thank you
for summer
and winter,
seedtime and
harvest.*

Dear God,
We are only
human beings,
and yet you
care for us.

The tallest tower in the world

ONCE UPON A TIME, all the people in the world spoke the same language. They were nomads who lived their lives traveling from place to place and scratching what they needed to survive in an untamed world.

At length, their journeying brought them to the plains of Babylon. There they settled and grew prosperous. They had time to think and to make new discoveries about their world. One discovery was to change everything.

"Look how hard this mud has baked in the sun," said one. "See – here is a piece that has become as hard as rock."

"And this piece," said another, "is curiously shaped. See – it dried in the crook of a fallen branch and has kept the shape of it."

"If we shaped the mud while it was wet, we could bake mudstones that were just the right shape for building walls – like our stone walls, but easier."

"Yes! We could make bricks! Think of what we could build with bricks!"

When they had grown skillful in making bricks, they decided to build a wonderful city, with a tall, tall tower that would reach to the sky.

"Then we'll be famous!" they said to one another. They began to build a huge tower, tier upon tier upon tier.

"Not too long to go now," they congratulated themselves. "Soon we will have built the tallest tower in the whole wide world."

Mixed-up talking

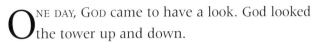

ONE DAY, GOD came to have a look. God looked the tower up and down.

There was no denying it was tall. But God noticed something else.

"These people have grown too clever," said God. "Their success has made them bold. Soon they will be able to do anything they want. It's time to show them they are not gods."

The next time everyone gathered to work on the tower, something rather puzzling happened.

One group of workers heard another group using strange new words as they talked to each other.

"What are those fellows talking about?" they wanted to know. "Have they got some secret? Are they plotting something against the rest of us?"

A third group shook their heads and muttered to themselves. They couldn't understand either of the two groups.

"It's not fair!" they said. "There's something going on and we don't know about it! How can we trust people who won't talk to us straight? We don't feel safe working alongside them any more."

Up in heaven, God smiled. "Such a simple thing," said God, "to mix up their languages. How they babble on! Now all their proud boasting about building the tallest tower in the world will come to nothing."

It was true. The groups of people began to shout at one another and, with no understanding between them, they began to fight. "That's it!" each group exclaimed. "We've had enough of secret words and secret plans. We're going to live by ourselves."

Soon a great movement of people began. Different groups traveled to different places and cherished their own language and identity more than any other. Soon the world was a multiplicity of nations. And that is why the Tower of Babylon was only half finished.

Dear God, You alone are great. You deserve our worship.

Dear God,
Speak to me
and show me
the way
I should go.

God calls Abram

ᘒ

ABRAM'S FAMILY TREE went back to the time of Shem, who was one of the sons of Noah. However, Abram was less impressed with the past than he was concerned about the future: would he have descendants who could inherit his wealth? Would the family tree go on?

One day, he heard God speaking to him: "Abram! Leave your country. Leave your relatives. Leave your home.

"Go to a land I am going to show you. You will have children there, and your children will have children. Your family will become a great nation. They will bring my blessing to the world."

Abram knew he must obey. At once he gathered together his close family: his wife, Sarai, and his nephew, Lot. He gathered his wealth and summoned his slaves. They left the city of Haran and all its comfortable living and set out for the land of Canaan.

It was a bold adventure. Abram and his family lived as tent-dwelling nomads: they were always on the move in search of pasture for their flocks. There were good years and bad years, but in time both Abram and Lot grew wealthy. Their flocks were so large that they could not find enough pasture for them all in one place. Arguments broke out.

"We are family," said Abram. "We should not quarrel. Lot, you choose part of the land for yourself. I'll go the other way." So Lot went south to the valley that was watered by the River Jordan. Abram stayed in Canaan, at a place called Hebron.

"Look around," God said to him. "I am going to give you all this land. It will belong to your family forever."

Hope after disaster

❧

Dear God,
Help me to
learn to trust
you.

DOWN IN THE Jordan Valley, four kings met together. They wanted to talk about battle plans. There were five wealthy cities that they hoped to plunder. Greed made them bold.

Not far away, the kings of the five cities met to make their own plans. How were they going to defend themselves? They gathered their armies and marched to war.

On the day of the battle, the armies lined up against each other. The fighting was fierce, but it was the invaders who got the upper hand. The five kings tried to make their escape, but there were huge tar pits in that country, and the kings of Sodom and Gomorrah perished in the morass.

The victorious kings saw their chance. They hurried to Sodom and Gomorrah, killing and looting as they went. Lot was captured during the battle in Sodom and robbed of all his possessions.

One man who escaped from the mayhem came and told Abram, "Your cousin has been greatly wronged! He has been robbed and taken prisoner! Surely you will come to his aid!"

At once, Abram gathered his own fighting force. They attacked the enemy by night and defeated them utterly.

The kings came to celebrate Abram's victory: "You have rescued us! You have won back all the wealth we lost," they cried. They laughed and drank and enjoyed themselves.

Abram himself did not feel elated by the victory. Disappointment clouded his life. "I still have no son," he sighed.

Then he heard God's whisper. "Come outside. Look at the stars in the sky and try to count them. Your family will grow and grow until there are more of them than there are stars."

Abram trusted God, and because of this God accepted him.

Dear God,
When people
are treated
cruelly, you
see all that
happens. Look
on them with
kindness, and
bless them.

The God who sees

ABRAM'S WIFE SARAI was downcast. Through all the years she had remained childless, and she knew that Abram longed for a son. She decided on a plan.

"I have an Egyptian slave woman named Hagar," she reminded him. "Everyone knows the custom that you are allowed to sleep with her; then she can have a child for you."

Abram agreed, and Hagar became pregnant.

Her new status made Hagar feel very important. She began to act as if she were more important than Sarai, and Sarai was angry. In her anger she decided to treat her slave as cruelly as she dared. In the end, Hagar ran away.

At a place in the desert where there was a spring of water, one of God's angels met Hagar. "You should go back to your mistress," said the angel. "God will bless you. You will have a son and you will name him Ishmael. He will have many enemies, but he will live to be the father of a great nation."

Hagar was amazed. "Have I really seen God and lived to tell about it?" she marveled. "This is truly a God who sees what is happening here on earth."

Bravely, Hagar made the journey back to Sarai. The months passed and she was overjoyed to have a son whom she named Ishmael.

And the well where Hagar met the angel was given this name: "The Well of the Living One Who Sees Me."

Sarah laughs

A BRAM WAS NOW ninety-nine years old. "You must go on trusting me," said God. "Your name will no longer be Abram but Abraham: the father of many nations. Your wife's name will no longer be Sarai but Sarah: princess. She will be the mother of many nations."

Abraham shook his head. "We are both old," he argued. "Why not let Ishmael be my heir?"

"The promise I made to you so long ago will come true through Sarah's son," replied God. "You will name him Isaac."

Abraham accepted God's promise.

Not long after that, three visitors arrived.

Abraham hurried to greet them. "Please have some water," he said, "and a meal to strengthen you." He rushed to Sarah and asked her to begin cooking.

Abraham gave the men the food while Sarah stayed in the tent.

"Where is your wife?" they asked, and Abraham told them. They beckoned to him to come nearer.

"In nine months' time, she will be a mother – and you will be the father of a son!" they whispered.

Sarah overheard. At my age! she thought. Those men know nothing! The thought of their foolishness made her laugh out loud.

God spoke to Abraham: "Why did Sarah laugh? Does she not believe I can give you and her a son?"

When Sarah realized that Abraham knew of her scornful reaction, she was afraid. "I didn't laugh," she exclaimed. "I didn't!"

"You did," came the reply. And it was God speaking.

The wicked cities

Dear God,
Please take
care of good
people in a
wicked world.

WHEN THE VISITORS set off again, Abraham walked with them to send them on their way. "We are going to visit Sodom near Gomorrah," they said. "We need to find out if those cities are as wicked as people say. If they are, then they will be destroyed."

Abraham pleaded with God. "You cannot destroy innocent people who happen to be living among wicked people," he argued. "What if there are fifty good people there?"

"Then I will not destroy them," agreed God.

Abraham continued to plead. "What if there are forty-five? Or forty? Or maybe just thirty?"

"Then I will not destroy the cities," said God.

"Would you save just twenty? What if there are only ten good men?"

"Then I will not destroy the cities," said God.

Two of the travelers went into Sodom. They discovered that there was only one good man: Abraham's nephew, Lot. He welcomed them into his house and kept them safe.

"Lot," the visitors warned him, "you are in great danger here. The city in which you live and neighboring Gomorrah are going to be destroyed. Gather your relatives and flee to a safer place."

At dawn, the two visitors grew even more anxious. "We must all get out – and now, really, there is no time to lose."

"I'm still not quite sure," Lot began, but the visitors grabbed him and his wife and two daughters and virtually dragged them out into the countryside. As they ran, a storm of burning sulfur fell on both the cities.

Lot's wife was dismayed. She turned to look at the ruins of their home. As she did, a hail of salt fell upon her and covered her completely.

Laughter and weeping

GOD REMEMBERED THE promise to Abraham and Sarah, and at long last they had a son.

Sarah was delighted. "God has brought me joy and laughter," she said. They named the boy "Isaac," and the name itself means "he laughs."

As her son grew, Sarah began to worry. "Send Hagar and Ishmael away," she whispered to Abraham. "I don't want Ishmael inheriting what really belongs to our Isaac."

Abraham was dismayed at what Sarah said. After all, Ishmael was his son too.

God told him to let Sarah have her way. "Let the boy and his mother go," agreed God. "My promise to you will come true through Isaac's children; but I will take care of Ishmael's children too."

The next morning, Abraham sent Hagar and Ishmael away with just a little food and a leather bag of water. She walked and walked through the dry and dusty wilderness. They soon drank the water. Almost at once, they were thirsty again.

In despair, she put her child down in the shade of a bush and went off a little way. She buried her head in her hands. "I don't want to see him die," she sobbed.

God heard her weeping. "Go and get your son," said God. "He will be the father of a great nation."

Hagar looked up in astonishment. The desert shimmered in the heat. Then she heard God speaking again. "Look around you," said God. "Really look."

Hagar scanned the barren landscape. Then she laughed aloud for joy. "There's a well!" she cried. "We can survive out here! We can make a new life for ourselves… and Ishmael can learn to hunt… and everything will be all right!"

The years went by and Ishmael grew to be a man. He married an Egyptian woman. Hagar knew that God's promise to her was coming true.

Dear God,
You help those
who are in
despair. You
give them new
hope.

Abraham and Isaac

🐦

SOME TIME LATER, God put Abraham's faith to the test. "Take your son Isaac," said God, "the son you love so much. Go to a mountaintop in the land of Moriah. Sacrifice him to me there."

Abraham did not question what he heard. The practice of child sacrifice was not uncommon among some of the neighboring peoples. The next morning he cut wood for the fire, loaded the donkey, and set out for the mountain with Isaac and two servants. He had told them about a sacrifice; he had not explained more.

As they came near the mountain, Abraham told the servants to wait with the donkey while he and Isaac went on to carry out the ceremony.

Isaac carried the wood. Abraham carried a knife and a pot of hot coals with which to start the fire.

"Oh – you know what we've forgotten," said Isaac. "We don't have the lamb for the sacrifice!"

"God will provide one," replied Abraham tersely.

The two of them walked on. On the mountaintop, Abraham built a stone altar and laid the wood on it.

Suddenly, harshly, he grabbed Isaac, tied him up and laid him on the altar. He raised his knife.

"Abraham," called God.

"Here I am," replied Abraham.

"Don't hurt the boy," said God. "All of this has shown me that you are willing to obey me."

Abraham lowered the knife. He looked around. Behind him, a wild goat was caught in the thorns. Abraham untied his son and sacrificed the goat. His beloved son was safe.

"From now on," said Abraham, "this place will be called 'God Provides.'"

"From now on," said God, "you can be sure that I will bless your son and his children for generation after generation."

A wife for Isaac

❧

20 January

❖

Genesis 23–24

WHEN ISAAC WAS a young man, his mother Sarah died. Abraham buried her with great respect. He began to think about the future. What was going to happen to all his wealth? What was going to happen to Isaac?

He called a servant. "Come over here! I want you to make a solemn promise with God as our witness. Go back to my relatives in my old homeland and find a girl among them who can be Isaac's wife. Bring her back here, to Canaan."

The servant agreed willingly, but as he and the caravan of camels made their way along the dusty roads, he began to worry about the promise he had made. "O God," he prayed. "Help me carry out this task."

By the time he reached the city to which he had been sent, he had worked out a plan. "O God," he said. "Here I am at the well, where the young women will come to draw water. I will ask one for a drink. If she says she'll bring water for my camels, I'll take that as a sign she's the girl for Isaac."

Before he had finished his prayer, a young woman arrived with a water jar. He waited until she had filled it and then asked for a drink.

"Of course," she replied. "After that, I will get water for your camels."

Everything had worked out perfectly. When the task was done, the servant brought out some gold jewelry. "This is a gift for you," he said, "but I have more questions to ask. What is your father's name? Is there room in his house for me to stay as his guest?"

The girl gave her answer, and it was exactly what the servant wanted to hear: the girl's family were Abraham's own relatives, and the servant was welcome to stay with them.

*Dear God,
Guide us in the
plans we make,
and bless them.*

Dear God,
May you be
in charge of all
the important
turning points
of my life.

Rebecca

THE YOUNG WOMAN, whose name was Rebecca, was astonished at the gifts she had been given. She ran, breathless with excitement, to tell her mother.

"Listen! The man gave me gold jewelry and asked if he could go and visit Father. Surely that can only mean one thing," she exclaimed.

Rebecca's brother, Laban, had noticed the jewelry, and he hurried off to find out what was going on. He and his father listened as the servant told of the task he had been set: to find a wife for their relative, Abraham.

"Well, it is truly amazing that God led you to us," they agreed. "It must be part of God's plan that our Rebecca should marry your master's son."

"Indeed," said the servant. "Remember that my master is wealthy, and he has provided me with all you could want for making the proper arrangements." He brought out splendid gifts for the family, and the finest gold ornaments and clothing for Rebecca.

Rebecca's father and brother nodded. "We are pleased with the offer," they said. "Now we must ask Rebecca what she thinks."

Rebecca was delighted. "I'd be happy to go and meet this young man as soon as you like!" she said.

With the blessing of her family, Rebecca and some of her servants got ready to travel to Canaan with Abraham's servant. Half giggling, half tearful, they climbed up onto the camels and waved farewell.

Isaac was delighted to see his bride-to-be arriving. Very soon, he knew he was also in love with her.

Jacob and Esau

❧

WHEN ABRAHAM AT last died and was buried next to his wife, Sarah, Isaac inherited all his wealth. God blessed him just as he had blessed Abraham, and Isaac prospered.

In time, his wife Rebecca became pregnant and had twin boys. The first to be born was reddish and covered in hair. She named him Esau, from a word in her language that sounded like "hairy." The second son was born clutching his brother's foot. She named him "Jacob," from a word that sounded like "heel."

Esau grew up strong and active. He loved to be outdoors and he became a skillful hunter. That made Isaac very fond of him: Isaac loved eating the meat from the animals that his elder son brought home from the kill.

Jacob preferred the comforts of staying at home. He was quiet and thoughtful, and that made him his mother's favorite.

One day, Jacob was at home cooking a pot of bean soup when Esau came back from hunting.

"I'm starving!" he exclaimed. "Let me have some of that soup."

"Perhaps," replied Jacob, keeping his brother away from the food. "But only if you promise I can have all the privileges that you have as the eldest son: I'd rather like to be the one who inherits our father's wealth."

"So what!" exclaimed Esau, and he flung himself down to rest and groaned with weariness. "Who cares about what we each get when our father dies? I'll die of hunger if I don't eat right away. Yes, you can have whatever you like."

In this unthinking way Esau gave away the valuable rights that were his by birth – and all for a bowl of soup.

*Dear God,
Thank you that
each one of us
is your special
child.*

Dear God,
Give us the
strength to
overcome anger
with love.

The stolen blessing

ISAAC GREW MORE and more wealthy as the years went by. He also grew frailer. In the end he went blind.

One day, he called for Esau. "I won't live much longer," he said, "but I'd love one more of those tasty meat stews before I die. It will be one last thing for me to enjoy, and then I will give you my final blessing."

Esau took his bow and arrows and went hunting.

Rebecca had been listening. "Hurry," she said to Jacob. "Bring me two young goats. We must make a meat stew for your father before Esau gets back. You can take it to him pretending to be Esau. Then he will give you his final blessing – and that's worth something."

"But it's not going to work," protested Jacob. "Our father will feel the difference between Esau's great hairy arms and mine. He'll end up cursing me."

"Just do what I say!" hissed Rebecca. "I have a plan."

Jacob brought the goats. Rebecca cooked the stew and dressed her son in the goatskins. Jacob carried it to his father, trembling with anxiety at the trick he was supposed to be playing.

"Is that really you, Esau?" asked Isaac. "You sound more like Jacob! Come… let me feel you… ahh, yes, I'd know those strong arms anywhere. Let me say the blessing prayer. I want you to prosper and be head of the family forever."

So the blessing was given. It was not until Esau came home from a successful hunt and carried a rich, savory stew to his father that the cheating was discovered.

"I've already given the final blessing," cried Isaac in dismay. "It must have been your brother. He has taken what was yours."

Esau was wild with fury. There was nothing his father could say that would calm him.

"I shall get revenge!" Esau said to himself. "As soon as our father has died, I shall kill that lowlife cheat. He can't expect mercy from me."

Jacob runs away

❧

24 January

❖

Genesis 27–28

REBECCA HURRIED TO warn Jacob. "You must escape!" she whispered. "Esau wants to kill you!"

Then she bustled off to Isaac. "You've never understood how disappointed I am that Esau married a girl from outside our people," she whimpered. "Please let Jacob go back to where I come from to find a wife." Isaac agreed to let him go.

That gave Jacob the chance to escape, and he set out alone. He felt tired and dejected as he made camp that evening, with only the hard ground for a bed and a stone for his pillow. As he slept, he dreamed: he saw a stairway reaching from earth to heaven and angels going up and down it. God was there beside him, speaking:

"I am the God of Abraham and Isaac. I will make this land your home. I will bless your family through all the generations, and they will bring my blessing to the world. I will be with you wherever you go, and I will bring you back to this land."

When he woke up, Jacob felt encouraged. He picked up the stone on which he had rested his head and set it in the ground upright. "This must be the place of God," he said. "I name it 'Bethel.'" Then he called out to God, "Here's a promise. If you bring me safely home again, you will be my God."

There was silence. Jacob sighed, turned on his heel and strode off. It was still many miles to his mother's home country.

*Dear God,
Show us heaven
on earth.*

*Dear God,
Whether time
seems fast or
slow, may I
always work
diligently.*

Uncle Laban

ה

JACOB HAD LOST track of how far he had come. He had no clear idea of where he might find his mother's people anyway.

Then one day, he came across some shepherds who were gathering by a well so they could get water for their sheep.

"I don't suppose you've heard of a man called Laban, have you?" he asked.

"We certainly have," they replied. "He's from the same town as us. Look – that's his daughter Rachel, bringing his sheep to the well."

Jacob could hardly believe his luck. He ran to greet the girl and began to cry with sheer relief and joy. "I'm your cousin," he said. "I'm Rebecca's son. I've… come home! Perhaps I can be part of the family."

He smiled shyly. Rachel was beautiful.

Rachel ran to tell her father, and Laban was delighted to see his nephew. Jacob stayed for a whole month as a guest. "You're welcome to stay," said Laban, "but you shouldn't work for me for nothing. What can I give you that you will accept as wages?"

Jacob sighed. "I will work for you for seven years if you let me marry Rachel," he said.

Laban laughed. "I like the deal," he said. "I like it very much. I hope you don't find the waiting too long."

Jacob didn't. It seemed to him that the time flew by. After seven years, Laban organized a wedding feast. The bride was draped in jewelry and veils, and when night fell, Laban led her to Jacob, and Jacob made her his wife.

Cheated

❧

JACOB WOKE IN the morning next to his new wife. The morning light shone through the curtains. He turned to look at her.

What he saw made him howl with rage. He flung on his clothes and stormed off to find Laban. "Where's Rachel?" he shrieked. "I worked seven years to marry her. You brought me her sister. You filthy cheat."

Laban did not look in the least surprised at the outburst; nor did he seem bothered. He motioned to his servants to continue with their duties: as the father of the bride, it was his duty to provide the community with celebrations for a week and he wasn't going to disappoint them. Then he turned to Jacob with a calm smile.

"Local custom, my boy," he said. "One has to respect these things. Leah is older. It's only proper she should marry first."

"But Leah is such an ugly –"

"Calm down, young man. My elder daughter has lovely eyes, everyone says so. Wait until the days of feasting are over, and you shall have Rachel too."

He paused for a moment to sip his drink. "Of course, you will have to work another seven years after that to conclude the arrangement in the proper way, but at least you'll have Rachel."

Jacob had nothing to bargain with. He glowered at his uncle, but Laban simply turned back to the business of the day's entertainments.

Jacob watched him, silent. "Fine," he said at last.

Dear God, May I never cheat; may I never be cheated.

33

*Dear God,
When family
arguments
rage, be with
me still.*

Jacob and his sons

🐌

JACOB WORKED FOR Laban for many years. In that time, Leah bore him six sons. As was the custom, he also had children from his wives' slaves: two from Leah's slave and two from Rachel's.

For a long time, Rachel remained childless. Then, at last, she had a son. She named him Joseph.

The birth marked a turning point for Jacob. He went to see Laban. "I've served you well," he said. "Now I'd like to take my family and go back to the country where I was born."

"Hmm," said Laban. "I suppose I should let you go. What shall I pay you to settle up?"

"Oh, I've thought of a simple plan," said Jacob. "I've helped build up your flocks of sheep and goats. When I leave, let me take the ones that are black or speckled."

Laban chuckled. "Agreed!" he said.

Both men knew about breeding sheep and goats. Now that the deal was struck, it was up to whoever was cleverer to see who got the better of it. To Laban's dismay, Jacob had clearly worked out exactly how to mix up the rams and the ewes, the billy goats and the nanny goats. Laban and his sons were furious as Jacob amassed huge flocks while theirs dwindled.

The matter flared into a huge family quarrel.. After much bitterness, Laban and Jacob agreed to part.

Brothers

As he traveled back to Canaan, Jacob felt worried. He was far from popular with the relatives he was leaving behind. Ahead of him was the country where Esau lived… the brother who had sworn to kill him.

"Remember your promise," he prayed to God. "Save me from my brother."

Even though he prayed earnestly, he did not feel confident. "Perhaps I can win his favor by giving him gifts," he thought. "I shall make a selection of animals from my flocks. Then I can send my servants ahead with the animals to see if Esau can be made to relent."

That night, a man came and wrestled with Jacob. The two fought and fought – but the stranger could not win. As dawn began to break the sky, the stranger addressed his opponent.

"I am giving you a new name. You have fought with God as well as people, and you have won. Your name will be Israel: the one who struggles with God."

In the half light, Jacob knew the stranger could be none other than God.

Then the sun rose in the sky. Jacob saw Esau coming with his fighting men. Jacob felt the cold chill of fear. With a dry mouth he began giving orders: "Quick – the slaves and their children must go first, then Leah and her children, then Rachel and Joseph last. When you meet him, bow: bow really low, really really low."

Jacob led the way. Esau saw him. First he stopped… then he ran toward his brother and hugged him. "So here you are," he cried heartily. "At long last. And who are these people? Your family. My goodness! So what was that animal parade all about, the one I've just seen?"

"Gifts for you, brother," replied Jacob, weakly.

"I don't need that," laughed Esau. "I'm rich enough."

In the end, Esau took the gifts just to keep Jacob happy. The past was forgotten. Jacob and Esau were brothers again.

Dear God, May those who quarrel learn to forgive and be forgiven.

Dear God,
May we not
think of
ourselves as
more important
than we are.

Jacob's sons

ès

JACOB MADE HIS home in Canaan. He already had eleven fine sons, and was delighted when Rachel became pregnant again. However, tragedy struck when she died in childbirth. Jacob consoled himself by treasuring the newborn son, Benjamin.

"I do love Rachel's children," he said to himself. "Joseph most of all. I wish I could make him my real heir… even though the custom is for the firstborn to inherit."

The more he thought about it, the more he wanted to do something about it. In the end, he had a beautiful robe made for Joseph – one that would show everyone just how important Joseph was in the family.

Joseph's ten older brothers got the message loud and clear. "This is just so unfair," they muttered to themselves. "It's the worst kind of favoritism. Joseph's bragging and boasting doesn't make it better either."

Joseph did seem to think very highly of himself.

"I had a dream," he told his brothers. "We were harvesting wheat. Then my sheaf stood up and yours bowed down to it."

"Oh did it really, baby brother? Well, remember it's just a dream. We're not sheaves and we're not going to bow down."

Joseph sauntered away. His dreams seemed very real to him. Then he had another dream.

"Listen to this," he told his brothers. "I saw the sun, the moon and eleven stars bowing down to me," he said. "I'm going to tell our father about that – to see if he thinks it means what I think it means."

But his father's response was not what he was expecting. Jacob was angry. "Do you think that I and your mother and all your brothers are going to bow down to you?" he asked. He glowered at his son… but he couldn't help thinking: maybe Joseph really was destined for great things.

The brothers' revenge

ONE DAY, JOSEPH'S ten older brothers were away from home looking after the family's flocks.

"I want you to go and find them, to make sure they're all right," said Jacob to Joseph.

The young man set out. He was wearing his wonderful coat. His brothers could see him coming from far away.

"Here comes the dreamer," they jeered. "Hey… what a chance to get rid of him. He's all alone in the wilderness and, well, that's a dangerous place. Who knows what animal might attack. We could tell a good story."

Reuben shook his head. "Let's just throw him down a dry well," he argued. "That'll teach him a lesson."

"Great idea!" The others cheered and grinned as their victim approached. When Joseph came near, they ripped his wonderful coat off him, threw him into a pit and sat laughing as they ate their meal. Reuben wandered off alone. He planned to rescue Joseph as soon as he could.

Suddenly, the nine brothers saw a caravan of traders going from Gilead to Egypt.

"Let's sell Joseph," said the brother named Judah. "Then we'll be rid of him forever without the nagging worry of having left him to die."

The others readily agreed: for twenty pieces of silver they would sell their brother into slavery.

Later, Reuben sidled up to the pit. "It's empty," he whispered in horror. "What has happened? This is dreadful news!"

He shook his head in dismay when the others explained. "What shall we tell our father Jacob?" he wanted to know.

"The wild animal story," they suggested. "It's believable. It's final."

They killed one of the flock and dipped Joseph's coat in the blood. Then, trembling with genuine fear, they took it to Jacob. "Is this cloth from Joseph's coat?" they asked.

Jacob looked. He froze with horror. Then he uttered a long, unearthly cry of pain. "My son! Torn to pieces by some wild animal! Aiieee!"

Dear God, Make me brave enough to say no to wicked plans.

Dear God,
May I resist the
temptation to
do anything I
know to be
wrong.

Potiphar and his wife

෴

FAR AWAY IN EGYPT, the captain of the palace guard smiled to himself. "I'm very pleased with that new slave I bought," he said. "I shall make him my personal servant. He can take care of my household, and I'll have time for more interesting things."

The captain, whose name was Potiphar, was not the only one who was pleased with Joseph. His wife had began to notice what a handsome young man he was. "I could wish he loved me," she giggled to herself. "I could love him more than Potiphar."

One day, she told Joseph what she wanted.

"No!" replied Joseph sharply. "If I agreed, I would be doing wrong to my master and to God!"

Day after day, Potiphar's wife tried to make Joseph love her. Time and again, he refused.

Potiphar's wife decided on a plan.

One day, her servants heard frantic screaming coming from her bedroom. "Help, help," she gasped. "That terrible Joseph… he came into my bedroom and… oh, it's too awful! He wanted to kiss me and… more." The woman was a good liar. "Look – I made him run away but you can see he left his clothes in here!"

The servants were shocked. When her husband heard the story, he was furious.

"There's only one place for you!" he shouted at Joseph. "You can go to prison and stay there until you rot!"

The Egyptian jail

THE EGYPTIAN JAILER was delighted to have Joseph in his charge. "He's so reliable," he murmured happily to himself. "I can leave him in charge of everything. His God must be looking after him!"

After Joseph had been in prison for some time, two new prisoners arrived. One had been the steward in charge of the king's wine cellar; the other had made the king's bread.

One morning, Joseph found them looking fearful. "We have both had puzzling dreams," they told him, "puzzling and disturbing."

"My God can help me explain dreams," said Joseph. "Tell me what you saw."

The wine steward began: "I dreamed of a grapevine. It grew leaves and flowers and then grapes appeared. I took some and squeezed them into the king's cup."

"It is a sign that the king will pardon you," said Joseph. "When you are free, please remember me and use your influence to help get me out of here. I haven't done anything wrong."

The baker was eager now to tell his dream. "I was carrying three baskets of cakes to the king," he said. "Birds were swooping down to peck at them and I couldn't keep them away."

"Oh," said Joseph. He lowered his head sorrowfully. "I'm afraid I have bad news. Your dream foretells your execution in three days' time."

The baker eyed him warily. "Could you be wrong about that?" he asked. Joseph did not dare to answer.

Three days went by. At his birthday banquet, the king gave his judgment. Joseph watched the two men leave prison: one for death, one for life.

"As for me, I'm still here," sighed Joseph. He shook his head sadly.

Dear God, May you continue to bless me even when times are hard.

*Dear God,
I pray for
those who are
in prison and
who long to
be set free.*

Forgotten

ॐ

TWO YEARS WENT BY. The wine steward tried to put all his memories of jail behind him. He busied himself in his work at the royal palaces. He was always anxious to please the king.

Then, one day, the king of Egypt himself had two puzzling dreams. He summoned all the wise men and wonder-workers in the land, but none of them could tell him what the dream meant.

"Fools," barked the king. "The dreams are making me very anxious. I think you know what happens around here when I'm in a bad mood, don't you?" He glared at the advisers who had gathered around him.

News of his displeasure spread through the palace like wildfire. The wine steward trembled with fear. "What can I do… what can I do?" he fretted. Then he remembered – and he hurried to the king.

"There is a Hebrew slave in your prison who can explain dreams," he said. "He foretold the day that you in your great mercy would pardon me… and he explained other dreams too. He told the truth, even if it meant bringing bad news."

The king listened to the steward's story. Then he sent for Joseph.

The prisoner was escorted from the prison to the palace. The slaves who were ordered to take care of him could not have been more helpful. "Here are bowls of water," they announced, "and a razor, a comb, clean towels… and fine linen clothing."

"You want to make a good impression," whispered the slave in charge. "The king can be a little… unpredictable."

The king's dream

J OSEPH CAME AND bowed before the king.

"So," said the king. "I've been told you can interpret dreams."

"Not I," said Joseph boldly, "but my God."

"Just listen," said the king. "In my first dream I was standing by the River Nile. Seven cows came up from the river and began grazing. They were fat and sleek. Then seven thin cows came and ate the fat ones, but they stayed as bony as before. Then I woke up. That's the first dream.

"Now, here's the second dream. I saw seven heads of grain on one stalk, all plump and ripe. Then seven more heads sprouted. They were thin and parched and they swallowed the plump ones."

The king lounged back on his throne. "I've consulted the usual range of so-called wise men. They didn't have a shred of advice."

Joseph gave his answer confidently: "The two dreams mean the same thing. God is going to give seven years of abundant harvests; then will come seven years of famine. You need to choose a wise and able person to store crops from the good years so you have enough for the bad years. In this way, Egypt will not starve."

The king listened thoughtfully. He consulted his officials. It did not take long to agree on an important decision.

"It is clear to me that God has made you wiser than anyone else," he told Joseph. "I am putting you in charge of gathering of food stores. It is your job to save us from the threatened disaster."

Dear God, May your wisdom give me understanding.

*Dear God,
May I live my
life so I am not
ashamed of
anything I
have done.*

Famine

J OSEPH WAS THIRTY years old when he began to
serve the king of Egypt. He was given the
second royal chariot to ride in, and a processional
guard to walk ahead of him wherever he went.

For seven years, Joseph toured the length and
breadth of the country to make sure that people
were building up stores of grain.

Then famine struck. In Egypt, everyone could buy food from the
storehouses. In the land of Canaan, Jacob and his family feared they
would die of starvation.

"Go and buy grain from Egypt," said Jacob to his sons. "Young
Benjamin will stay here. I don't want to lose him like I lost Joseph."

The brothers went. They bowed low to the official in charge of the grain
stores, unaware of who he was.

My brothers! thought Joseph. But no Benjamin. Why not?

Then he spoke aloud, and harshly. "Where do you come from? I think
you're spies!" He spoke in Egyptian, and an interpreter translated.

"No sir," the brothers replied. "We come from Canaan. Our father had
twelve sons – one is at home with him, and another is dead. We simply
want to buy grain."

"I don't believe you!" said Joseph. "One of you can go and get that
brother to prove your story. If he fails to do so, I'll have the rest executed!
Guards – throw them all in jail while I think through the strategy."

Three days later, Joseph summoned the brothers back. "Listen!" he
snapped. "I'm going to show what a decent, God-fearing man I am. I'm
going to pick just one hostage. The rest of you can have the grain you
came begging for. But you have to bring that young brother back to me."

The brothers nodded gratefully.

"We're getting the punishment we deserve for what we did to Joseph,"
whispered Reuben. The others nodded in shame.

None of them knew that Joseph understood every word. As Joseph
swept grandly out of the room, they didn't suspect for one moment that
he was hurrying away to cry.

A terrible choice

❧

NINE WEARY BROTHERS told their father the bad news.
"I am sorry, Father," said Reuben to Jacob. "The Egyptian governor picked Simeon as a hostage and said we must take Benjamin back to Egypt to prove our story."

"We paid for the sacks of grain," added another, "but found the money we had given was put back in the sacks. That makes it look as if we stole the goods. We have to go back to show we were honest."

"Joseph is dead, Simeon is gone – I will die if I lose Benjamin," said Jacob. "He cannot go."

But the famine dragged on and on. Once again the family was running out of food.

"We'll have to go back," pleaded the brothers.

"I'll take care of Benjamin," said Judah. "I promise on my life to keep him as safe as I can."

Jacob faced a terrible choice. "Well, if you have to take Benjamin, at least take money and the best gifts we can afford to please the governor," he wept. He watched in anguish as his sons took the long road to Egypt.

The brothers were fearful of meeting the governor again, and so they were astonished to be given a warm welcome. No one had missed the money. Simeon was well.

They got their gifts ready to give to Joseph, and bowed down in front of him.

"Tell me your news. You said your father was old – is he well?" Joseph asked eagerly. "And is this the youngest brother you told me about?" He turned to Benjamin – his only true brother.
"God bless you," he said.

Then Joseph fled from the room and wept. When he had washed his tears away, he ordered his servants to bring in a feast. Benjamin was served much more food than anyone else!

Dear God, Help us all to mend our quarrels.

Dear God,
If I am wrongly
accused, help
me uncover the
truth.

The silver goblet

ã♣

THE TIME CAME for Joseph's brothers to go back home. Joseph's slaves worked hard through the night to fill the brothers' sacks with grain and load their donkeys so the party could set off at dawn.

"Here's something extra the master wants put in," whispered Joseph's personal servant to a slave. The object was buried deep in one of the sacks.

At first light, the brothers collected their belongings and set off joyfully. They had not gone far when they heard someone running. One of Joseph's servants raced up to them. "Why did you steal my master's silver goblet?" he exclaimed. "It is very special!"

"We have done no such thing!" replied the brothers. "Search all you like. If you find we are lying, you can punish the thief severely."

The servant searched carefully. He began with the eldest brother's sack, then the one belonging to the second eldest, and so on.

He had almost finished sifting through the grain in Benjamin's sack when he felt something... Slowly he pulled something out: a gleaming silver cup.

"Guilty!" he exclaimed.

The brothers could not believe what was happening and exchanged fearful glances as they let themselves be led back to Joseph's house.

"If one of us is guilty, then let us all be guilty and share the punishment," they pleaded.

"Oh no," replied Joseph. "Benjamin is the thief, so Benjamin must stay and the rest of you can get out of my sight forever."

"But our father will die of sorrow and –"

"Am I supposed to care about that?" exclaimed Joseph. He turned to go.

A joyful reunion

❧

*Dear God,
Though people
plan evil, may
you make
everything work
together for
good.*

JUDAH HUNG HIS head. Years ago, he had sold Joseph as a slave. Was he going to watch Benjamin be taken? Was he going to break the promise he had made to his father to keep the boy safe?

He went up to Joseph. "Please, sir," he said. "We made a promise to our father. He was always especially fond of the sons born to his wife Rachel. One has been dead for many years; Benjamin is the other. Our father will die without him. Let him go home, and let me be your slave in his place."

Joseph felt tears welling up in his eyes. He waved to his servants to get out of the room. Then he broke down and wept.

"I am your brother Joseph," he sobbed. "Don't blame yourselves for what happened so long ago. It was really God who sent me here so I could rescue the family now. I am the ruler of Egypt. It is within my power to invite you all to come and live here and be safe!"

The brothers were amazed! They could hardly believe the news. It was like a dream come true. They hurried back home to tell their father.

At first the elderly Jacob could not take in the news. He kept asking his sons to tell the story over again until he had fully grasped it. Then at last he said, "This is all I could ask for! I must go and see him before I die."

The entire family came to Egypt: Jacob, also known as Israel, lived to a ripe old age there. His twelve sons prospered: Reuben, Simeon, Levi, Judah, Issachar, Zebulun, Gad, Asher, Dan, Naphtali and, of course, Joseph and Benjamin. They had children and grandchildren.

Joseph was content. Although his brothers had plotted evil against him, God had turned it into good.

Dear God,
I will not do
wrong things,
even if powerful
people say
I must.

A change for the worse

❧

THE GREAT-GRANDCHILDREN of Israel had children and grandchildren. The family became a nation: the people of Israel.

A new king who had never heard of Joseph came to power.

"I am highly suspicious of these Israelites," he said to his advisers. "There are too many of them. They could plot with our enemies to take over the country. I intend to make them slaves to keep them under our control!"

So he put slave drivers in charge of the Israelites. They whipped them and beat them if, for even a moment, they rested from building the king's fine new cities.

But the Israelites were strong, and they continued to have fine, healthy children.

So the king called the two midwives who helped the Israelite women when they gave birth. "Some babies die young, don't they?" said the king. "Well, I'd like you to make sure that the baby boys born to the Israelites ALL die young. You can let the girls live." He waved them away.

The midwives were horrified. "That's not what God would want," they agreed. "We simply won't do the king's dirty work."

The king summoned the midwives a second time. "Why are you letting the boys live?" he asked. "Why can't you do what I ordered?"

"Oh, the Israelite women have babies so quickly," the midwives told the king, feigning dismay. "By the time we arrive the dear little things are screaming. We can't pretend they suddenly stop breathing."

The king frowned and waved them away. Then he issued a new order – and this time to his soldiers: "Every baby boy born to those foreigners must be thrown into the River Nile."

The baby in the basket

I'M NOT GOING to let our new baby boy drown in the river." The mother was almost sobbing as she spoke to her little daughter Miriam. "We must save him somehow, and I need your help."

The mother had a plan. She made a basket and covered it with tar to make it waterproof; then she put the baby inside and left it floating in the reeds down by the river. Miriam stayed close by, keeping watch.

A while later, the king's daughter came down to the river to bathe. Her servants waited on the bank as she stepped into the river and let herself float in the sun-warmed water. Suddenly she stood up and turned to them. "What's that in the reeds over there?" she asked.

A servant went to get it. They lifted the lid and saw…

"A BABY!" the princess squealed with delight. "It must be one of the Israelite baby boys. His mother has put him in the river as the law requires… but in this clever little boat. Oh, what a sweet idea."

The baby began to wail. "There, there, poor darling," said the princess. "Don't you cry. I'm going to keep you safe!"

Miriam crept forward. "If you need someone to nurse the baby," she said, "I know someone who… who's just finished nursing her own baby."

The princess smiled. "Yes, please," she said.

Miriam brought her own mother. "I will pay you to look after this baby for me," said the princess. "When he's old enough, he shall come to the palace as my son. I want him to be called Moses."

*Dear God,
Help me to find
clever ways to
overcome
bullying and
unkindness.*

47

Moses the prince

૨♠

MOSES GREW UP as a prince in the royal palace. There were servants to take care of his every need, and he didn't have to worry about anything.

However, he always knew that his real parents were Israelites and, when he was a young man, he went to see how his people lived.

He was shocked at what he saw. "It is bad enough that they are slaves," he said to himself, "but the slave drivers are crueler to them than I had imagined. They treat the Israelites as if they were less than human."

Suddenly he heard frantic cries for help, and he ran to see what was going on. An Egyptian was beating a slave mercilessly. Harder and harder he struck the man, until the slave fell silent – and dead.

Moses felt rage welling up inside him. He looked round. No one was looking. He leaped out, grabbed the Egyptian and killed him on the spot. Then, suddenly frightened, he hid the body in the sand.

The next day he went back to find out more about his people. This time he saw two Israelites fighting. "Why are you two hurting each other?" he asked. "Don't you have enough trouble with the cruelty of the Egyptians?"

The two men turned to look at him: a long, cold, sneering stare. "What gives you the right to judge us?" hissed one.

"And what are you planning to do to make things better?" snarled the other. "Kill us like you killed that Egyptian?"

Moses knew the awful truth: there were witnesses to his crime.

He fled from Egypt.

Moses the shepherd

ॐ

MOSES RAN AWAY to the land of Midian. He knew he was an outlaw to both the Israelites and the Egyptians.

At last, weary and dispirited, he sat down near a well to rest.

As he sat there, seven young women came to draw water for their family's flocks of sheep and goats. As they began their work, some shepherds came along leading their flocks to the well.

"Out of our way, we want to use this well now," they shouted. They jeered and jostled to make the women go.

Moses stood up from the shadows. "The women were here first," he shouted to the men. "Let them have their turn."

He leaped down, ran straight to the well and began drawing water for the women. He worked with fierce determination. The shepherds eyed him warily. "We can come back later," they mumbled. Then they called out to their sheep and led them away.

When their flocks had all been watered, the young women hurried back home.

"You're back early," their father, Jethro, exclaimed. "Yes," they said. "An Egyptian man was at the well and he defended us when some shepherds tried to take our turn!"

"Then where is this man?" asked Jethro. "Bring him here as my guest!"

Jethro welcomed Moses into his household. In time, the young man married one of Jethro's daughters, Zipporah.

Moses began a new life as a shepherd.

*D*ear God,
*Keep me safe so
that I may live
my life for you.*

Dear God,
You are the God
who is, the one
whose name
is I AM.

The holy mountain

ONE DAY, MOSES took his family's flocks out to find pasture. There was little for the animals to graze, so they had to keep on moving further and further into the wild country.

He reached a place called Sinai, where there was a tall and rocky mountain that seemed to reach to heaven itself.

Suddenly, there in front of him, he saw a strange sight. "Are my eyes playing tricks, or is that bush on fire?" he murmured. "I can see flames, but the bush isn't being burned up."

As he went closer, God called to Moses from the middle of the bush.

"Moses! Stop where you are. Take off your sandals, for this is holy ground. I am God – the God of your people, the God of Abraham, Isaac and Jacob."

Fearfully, Moses did as he was commanded, and he pulled his cloak over his face so he could not see.

"Listen," said God. "I have seen how much my people are suffering. Now I am sending you to the king of Egypt to ask him to let them go."

Moses shook his head. "The king won't listen to me," he protested. "And neither will the Israelites. If I say, 'The God of your people has sent me,' they will reply, 'What is this God's name?' – and I don't know what to tell them."

God replied, "I am who I am. You will say, 'The one who is called I AM has sent me to you.'"

Help from God

EVEN THOUGH GOD had spoken to him, Moses was hesitant.

"But… but…" he said, struggling to find his words.

God waited.

"What if the Israelites don't believe you have sent me? What if they say I'm making up my story?"

"You are holding a stick," said God. "Throw it to the ground."

Moses did so. At once it began to wriggle. It was a snake! Moses stepped back in alarm.

"Now bend down and pick it up by the tail," said God. Moses crept forward. He lunged to grab the snake. As soon as he touched it, he found he was simply holding his stick again.

"You see," said God. "I am giving you power to perform wonders like this. They will convince people that I have sent you."

"But… but…" Once again Moses struggled to put a sentence together.

God waited.

"Listen to how I'm stumbling over my words, even now. You know I'm not a good speaker. I'm not the right person for the task."

"I will help you to speak well," said God.

"But…"

God waited.

"Please send someone else!" pleaded Moses.

God's reply was quiet, but it was also strong: the voice of a God who must be obeyed. "Go to your brother Aaron. You will tell him what to say, and he will speak for you."

Moses went home. He agreed with Jethro that he would take his family to Egypt. On the way there, he met Aaron.

Dear God, May I trust in your power to help me to do what is right.

*Dear God,
When it seems
that you have
forgotten me,
I will listen
again to the
stories of how
you help your
people.*

The king of Egypt

🐚

MOSES WENT TO get Aaron and together they went to the king of Egypt. The pharaoh looked down haughtily at the two men in front of him. Apparently they wanted to talk about some nonsense to do with his slaves. He waved his hand, indicating that they could speak.

Moses and Aaron began: "The Lord, the God of Israel, says this: 'Let my people go. Let them go into the wild country beyond Egypt for a special festival to worship me.'"

The king sneered as he replied. "The God of Israel? I neither know nor respect a god with this name. I will not let the Israelites go anywhere!"

Moses and Aaron stood their ground. They tried to convince the king that disasters would follow if he did not obey God, but the king only grew angrier.

On the same day that he dismissed Moses and Aaron from his sight, he called his slave drivers and foremen. "Make those Israelites work harder," he ordered. "Why have we been supplying them with the straw they need to make the mud bricks bind together well? Let them find their own straw – and still make the same number of bricks! That will keep them busy. Then they won't have time to listen to these two troublemakers."

The extra work wore the Israelites out. "You have made everything worse!" they complained to Moses and Aaron.

Moses complained to God. "Why did you send me here? The king has not listened to me. Now the people are treated worse than ever, and you have done nothing!"

Tricks and wonders

❧

ONCE AGAIN, GOD spoke to Moses: "I made a promise to Abraham, Isaac and Jacob. The land of Canaan is the place where their children and their children's children will live in freedom. Go back to the king. Tell him to let my people go."

Moses and Aaron knew in their hearts that they must obey God. They knew, too, that God had given them the power to work wonders. Nervous but resolute, they went.

Once they were in the king's presence, Aaron threw his stick to the ground. It turned into a snake.

"Look," they said. "There is proof we have authority from God."

"Oh, that old trick," sighed the king. He called for his magicians. "I want these troublemakers over here to understand just how ridiculous is their claim to supernatural authority," he told them.

The magicians threw down their sticks and at once the gleaming wood turned to wriggling snakes.

The king laughed and turned to Aaron, ready to pour scorn on him. Aaron had his eyes fixed on the ground, and the king followed the line of his gaze.

Aaron's snake was swallowing the magicians' snakes.

The room was silent.

One by one, everyone turned to look at the king.

"Just get out of my sight," ordered the king.

*Dear God,
Help me not to
be dismayed by
the trickery of
those who do
not respect you.*

Dear God,
I will learn
from the
stories of your
people how to
be patient.

The disasters begin

GOD SPOKE TO Moses again. "Tomorrow, I want you to take the stick that turned into a snake and go down to the River Nile. You will meet the king there. Warn him that if he does not let my people go, you will turn the river to blood."

The king shook his head and turned away when he saw Moses and Aaron yet again. He paid no attention to their pleading. He dismissed their warnings about what God would do.

Aaron lifted up the stick. At once the river turned red.

"Now your people will not be able to collect drinking water," warned Moses. "The fish will die. The river will begin to stink."

The king turned away. "My magicians can do that trick too," he sneered.

Then seven days went by. The Egyptians had to dig channels along the riverbanks to find clean water. The king ignored the problem.

"Go back," said God to Moses, "and warn the king to let my people go, or another disaster will strike. The country will be overrun by frogs."

Once again the king refused to listen. But all over Egypt the frogs were driving people to despair. Even the palace cook had to shriek at the slaves to come and get the frogs out of the ovens and out of the cooking pans.

The king merely wanted his meal on time. He refused to notice the slaves who were sweeping his bedroom floor clear of frogs that night. Only when frogs hopped onto his bed did he take any notice.

He summoned Moses: "If your god has sent these frogs, then pray to your god to take them away. Then I will let your people go."

"I will do so tomorrow," replied Moses. "Then you will begin to respect the God of my people."

Moses prayed. The frogs went back to the river.

"Good," said the king. "But your people stay, after all."

Disaster follows disaster

GOD SPOKE TO Moses again.

"Tell Aaron to strike the ground with his stick. The dust will turn to gnats."

The king was furious as he swatted at the insects hovering around him. "This is just another bit of trickery," he snapped at his magicians. "You can do the same, can't you?"

The magicians tried to use their secret arts to make gnats appear from the dust, but they did not succeed. "It must be the Israelite god who has done this," they told the king.

"Nonsense," the king retorted.

The next disaster was a great swarm of flies. They hummed and buzzed over the land of Egypt.

After that, all the animals in Egypt were struck down by a mystery illness. A further mystery was that the animals belonging to the Israelites stayed well.

Then all the Egyptians and their animals suffered a terrible skin disease, with sores that were slow to heal.

A massive hailstorm flattened the crops. The flax and the barley were ruined. Then in from the desert came a plague of locusts – great swarms of insects that shut out the daylight and ate every plant in sight.

Darkness covered the land like a thick blanket. For three whole days it was darker than a moonless night.

"Oh, you and your people go and have your ridiculous festival!" said the king to Moses. "But don't take any of your flocks. Leave them here."

"We will need animals to offer as sacrifices," Moses protested.

"Then you can't go," shouted the king. "Get out of my sight."

Dear God, Sometimes, in the dark, I wonder if good things will ever happen.

Dear God,
Guide me by
day and by
night.

The final disaster

MOSES HEARD GOD speaking to him again, and he bowed his head as he realized the solemnity of what God was telling him.

"The Egyptians will suffer only one more disaster. Then you will be able to lead the people to freedom.

"You must tell the Israelites to be ready to leave for a new land. On the chosen night, every family must take a lamb or a goat and kill it to eat. They must mark the doorposts of their houses with its blood.

"Then they must roast the animal for supper. They must make bread quickly, without yeast, and a salad of herbs they have gathered.

"When they eat the meal, they should have their sandals on so they are ready to begin the long march to freedom.

"That night, death will strike all over Egypt; but death will pass over the houses marked with blood."

The people did as Moses instructed. At midnight, the sound of weeping was heard all over the land, as disaster struck every unmarked home.

At last the king and the rest of the Egyptians knew that the God of Moses must be respected. They hurried to speak to the Israelites.

"Go, leave us alone before anything worse happens," they begged. "Look, we have gold and silver ornaments to give you. But please, please, please: be on your way at once."

"Hurry," said the Israelite mothers to their children. "Here's bread dough not yet baked. You must help put it into pans, and we'll take it with us."

The people gathered their possessions, rounded up their flocks and left.

God put a pillar of cloud in front of them to guide them during the day. In the night, it became a pillar of fire.

Crossing the sea

WHEN THE KING of Egypt realized that he had actually allowed the Israelites to make their escape, he was furious all over again.

"We need them as slaves!" he shouted to his attendants. "Get my chariot ready! Summon the army! We will capture them!"

The king's charioteers raced out across the dusty plain. The people of Israel were camped by the Red Sea. They heard the sound of galloping hooves. In the far distance, they saw the army coming toward them.

"We're going to die!" they wailed. "Oh, why didn't we stay in Egypt?"

"Don't be afraid," replied Moses sternly. "God will save us."

He walked to the edge of the Red Sea and lifted up his stick.

A strong east wind began to blow. It blew so hard that the sea began to move back like an ebbing tide.

As night fell, the pillar of cloud that had led the way ahead moved to the back of the Israelite camp. The Egyptians could not see their way in the misty dark.

Ahead of him, Moses saw that the wind had made a dry path through the sea. Quietly, urgently, he ordered everyone to move on.

"Look!" shouted one of the Egyptian guards. "They're escaping!"

"Follow them!" ordered the king.

The chariots trundled forward. The ground that had been covered by sea was soft. The wheels sank into mud.

When the Israelites reached the other side, Moses lifted up his stick. As he did so, the waters flooded back and swept the Egyptian army away.

Dear God,
You are faithful
to your promises.
You work
miracles to save
your people.

*Dear God,
You are my
defender. You are
the one who
helps me.*

Food in the desert

🐦

THE ISRAELITES WERE free! But their troubles were not yet over. They found themselves alone in the dry and stony wilderness that lay between Egypt and Canaan.

"There's hardly any water out here," they moaned. "Whatever will happen to us in this dreadful place?"

The people were slow to discover that God was determined to keep them safe. Even when God gave Moses miraculous power to make bitter water pure enough to drink, they remained fearful when they found a shady oasis.

As they moved on from one plentiful oasis, the people began to complain again.

"Oh, do you remember the vegetables we used to have in Egypt? Garlic and onions, leeks and cucumbers –"

"– and juicy watermelons."

"Oh yes. All those things we could grow down by the river. Do you remember fishing as well… all those fish we could catch for free, and the delicious suppers we used to have watching the sun go down?"

"It wasn't so bad in Egypt, was it? Here, we have hardly any food."

Despite their complaining, God was there to help them.

In the evening, a flock of quails flew into the camp, and the Israelites caught them for food. In the morning, as the dew melted, they found thin pieces of something like delicate flakes of frost on the ground.

"God has provided this for us to eat," explained Moses. "You will be able to collect enough each day, and twice as much on the sixth day. Then we can enjoy the seventh day of rest, as commanded in the beginning."

Over and over again, God took care of them. Over and over again, God gave Moses the encouragement he needed to keep going.

The Ten Commandments

❧

A FTER DAYS OF journeying, the Israelites reached the foot of Mount Sinai. Moses left people he could trust in charge of everyday matters and went up the mountain alone to meet with God.

Sinai was a mysterious mountain. Sometimes, in the midst of thunder and lightning, it would be covered in smoke, and there would come a terrifying sound like that of a great trumpet. In the swirling mountain mists, God spoke to Moses. God gave him laws that would help the Israelites to live as God's own people.

Some of the laws were about the right way to worship God: how to conduct the ceremonies and the festivals in a way that showed respect for God's holiness.

Others were laws about the right way for people to treat one another: within the family, within the community and beyond it.

Among the laws God gave were ten great laws, the Ten Commandments.

I am the Lord your God. I brought you out of Egypt, where you were slaves. Worship no god but me.

Do not make objects to worship as if they were gods. Nothing in the world deserves more respect than me.

Do not say you are acting in my name when you have no right to do so.

Every seventh day is the sabbath. It is a day of rest. You must not do any work, and you must allow everyone in your household to rest too.

Show respect to your father and mother.

Do not murder.

Do not commit adultery. Husbands and wives must be faithful to one another.

Do not steal.

Do not tell lies that accuse people of doing wrong things.

Do not allow yourself to dream of owning the things that belong to someone else.

These few words told the people all they needed to know to live wisely.

21 February

❖

Exodus 18–20

Dear God, May I learn to worship you as you deserve; may I learn to treat others as I should.

The golden calf

AT THE FOOT of the mountain, the people grew tired of waiting. "Moses has been away for too long," they complained to Aaron. "He isn't our leader anymore. Make us a god – a new one."

Aaron felt he had to do something. He told the people to bring their gold jewelry, poured it into a mold and made a gold bull calf.

The people were delighted. "This is our god, the one who led us out of Egypt," they cheered.

The following day began with religious ceremonies. Then everyone sat down for a feast.

"Bring out more wine!" someone shouted. Everyone cheered as the stocks of wine were opened. Soon the feast turned into a wild party.

Up on the mountain, God spoke to Moses, and God's voice was quiet and angry. "Hurry: go back down. The people have made a new god for themselves. They have abandoned all that is holy. They will no longer be my people."

Moses pleaded with God. "Please do not destroy them. Remember the promises you made to Abraham so long ago and honor them!"

He hurried down, carrying two tablets of stone on which were written the great laws God had given to guide the people.

As he came near the camp, he heard the singing and shrieking. He saw the mayhem. He saw the golden calf.

Furious, he threw down the stone tablets and smashed them.

Moses' anger

❧

MOSES STRODE PAST all the revelers. He was blazing with anger. He tore down the golden bull calf from its pedestal and flung it into the fire. Soon it was no more than a puddle of metal.

He spoke sharply to Aaron, rebuking him for leading the people astray, and he dealt sternly with the people. "Is he going to punish all of us?" they whispered fearfully. "Do you think he'll be very severe?"

Moses strode off to the mountain to talk to God: "Have pity on your people," he prayed. "Don't abandon them. Please forgive them."

In the end, God was moved by Moses' prayers. God told Moses to cut two more tablets of stone and bring them to the top of Mount Sinai.

Once again, Moses came and waited amid the swirling mists. There, in a landscape that was shrouded in mystery, God came and met him.

"I am the Lord," said God. "I am full of compassion and pity. I love my people and will be faithful to them. I really do keep my promises."

Then God gave Moses the laws again, and they were written into the stone as a reminder that they were intended to last forever.

"Take these laws to the people," said God. "They are part of the agreement I am making with the people. They must obey these laws, and I will take care of them."

When Moses went back down the mountain, the people saw that his face was shining. They knew for sure that he had been in the presence of God.

*Dear God,
You are holy.
Everyone should
stand in awe
of you.*

A place of worship

24 February

❖

Exodus 25, 28

*Dear God,
Thank you
for your
compassion
and pity, for
your love and
faithfulness.*

EVEN THOUGH THE people were still desert nomads, the time was right for them to build a place of worship. God gave instructions for a special tent that they could take with them wherever they went. "We must worship God in the way that God deserves," Moses explained to the people. "I want you to give whatever you can afford to build it."

The people brought their offerings of gold, silver and bronze; of linen and wool; of leather and wood; of oil and incense and precious stones.

The best craftworkers among the people were chosen to create the tent – the tabernacle. Some made the frame and coverings for the tent itself. Others made the curtains for the inside. There was a golden altar where incense could be burned and a magnificent golden lampstand of intricate design.

Priests were appointed to be in charge of the worship, and special clothes were made for them. For the high priest there was a special breastplate: it was set with twelve jewels, one for each of the tribes descended from the twelve sons of Israel, and a reminder that all of them were immensely precious to God.

62

The covenant box

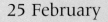

❖

Exodus 25, 37,
Deuteronomy 11

THE MOST IMPORTANT item that was made to go inside the tent of worship was a box. It was of modest size and sturdily crafted in acacia wood. What set it apart was its covering of pure gold inside and out, and a border of intricate design. A gold ring was affixed to each of its four legs so that a carrying pole could be inserted on either side; in this way, no one would have to touch the sacred item.

The lid of the box was also made of gold, and two creatures with outstretched wings were hammered out of the same metal and fixed on top. Into this box, this ark, Moses would put the tablets of stone on which the Law was written. It was the sign of God's agreement with them – God's covenant. If the people kept the laws, God would be their God; they would be God's people.

"Love the Lord your God and always obey all his laws. Remember today what you have learned about the Lord: you saw what he did to the king of Egypt and to his entire country; you know what the Lord did for you in the desert before you arrived here.

"Trust in the Lord, and do good."

Dear God, Teach me to treat with respect the things that are sacred.

The presence of God

A T LAST, ALL the work on the tabernacle was complete. Moses put the tablets on which the commandments were written into the covenant box, and it was carried into the farthest end of the tabernacle. The curtain fell back in place, screening the holy place from view.

In the main room of the tabernacle, the lamps in the lampstand flickered gold. Sweet-smelling smoke rose from the incense on the altar.

Outside, the priests made offerings to God.

In the midst of all the ceremony, a cloud came and covered the tabernacle and filled it with the dazzling light of God's presence.

As long as the cloud stayed over the tabernacle, the people camped in the same place. Only when the cloud moved did they move on.

In this way, the people could be sure that God was always with them.

The fertile land of Canaan

At one time, Moses and the people came close to the land of Canaan.

"This is the land that will be your home," said God to Moses. "Pick a brave leader from each of the tribes of Israel and send them to explore it."

The men set off, and for forty days they secretly visited Canaan.

They saw the strongly built cities, each surrounded by a high wall and guarded by powerful soldiers. In one place, there lived a tribe of people who were amazingly tall – giants compared with the Israelites – fearsome warriors.

They also saw fields where crops had been harvested and vineyards where plump grapes were ripening in the sun. In one fertile valley they saw the biggest bunch of grapes ever!

"Let's take it back to show everyone," said a man named Joshua, and everyone agreed.

The bunch of grapes was so heavy the men had to sling it on a pole so that two of them could carry it on their shoulders. Laden with this and baskets of fruit, they returned to Moses to tell everyone of what they had seen.

Even after they had given their report, the Israelites could not make up their minds what to do. The land was clearly fertile, but the people who lived there were going to fight for their homes.

"If God is with us, then we will be successful," Joshua tried to persuade them.

But the argument went the other way. "Then the people will have to live out here in the wilderness," said God to Moses. "Most of them will never enter Canaan."

Dear God,
When you are
with me, I need
not be afraid
of any challenge.

*Dear God,
Help me to be
determined and
confident as I
live my life
for you.*

Moses sees the land

FOR FORTY YEARS, the people of Israel lived as nomads in the wilderness. Children were born there. Parents grew old.

Moses himself grew old, and he decided to choose the person who would lead the nation after him. "Listen," he announced to the people, "Joshua will be your leader. Be determined and confident as you go forward into your new land. God will not fail you or abandon you.

"Make sure you obey all the commands I have given you. Teach them to your children, so that they may faithfully obey all God's teachings. Obey them, and you will live long in the land across the River Jordan that you are about to enter."

After he had finished speaking, Moses went up to the top of Mount Nebo. In the far distance he could see the tall trees that grew around the springs of water in Jericho. By a miracle, God showed him the whole land of Canaan, from north to south and as far as the western shore where the great sea glittered. Then Moses died there, on top of the mountain.

For thirty days, the people mourned his death, and then they looked to Joshua to lead them into Canaan.

Rahab and the spies

"GET READY TO move into Canaan," announced Joshua. "The time has come!"

First, Joshua sent two spies to Jericho. They found it easy enough to enter the city during the day, when the gates were open for people to come and go. However, they wanted to stay until after sunset. For that, they needed a place to hide.

A woman named Rahab proved to be their ally. "You can stay in my house," she assured them. "Come – I know where you can hide."

Even as she did so, the king's guards hammered on the door. "Bring out those men who are with you!" they ordered. "They are spies."

"They're not here," Rahab protested; but the guards pushed their way into her house and began looking around suspiciously. "They did come here," she continued, "but they left before the city gates were closed. They can't have gone far."

The soldiers exchanged glances. They'd looked through all the rooms. "In that case, they'll be heading back to their camp the other side of the Jordan," they agreed. "After them!"

As they clattered down the street, Rahab rushed back onto the flat roof of her house. It was piled with great heaps of flax stalks that she had spread out to dry.

"Come out," she whispered to the men. "I know you and your people are going to defeat us here in Jericho. You must promise that when you do, you will treat my family as kindly as I have treated you."

The men promised. "Now run to the hill country," whispered Rahab. "The guards have gone out on the road down to the River Jordan. My house is built into the city walls, and I can let you down on a rope to the outside. Hurry!"

*Dear God,
Help me to resist
those who seek
to harm others.*

Crossing the River Jordan

May everyone on earth know how great is God's power.

THE SPIES RETURNED to the camp and gave their report.

"The people in Jericho are terrified of us," they said. "We are sure God wants us to make this land our own."

Joshua felt encouraged. He also believed God was telling him what to do next. "Tell the priests to lead the way toward Canaan, carrying the covenant box. I will work a miracle that will make the people respect you as their leader. They will know that I am with you, as I was with Moses."

The priests did as Joshua commanded. They walked ahead of the people down to the banks of the River Jordan.

There they stopped. The river was in flood: its swirling waters were brown and menacing.

"Carry the box into the river," ordered Joshua.

Grimacing slightly, the priests stepped in. To their amazement, the water slowed to a muddy trickle. High upstream, the torrent of water began to form a huge lake; but where the priests stood with the covenant box, the riverbed drained dry.

The people hurried across. Joshua told each of the twelve tribes to choose a man to collect a large boulder from the riverbed and bring it to the camp. These stones would remind the people of what God had done. Joshua also took twelve more stones and laid them on the riverbed where the priests were standing.

Then Joshua told the priests to carry the covenant box out of the river.

Once they were safe on the opposite bank, the water came rushing down in a huge and devastating surge.

The battle of Jericho

❧

JOSHUA LOOKED TOWARD the city of Jericho. Its walls were high and strong. The heavy gate was locked. Armed soldiers kept watch from the towers on either side.

"Do as I tell you," God told him. "The city will be yours."

The following day, the soldiers guarding Jericho saw what they had dreaded and gripped their weapons. "Here comes the attack," they murmured to one another.

A column of Israelites was marching toward the city. First came a band of soldiers; next, seven priests, all blowing trumpets. Behind them came people carrying a gold box with great ceremony. After that came yet more soldiers. They marched around the city and then returned to camp.

"Too scared, most likely," the soldiers in Jericho laughed. "Or maybe that was a training exercise for their ragged little army."

The same thing happened six days in a row. The soldiers in Jericho were puzzled, and they were growing more than a little anxious.

In the Israelite camp, Joshua gave a passionate speech. "God has given us the city," he proclaimed. "You will play your part tomorrow."

On the seventh day, at daybreak, the Israelites came to Jericho again. They marched around the city once. Then a second time.

"Oh, a new training exercise for today," scoffed the city guards.

The Israelites kept on marching. They completed the seventh circuit, and the priests blew a mighty blast on the trumpets. The people shouted.

Slowly at first, and then with gathering speed, the city walls collapsed. The Israelites took the city. Only Rahab and her family were spared.

Dear God,
Nothing can
stand in the
way of what
you want.

*Dear God,
May I and all
my family
choose to do
what is good
and right.*

A place to call home

ॐ

ONCE THE ISRAELITES had made Jericho theirs, they began to capture other places. Joshua encouraged his soldiers to fight bravely. He also made sure that God's laws were read aloud as God had commanded: he knew that the nation needed to stay faithful to God.

Little by little, land was won. At Ai, the victory seemed to depend on Joshua's military strategy. With the people of Gibeon it was possible to agree on a treaty. In the battle against the Amorites, the sun stood still – as if by a miracle – until the victory was secure.

By the time Joshua was old, he knew that God's promises had all come true. The land belonged to the people of Israel. Everyone had a place to call home. They were able to live in peace.

Joshua called the people together one last time. "I will not be alive much longer," he said. "I want you always to remember the things that God has done for you. I want you to live as God's people and obey God's good laws. The other nations who live among us worship other gods. Sometimes, you may be tempted to follow their example. As for me and my family, we will serve the Lord, our God."

"We will never forget what God has done for us," replied the people. "We will be faithful to God."

"Then you will have to live in the right way," said Joshua. "You must remember that our God is a holy God."

"We will!" declared the people. "We will be faithful to our holy God."

Other gods

❧

WHILE JOSHUA WAS leader, the people were faithful to God. When he died, they forgot their promise.

"There can't be any harm worshiping the gods of the people who used to live in this land," they said to one another. "In fact, the local gods might be useful to us: they're supposed to be the gods of the weather and crops and practical things like that."

So the people began to make statues of the god Baal and the goddess Astarte. They bowed down to them and said prayers to them.

God was angry. "Because they have broken their agreement with me, they are no longer my people," said God. "They will learn their mistake the hard way. Enemies will attack them and defeat them."

One of their enemies was the gluttonous King Eglon of the Moabites. The news that came to him about the Israelites caused him to rub his fat hands with glee.

"Hee hee hee," he giggled, his rolls of fat shaking as he laughed. "I shall make a pact with the Ammonites and the Amalekites. We three tribes together will be able to defeat those bothersome Israelites. We could even steal Jericho back! Hee hee hee."

The three nations went to war against the Israelites and crushed them. The fighters laughed and congratulated themselves as they wandered triumphant among the palm trees of Jericho. The Israelites were dismayed.

"Why is this happening to us?" they cried. "God gave us Jericho in the time of Joshua, as a sign that the land is for us to live in. What has gone wrong, what have we done to deserve this?"

No sooner had they complained than they knew the answer. "We have not been faithful to God," they wept.

Dear God, May I stay faithful to you and your laws and trust in you to take care of everyday worries.

*Dear God,
When I am in
danger, thank
you for providing
people who are
brave enough to
help me.*

Ehud and Eglon

❧

THE ISRAELITES KNEW only too well what they needed to do to escape further disaster. They cried out to God. "Forgive us, O Lord," they prayed. "Help us! Send someone to save us! We will be your people; you will be our God."

God loved the people of Israel and chose a man named Ehud to be their hero. Ehud was confident about how to put things right.

"King Eglon will begin to trust us if we send gifts," he said. "A defeated people should always send tribute to their new ruler, and I am willing to take it to him. I will convince him that we have been truly humbled by his great victory."

A band of men set out with Ehud to carry the gifts, and they delivered them to the king personally, with much bowing and attentiveness. Eglon was delighted.

As the envoys returned home, Ehud told his men to keep going. "I, however, must go back," he said. "There is one thing I have yet to say to Eglon."

Furtively Ehud made his way to the king. He managed to persuade the guards to let him go through to the rooftop pavilion where the king was resting. "Your Majesty," he said, keeping his voice low, "I have come back alone and undefended with a secret message for you." He glanced sideways at the servants who stood around waiting on the king. "It is for you alone," he added.

"Aha!" said King Eglon. He settled his ample body on his chair and looked Ehud up and down. The man was clearly unarmed. There was no bulge in his clothing where a sword might have hung. He waved the servants away. "I'm always ready to listen to secrets," he said.

Ehud's revenge

E HUD WENT UP close to King Eglon. "The message is from God," he whispered. He paused to plan his next move. As a boy, he had been laughed at for being left handed. Now it was his main advantage. He reached with his left hand into his clothes and drew out a double-edged sword.

"Here it is," he hissed. He plunged the blade all the way into Eglon's fat belly. The weapon was lost among the rolls of fat. Ehud smiled grimly at his victim, left the room and locked the doors. Then he fled.

Meanwhile, King Eglon's servants were getting nervous. Why hadn't the king called them back to their duties? He would be in a terrible rage if he thought they were slacking.

"Let's go back to the room," they agreed.

They went and found the door locked. "Oh – you know what that must mean. He's going to the toilet. We'd better wait quietly."

They waited and waited. They listened at the door. Silence.

"Come on, we'll have to check if he's all right. We'll have to break the door down."

As they tumbled through the splintered wood they found King Eglon dead on the floor.

Ehud had not been idle. He hurried to the hill country. There he raised a trumpet to his lips and blew a mighty blast. It was the sound to summon the men of Israel to war. They swarmed down on the Moabites and defeated them utterly. The Israelites were safe again.

Dear God, Bless my strengths and my weaknesses so I can use them to serve you.

73

Deborah and Barak

*Dear God,
May I learn to
recognize when
the advice I am
given is truly
from you.*

AFTER EHUD DIED, the people of Israel forgot their promise to God. Once again they began to disobey the laws they had been given. Once again, God let their enemies defeat them.

A Canaanite king named Jabin swept to victory. He had the finest military equipment, including 900 chariots made from iron – by far the best metal for instruments of war. He was a cruel king who ruled by fear. No one knew when his death squads might appear.

It so happened that among the wise leaders of the people of Israel was a woman named Deborah. She was respected as a prophet of God and also as a judge who could decide difficult cases. God gave her special wisdom about how to help her people, and so she sent for a man named Barak.

"The God of Israel has chosen you to lead an army of 10,000 men," she said. "Take them to Mount Tabor. There, on the banks of the River Kishon, you will defeat the armies of King Jabin, led by his commander Sisera."

Barak glared at Deborah. He had years of experience as a fighter. Now this so-called wise woman was telling him to take on a much stronger enemy. He shifted uneasily.

"I'll go if you go with me," he said, rather morosely. "But if you don't go with me, I won't go either."

"All right," snapped Deborah, "but don't expect to be the hero when we win." She fixed the former warrior with a fierce stare. "Sisera will have been defeated by a woman."

Battle at Mount Tabor

❧

Dear God, May we learn proper respect for the natural forces at work in the world.

WHEN SISERA HEARD that Barak had gone to Mount Tabor, he called out all his men and all the 900 iron chariots and sent them to the River Kishon. Mount Tabor loomed above them, its slopes dark with 10,000 Israelite fighting men.

"Get ready for the attack," cried Sisera. "They'll be fierce, but they have nothing that will stand up to our chariot regiments."

Almost at once came the sound of clashing weapons. The battle was under way. From his own splendid chariot, Sisera gave the signal for the first line of chariots to charge. "Go, men, go!" he screamed. The chariots were hardly moving. "Take me closer," he said to his charioteer. "I'll make them move."

"I can't get the wheels going," gasped his charioteer. "They're stuck. The ground is soft. It must be a flood plain. We're not going to be able to… aargh!"

A missile struck the charioteer on the head and he slumped down. "Charge!" screamed Sisera… but his army was in complete disarray. His chariots were sinking, he could see the Israelites coming closer and he could hear the screams and groans of wounded men.

Sisera held his breath as he surveyed the grim scene. He pushed his charioteer's body aside and shook the reins. The horse reared and whinnied, but the chariot was sinking slowly into the ground.

"What now?" whispered Sisera to himself. "This is a disaster."

Suddenly his resolve crumbled. He leapt from the chariot and ran away.

Dear God,
Show me where
I should place
my loyalty.

Sisera and Jael

SISERA CREPT CLOSE to the nomad encampment, his heart still pounding from exhaustion and fear. He wanted to wait for a few moments and watch: he needed to be sure this was the clan of Heber the Kenite, who was on good terms with his master, King Jabin. To his great relief, he saw people he knew. Stealthily, he went to one of the tents and told a servant who he was.

Heber's wife Jael came to greet him. "Come in," she said. "Don't be afraid."

Inside the tent was dark. Jael lifted a heavy curtain. "Hide yourself in here," she whispered. "No one will know where you are."

Sisera nodded gratefully. "Can I have a drink of water as well?" he pleaded.

"I can do better than that," replied Jael. "You must have some milk to revive you."

"I'm in desperate need of help." As he drank, Sisera began to explain his predicament. He said, "If people come asking if there's anyone staying with you, say no."

Jael smiled. Sisera smiled back. Then he lay down and fell asleep.

Jael sat thinking for a moment. Her husband was at peace with Sisera's king, she knew. However, her people, the Kenites, were the descendants of Moses' brother-in-law. That made them relatives.

She got up and fetched a tent peg and a hammer. Then she went quietly up to Sisera and drove the peg through his head.

She didn't have to wait long before Barak came hunting for Sisera. Jael jumped up to greet him. "He's in here," she said.

Barak saw the once-proud general dead in his own blood. "Thank God," he said grimly. "That pretty much seals the outcome of today's battle."

Before the day was over, King Jabin's army had been completely defeated. Deborah sang a song of victory – a victory that gave Israel forty years of peace.

The call of Gideon

❧

THERE CAME A TIME when, as so often before, the people of Israel forgot to be loyal to God. As a result, the people of Midian gained the upper hand.

The Israelites were very afraid of these desert raiders. Time and again, they came and destroyed the crops the Israelites had planted; time and again, they came and stole sheep and goats and cattle.

"Why is God not looking after us?" the Israelites wailed. "Why are we having to hide in caves and up in the hills?"

A man named Gideon was asking himself the same question as he shook sheaves of wheat into a winepress. "If God were looking after us, then I would not have to go to these ridiculous lengths to thresh this wheat in secret," he said. He looked up to where the real threshing floor lay empty, on the windblown hilltop, then climbed inside the walls of the winepress and began to beat the stalks with a flail.

He heard someone speaking: "The Lord is with you, brave and mighty man." Gideon looked up.

"If I may say so, I don't think God is with us," he said. "Our enemies are causing trouble, and I don't see God doing anything to help us."

"It is for you to go and rescue Israel," said the stranger. "I myself am sending you."

Gideon was astonished. Who could it be who dared speak like this?

Dear God, Come to the rescue of those who fear violent enemies.

77

*Dear God,
Help me
believe what
you are saying
to me.*

Gideon asks for proof

GIDEON TREMBLED AS he looked at the stranger. What if it was God who was challenging him to rescue his people? But was it God? He wasn't at all sure.

Then he spoke aloud: "I can't fight the Midianites," he protested. "I'm the least important person in an unimportant family."

"You can do it," came the reply, "because I will help you."

Gideon hesitated. "Please, can you do something to prove you are God?" he said nervously. "Wait – I'll bring you some food as an offering."

He went home to prepare a meal and soon came hurrying back with a basket of meat and bread and a pot of broth.

"Put the meat and bread on this rock," ordered the stranger, "and then pour the broth over them."

Gideon did so, and then the stranger touched the sodden food with his stick. By a miracle, the meal burst into flames, and the stranger vanished.

Gideon trembled with fear. Then he heard God speaking. "Tear down the altars your people have built to worship other gods. Make a place to worship me."

Gideon obeyed at once. The Israelites were at first dismayed, but when they saw that the local gods took no revenge, they began to pay attention to their fierce new hero. They even agreed to follow him into war.

Then Gideon began to doubt. "Please, God," he prayed, "do something to prove that I am meant to rescue Israel. Look, I'm putting some wool on the threshing floor. If, by tomorrow, there is dew on the wool but none on the ground, I will be sure."

The next morning, Gideon was able to squeeze a bowlful of water out of the wool. He looked at the dry ground.

"Please, God," he prayed, "give me one more sign. Tomorrow, let the wool be dry and the ground wet."

In the morning, things were as he had asked.

An army of 300

THE DAY CAME when Gideon decided to lead his army into battle against the Midianites.

"You have too many fighting men," said God. "When you win, the people will think they did so without my help. Announce that anyone who is afraid may go home."

Twenty-two thousand soldiers took their chance to leave.

"Now take the 10,000 who remain down to the water to drink," said God.

Most of the men knelt down by the spring to drink. Three hundred stood and scooped up the water in their hands.

"Keep just the 300," said God. "Send the rest home."

As the sun went down, God spoke to Gideon again. "Tonight, you will attack the Midianites. Just do everything I say."

Gideon wanted to trust God; even so, he felt his heart sink as he crept downhill to spy on the enemy encampment. It was huge.

Then he heard one of the enemy telling a friend about a dream he'd had. "Do you know what I saw? A huge great loaf rolled into our camp and went smack into a tent. Left it flat!"

Gideon smiled grimly as he heard the surly reply: "That's bad news. It sounds as if God is going to let that Israelite leader beat us."

Gideon went back to his fighting men and divided them into three groups. He gave each person a trumpet and a jar in which to hide a flaming torch. In the dark of night, all three groups crept down to the edge of the enemy camp.

At Gideon's sign, the men blew the trumpets – a wild, wailing blast. They smashed their jars, held their blazing torches high and cried, "A sword for the Lord and for Gideon!"

In the dark, the enemy soldiers jumped up in confusion. Mistakenly they fought with each other. Then they fled.

Dear God, May I never grow proud of all that I think I can do, but rather may I trust in you.

79

Dear God,
When I feel
downcast, give
me hope for
the future.

Samson the strong

ᕫ

WITH THE MIDIANITES defeated, Israel enjoyed a time of peace. Yet, little by little the people forgot to be grateful to God. One by one, they set up places of worship to other gods. After Gideon died, everyone went back to their old ways.

They did not obey any laws; often they quarreled among themselves. Time and again they had to fight their enemies – sometimes winning, sometimes losing. In time, the nation of Philistines who lived on the coastal plain came and defeated them utterly.

Times were hard and the future uncertain, but one woman from the tribe of Dan had yet another reason to feel downcast. She had been married for years but had borne no children. As the years went by, she felt increasing despair that there was no future for her family, and no future for her nation.

One day, a mysterious stranger appeared. "You will soon have a son," he said. "While you are pregnant, you must not drink alcohol or eat the foods that God's laws forbid. When the boy is born, you must leave his hair uncut. He must be dedicated to God. He will rescue the nation from the Philistines."

The woman ran to her husband to tell the startling news: "I know we haven't ever had children," she said, "but someone from nowhere said I would. I think it was an angel! We are going to have a son and dedicate him to God."

Her husband, Manoah, did not believe her. Then the stranger came again. Manoah presented an offering of food. By a miracle, the stranger set it alight – and vanished.

Even so, the wonder Manoah felt at this display of power was nothing compared to his joy when, a few short months later, he and his wife did indeed have a son. They named him Samson. He grew up tall and strong, with dark hair that grew to his waist.

Samson's riddle

❧

SAMSON KNEW HE was strong. He also knew that his parents adored him. He grew up expecting always to have his own way.

One day, he met a Philistine girl. "I want to marry her," he told his parents. "You've got to arrange it for me."

His parents were unhappy. They wrung their hands and fretted. "It would be so much better to marry one of our own people," they argued.

"No," said Samson. "I know who I want to marry. I like her, and that's all that matters to me." He folded his arms and glared at his parents moodily.

"All right, all right, we will go to meet her," agreed his father.

The three of them set out for where she lived. As they walked through some vineyards, they heard a lion roaring.

"I'll go and see if I can find it," cried Samson. He went leaping over the vines in the direction of the sound. He grabbed the animal and killed it with his bare hands. Then he came sauntering back as if nothing had happened.

The rest of the visit was a great success. Samson was even more convinced about how much he liked the young Philistine girl. It was all arranged between the two families that Samson should marry her. A few days later, as Samson was going to make her his bride, he went to find the lion carcass again. "Who would have thought of that!" he laughed. "A swarm of bees inside, and honey in the honeycomb. That's unusual!"

Then he went on to the girl's house, where he and his father were giving the wedding banquet.

In the midst of the partying, Samson asked a riddle. "Here's a challenge for all you Philistine men," he laughed. "I bet you each a piece of the best linen and a change of the finest clothes if you answer it before this week of festivity is over. If you can't, you each have to give me the same prize. What's the answer to this riddle? 'Out of the eater, something to eat; out of the strong, something sweet.'

"Keep thinking! I'll give you seven days to guess the answer."

*Dear God,
When parents
and children
are not in
agreement,
help them
to find good
solutions.*

*Dear God,
May I learn to
understand
the curious
ways in which
the story of
your people can
unfold.*

Samson's war

🐋

FOR THREE DAYS the Philistines thought about Samson's riddle. It had left them completely puzzled.

On the fourth day, they went to Samson's wife. "You've got to get him to tell you the answer," they threatened, "or… let's just say that something very nasty will happen to your family."

She went to Samson in tears and begged him to tell her. "I haven't told anyone," he replied. "Not my father, not my mother… and I won't tell you."

The young woman wept and pleaded and fretted and nagged. After seven days of this behavior, Samson gave in. "Stop fussing and listen," he said. "It all has to do with my killing a lion. A swarm of bees came and made a home in the carcass. That's all it is. Now leave me alone!"

Samson's wife went and told the Philistine men.

They went and swaggered up to Samson: "About the riddle," they said. "What could be sweeter than honey? What could be stronger than a lion?"

Samson stared at them, anger welling up inside. He knew that his wife must have told them. In a rage, he stormed off to one of the five great Philistine cities. He attacked and robbed thirty people so he could give their clothes to his wedding guests as their prize. Then he left his wife and went back to his own home.

When his temper had cooled, he went to find his wife again. To his dismay, her father had married her to his best man. At once, his anger exploded all over again.

"Don't blame me for what I do next!" he cried.

Not long after, when the Philistines saw their cornfields ablaze and foxes running through them spreading the fire as they went, they were sure of one thing: Samson was behind it all.

In this way, a terrible feud began. It lasted twenty years, and in that time Samson killed many of his people's Philistine enemies.

Samson and Delilah

ONE DAY, SAMSON fell in love with another Philistine woman. She was named Delilah. The Philistine kings were delighted at the opportunity it gave them. They went and pleaded with her.

"You know how much trouble Samson has brought us," they said. "Only you can find out what makes him so strong – and how we can capture him. We will give you a huge reward."

Delilah was tempted by the offer. When she was alone with Samson, she began to wheedle. "Oh, you're so strong. What makes you stronger than anyone else in the world, my love? Could anyone ever tie you up?"

Samson laughed. "Oh, anyone could tie me up easily: seven new bowstrings would do it!"

Delilah passed the message to the Philistines and they gave her the bowstrings she needed. One night, she let some Philistine soldiers into her house and then went and tied Samson up.

"Samson!" she cried. "The Philistines are coming!"

Samson snapped the bowstrings at once. "Where?" he demanded. "Where?"

All he saw was men fleeing into the night. Delilah feigned terror and dismay. Her plot was still secret.

Not long after, she began to complain again. "You lied about the bowstrings," she said. "I wish you wouldn't lie to me."

"You're right, I did make that up," said Samson airily. "You'd need seven new ropes to tie me up."

Once again, Delilah arranged to betray him. She tied Samson with ropes: but when the Philistines came to arrest him, he simply broke free.

Samson laughed at his easy escape. "Look at my long, plaited hair," he said to Delilah. "You'd have to weave it into your loom to hold me down."

While he was sleeping, Delilah wove his hair tightly into her loom. "Samson!" she cried. "The Philistines!"

He jumped up and pulled his hair loose. Not one of the Philistines knew the secret of his strength. Not one of them could even guess.

Dear God,
May I never let
money lure me
into betraying
someone.

Dear God,
When I give my
loyalty, may I
stay faithful.

Samson the prisoner

❧

I WON'T LET HIM mock me! thought Delilah as she watched Samson sleeping. I'll get his secret, collect my reward and be free of him.

She nagged and nagged and sulked and nagged. 'If you really loved me, you'd tell me what makes you so strong,' she whined.

'Oh, change the subject!' snapped Samson.

Delilah kept nagging. Samson got fed up. 'Listen,' he said. 'Here's the truth. Never ask me again. I was dedicated to God when I was born. My long hair is the sign of it. That's what makes me strong. If my hair is cut, I'll be as weak as anybody.'

Delilah sent a message to the Philistine kings. 'I've found out at last! Come and capture Samson.'

When the Philistines were ready, Delilah lulled Samson to sleep, and a man came and cut his hair off.

Then she shouted: 'Samson – the Philistines!'

Samson leaped up and mocked the soldiers. 'You'll never get me!'

Only this time he was mistaken. The strength that God had given him was gone. The Philistines captured him. They blinded him, put him in chains and threw him into prison.

'Keep your strength up!' they mocked. 'You've got to grind the grain in the prison mill!'

Samson's final deed

❧

T HE PHILISTINES LAUGHED uproariously. 'That's the end of Samson! We should celebrate and thank our god Dagon for giving us the victory.'

They set the day for an extravagant festival. When it arrived, all five Philistine kings came to the temple, along with 3,000 participants. In the holy place, sacrifices were offered.

'We have the victory, Samson is our prisoner, Dagon has saved us!' everyone sang. Soon everyone was enjoying the party with abandon.

'Let's bring Samson here!' someone called. 'Then we can have some fun with him.' The partygoers cheered merrily.

Guards led Samson from the prison. They took him to the front of the temple, where two pillars stood close together. Blind and unsure of what was happening, Samson reached out. As he felt the pillars, he bowed his head. His roughly chopped hair had started to grow and he felt the locks fall forward. Samson remembered that he had been dedicated to God.

'Lord,' he prayed, 'please give me strength just one more time so I can get even with the Philistines.'

Slowly, powerfully, he began to push against the pillars – flesh and blood against cold, hard stone. Could God still help him?

There came a strange roar like the start of a rockfall. The pillars were cracking. They broke and fell.

Samson's final deed killed more of his people's enemies than anything he had done before.

19 March

❖

Judges 16

*Dear God,
If I should ever
be careless and
forget my
promises, may
I learn from my
mistakes and
have the
courage to try
again.*

Dear God,
Help me to
understand the
loneliness of
those who feel
they have no
family to
love them.

The story of Naomi and her family

ра

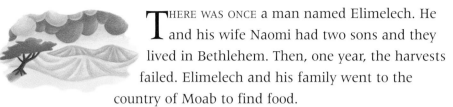

THERE WAS ONCE a man named Elimelech. He and his wife Naomi had two sons and they lived in Bethlehem. Then, one year, the harvests failed. Elimelech and his family went to the country of Moab to find food.

Years went by. They were years of hard work, but at least their toil brought them a living. Elimelech died, but Naomi was comforted by the fact that she still had a family to look after her as she grew old: her sons had both married Moabite girls.

Then both of the sons died without children. Naomi was inconsolable. She had lost all of her blood relatives.

In the midst of the tragedy, news came that the harvest was good in Bethlehem. Naomi decided to go there with her daughters-in-law, Orpah and Ruth. They had not gone very far when Naomi stopped. "It will be better for you to stay with your own people," she said to the young women. "May God bless you. May you both marry again and have a home."

"No, please don't say good-bye; we will come with you," they wept.

"Please do as I say. It is the sensible choice," said Naomi.

Still crying, Orpah kissed Naomi good-bye and went back to her own people. Ruth clung to Naomi.

"Let me go with you," she pleaded. "Your people will be my people, and your God will be my God." She looked up, her eyes glistening with tears.

In the end, Naomi agreed. The older woman and the younger woman walked side by side to Bethlehem. They arrived as the barley was being harvested.

Even though many years had passed, the community had not forgotten one of their own. "Look! It's Naomi!" people exclaimed.

"I was Naomi," came the terse reply, "but that name belongs to the time when life was good. Now I need a new name – something to match my bitter fate."

Ruth's harvest

RUTH DID HER best to take care of Naomi. "We need more food," she said to Naomi one day. "Let me go out gleaning grain. I know it's the custom here to allow the poor to gather the grain the harvesters leave behind."

Naomi agreed to let her go. Ruth got up very early so she would be in the fields as soon as the harvest workers arrived. She walked behind them picking up the heads of grain they had left.

Later, the landowner arrived. His name was Boaz. "Who is that young woman?" he wanted to know.

"She's the Moabite woman who came with Naomi," the workers explained. "She's been working as long as we have."

Boaz went over to her. "Don't pick grain anywhere but in my field," he said. "Stay with the women here. I have given orders that no one must bother you. And help yourself to water from the jars we have filled."

Ruth bowed low and thanked him. She was overawed by his generosity.

"I have heard that you are very kind to Naomi," continued Boaz, "and that you accept the God of Israel as your protector. May God bless you."

Boaz was utterly sincere in his concern. Later that day, he invited Ruth to share the meal that was brought out to the workers. He told the harvesters to be sure to leave plenty of grain for Ruth to gather.

Naomi was delighted when Ruth told her the news. "Boaz!" she exclaimed. "He is related to my husband! He is doing his duty by taking care of us."

Dear God, May I be loyal to any of my relatives who are in need.

87

*Dear God,
May I act in
ways that
everyone can
see are good
and right.*

Naomi's plan

SOME TIME LATER, Naomi decided on a plan. She explained it all to Ruth. "Today, I want you to dress yourself in your finest clothes. Go and hide close to where Boaz and his workers are threshing grain. At the right time, go up to him boldly. Remind him that you are a relative and that he should take care of you. Put him in a situation where he knows he has to marry you."

It was a risky plan: true, it made the most of the local customs about looking after relatives – but if it didn't work, Ruth risked being thoroughly embarrassed. Nevertheless, the young woman could see for herself that it offered the only chance the pair of them might ever have of security. And after all, Boaz had already shown that he was generous and kind. She played her part humbly and bravely.

Boaz was utterly taken aback when she proposed to him. Then he smiled with delight. "I am flattered that you should ask me," he replied. "I know that you are a fine person and everyone speaks highly of you. But did you know there is someone else in Bethlehem who is an even closer relative to Naomi and her family? He must give his permission."

In front of all the town elders, Boaz agreed with Naomi's other relative that the marriage would be right and proper. Boaz soon married Ruth, and they had a son whose name was Obed.

Naomi's friends were happy for her. She had a proper family again – people who loved her and who could look after her when she was old.

Obed became the father of Jesse, and Jesse became the father of David, who would become the most famous king of Israel.

Hannah's prayer

IN THE TIME before Israel had kings, there was a place of worship in Shiloh. A man named Elkanah was among the pilgrims who went there every year to make offerings to God.

His two wives went with him. It was a happy time for one, because Elkanah gave gifts to her and all her children. The festival left the other wife, whose name was Hannah, feeling deeply miserable: she, too, received a gift from her husband – but her one gift seemed so insignificant compared with the presents heaped on the others in the family. They only reminded her of the bitter disappointment in her life: that she had no children.

"Don't cry, Hannah," her husband used to say, "you are very precious to me as you are." But Hannah remained unhappy.

One day when she was feeling particularly sad, she went to the place of worship to pray. She wept as she told God just how unhappy she was. "Please let me have a son," she sobbed. "If you do, I will dedicate him to you for all his life."

The priest, Eli, watched her, and he frowned. Hannah was saying her prayers silently but she was mouthing the words. He could think of only one explanation: the woman had been enjoying the festivities a little too much, and now she was drunk.

"Go away from here until you've sobered up!" he said angrily.

"Please don't think bad things about me," said Hannah, still sniffing. "I've been praying like this because I'm so miserable."

"Oh," said Eli grudgingly. "Then may the God of Israel give you what you have asked for."

Hannah went away, feeling a little bit happier.

Dear God, You can bring joy to those who are sad.

The boy Samuel

*Dear God,
You will be
faithful to those
who are
faithful to you.*

THE FOLLOWING YEAR, Hannah did not go to Shiloh for the festival. She stayed at home to look after her little baby boy, Samuel. She felt happy as never before – she was a mother at last.

Only when Samuel was old enough did Hannah make the journey to Shiloh again. She took her little boy to Eli.

"Do you remember me?" she asked. "I was the woman who was praying so hard you didn't think I was in my right mind. I was praying for a child – and here he is. I promised that if God answered my prayers I would dedicate the child to God. Will you let him stay with you to help look after God's holy shrine?"

Eli welcomed Samuel. Every year Hannah made the pilgrimage to Shiloh and brought her son a new tunic she had made. Every year she noticed how well he was learning his tasks at the place of worship.

However, it soon became all too obvious that Samuel was a better helper than Eli's own sons. One day, another holy man, who was a prophet, came to Eli with a solemn warning: "You have not controlled your sons well enough. They are not fit to be in charge of the shrine after you die. God is going to choose someone else to be a priest – someone who will be faithful to God and God's laws for all his life."

The voice in the night

As Eli grew old and frail, he began to go blind. He had to rely on Samuel to take care of the place of worship.

One night, Samuel was sleeping in the shrine, just by the place where the covenant box was kept. The lamp cast a dim, gold light.

Suddenly, Samuel sat up. Someone had called his name.

He ran to Eli. "Yes, sir," he said. "Here I am!"

Eli was puzzled. "I didn't call you," he said. "Go back to bed!"

Samuel went and lay down. Then he heard his name again. He ran to Eli. "You did call me," he said. "Here I am. What can I do to help?"

"I didn't call last time and I didn't call this time," replied the old man. "Go back to bed and get some sleep."

A third time Samuel heard his name; Samuel was so sure of it, he went to Eli again, even though the old man seemed put out to be disturbed. "It must have been you calling," said Samuel. "There's no one else near the shrine at this time of night."

Only then did the old priest understand.

"Go back to bed," he said gently. "If the voice calls again, say, 'Speak, Lord, your servant is listening.'"

The voice spoke, calm and clear and persistent: "Samuel! Samuel!" The boy replied as Eli had said, and God spoke.

When Samuel heard the message, he hung his head. I dare not tell Eli, he thought to himself.

But in the morning, as Samuel was opening the doors to the shrine, Eli came to ask what God had said and there was no getting out of telling: Eli's sons had been abusing their privileges as priests and helping themselves to the offerings that people brought to the shrine. They were going to reap a dreadful punishment for their wrongdoing.

Eli bowed his head. "The Lord will do whatever is best," he said.

And God did indeed punish Eli's sons. It soon became clear that Samuel was a true prophet of God. Everyone in Israel respected him.

Dear God,
Help me to
know your voice,
and to listen.

91

Dear God,
May I show
respect for that
which is holy.

The power of the covenant box

৵

AROUND THIS TIME, the Philistines went to war against the people of Israel. There was a great battle, and the Israelites lost.

"Let's go get the covenant box from Shiloh," the Israelites agreed. "Then we will be sure that God will help us win!"

They sent messengers, and Eli's sons brought the covenant box into the army camp. All the Israelites cheered, certain as they were of victory.

When the Philistine spies found out why the Israelites were so exuberant, they were dismayed, and they hurried to warn the Philistine army. However, the fearful news gave the soldiers strength. They fought with utter desperation, routed the Israelites and captured the covenant box. Eli's sons were killed, and the news made Eli die of shock.

Triumphantly, the Philistines carried the covenant box into one of their temples. They placed it next to the statue of their god Dagon and marched away gleefully.

The following morning, the statue had fallen on its face. The Philistines set it up again, but the next day, the same thing happened. So they took the covenant box to another city – but wherever the covenant box went, there was some kind of trouble.

In the end, the Philistines knew they must return the covenant box back to Israel. They put it on an oxcart and drove it to the border.

There, in a valley, some Israelites were harvesting their wheat. Something gold glinted in the sunlight. They looked up and saw the shining covenant box.

The entire nation was overjoyed. "We must find a new shrine in which to keep this holy and precious object safe," they agreed. After so much disaster, they knew they must treat it with respect.

The people demand a king

THE PEOPLE OF ISRAEL all respected Samuel as a prophet and a judge. He gave wise advice and settled arguments fairly.

Samuel hoped his two sons would grow up to follow his example. In time, he made them judges too. Sadly, they were only interested in making money. They accepted bribes and did not settle cases honestly.

The leaders of the people went to Samuel. "You are getting old," they explained, "and your sons are not wise and fair like you. We want a king, like the nations all around us."

Samuel was unhappy about this. He prayed to God.

"It is not you they have rejected as leader," said God. "It is me they have rejected as king. Ever since I led them out of Egypt they have gone and worshiped other gods. So warn them what human kings are like, but let them have their way."

Samuel did so. "A king will make big demands," he told them. "He will order your young men to fight in his wars – some in his war chariots, some in the cavalry, some as foot soldiers facing the worst of the charge into battle. Others will have to work on his land, plowing his fields and gathering his crops. Your young women will toil to bring him luxuries – rich meals, delicate pastries and lavish perfumes.

"He will demand a tenth of your own produce in taxes. Your servants, your herds, your flocks – the king will take the portion he wants. In the end, you'll be sorry you asked for a king, but God will not help you then."

"We want a king," the people clamored. "A king will lead us to victory in war. That's what we want."

God spoke to Samuel. "Give them a king," said God. "I will tell you whom to choose."

Dear God,
There is no ruler
on earth who is
as wise and
generous
as you.

Samuel meets Saul

❧

*Dear God,
When I am
faced with the
unexpected,
may your
wisdom guide
me and
inspire me.*

S AUL WAS THE son of a wealthy family. He was tall and strong and well able to take his place working the family's land, aided by his father's servants.

One day, two of the family's donkeys wandered away. Saul and a servant went to look for them. They walked many miles without success.

"Let's go and ask the prophet, Samuel," suggested the servant. "He lives around here and he's bound to know: they don't call him a seer for nothing."

The young men hurried off to find him, little suspecting that Samuel was already expecting visitors: God had told him that he was about to meet the future king of Israel.

As they drew near, Samuel heard the voice of God. "This is the man I told you about. He is the one who will rule my people."

In many ways, Saul looked like a king. He was young and strong. He was also taller than everyone else, and very handsome. However, he had not harbored any ambitions of greatness. When Samuel hinted that Saul was going to be chosen for great things, he was astonished.

"I'm nobody," he said, "and my family belongs to the smallest tribe in Israel."

Samuel insisted that Saul come and stay with him. During the visit, he performed the ceremony of anointing: he poured olive oil over Saul's head as a sign that God had chosen him to be king. It left Saul more puzzled than ever.

"Listen," explained Samuel. "Everything is going to turn out as I say. First, you are going to meet some people who will tell you about the donkeys: they have been found. Later, you are going to meet some prophets who will come along the road singing and dancing. God's spirit will fill you, just as it fills them, and God will change you from the inside."

Everything Samuel said came true. The people who saw Saul singing and dancing began to whisper: "Has Saul become a prophet? What is going to happen next?"

Long live the king!

S AMUEL CALLED ALL the people of Israel to a great ceremony. "God is going to choose your king," he said. "I will cast lots. God will direct how they fall and you will see who is chosen."

First he cast lots to find out from which tribe the king was to come: the choice fell on the smallest tribe – the tribe of Benjamin.

Then he cast lots to find out from which family the king was to come: the choice fell on the family of Matri.

Finally he cast lots to find out which man from that family was to be king: the choice fell on Saul, son of Kish.

"Bring him here to me!" announced Samuel.

Astonishingly, Saul had gone missing. His relatives hunted everywhere but without success. The crowd began to murmur. "Samuel must be mistaken. Surely there must be someone else who is fit to be king."

But Samuel remained unmoved, and the search continued. At last, Saul's relatives found him hiding among the baggage that they had brought for the journey. They led him to the front of the crowd.

"Here is the man the Lord has chosen!" announced Samuel, his voice ringing like a silver trumpet. "There is no one else among us like him."

All the people shouted joyfully, "Long live the king!"

Dear God, Please direct me in the choices I make.

95

*Dear God,
Help all the
rulers of the
world to know
the right way
to overcome
wicked people.*

Saul goes to war

WHAT IS A KING supposed to do? Israel had never had a king before – and the job had simply been thrust upon Saul.

He went back home to the family's land. There was plowing to be done: he knew how that was done – he had been brought up to do it.

One day, as he was coming back home with the oxen, some messengers arrived. They were desperate for help – they needed to call on a leader who could demonstrate power and courage.

"The king of Ammon is threatening our people in Gilead," they said. "He besieged the town of Jabesh and was certain to defeat it. The men of that city asked to make a peace treaty, but the king demanded the most awful conditions. He agreed to make peace only if he was allowed to blind every man in one eye. He simply wanted to disgrace our nation.

"You are our king, the king of Israel. Surely you are not going to let such a terrible thing happen."

At once, Saul knew that God had chosen him to defend his people. Fired with anger, he sent messengers throughout the land of Israel commanding people to join his new army. Many thousands came, all ready to fight.

In the dark of night, Saul led his army into their battle positions. At dawn, the raid began – fierce, violent and determined.

By the time the noonday sun was high in the sky, Saul and his men had routed the Ammonites.

"Saul is truly our king," the Israelites cheered. "Did anyone say they didn't want him to be king? Bring them here to be punished!"

"No one will be punished today," announced Saul, "for this is the day the Lord has rescued Israel."

Then Saul and Samuel and all the people went to their holy place at Gilgal to thank God for the victory and to celebrate.

Samuel's warning

❧

EVERYONE IN ISRAEL was delighted at Saul's victory. Everyone was delighted to have a king.

Except, it seemed, for Samuel. He stood up to give a long speech.

"I'm an old man now," he began, "old and gray. I've been your leader from the time I was young, and have I ever done wrong? If anyone can think of some way in which I've wronged them, then let them speak."

"No, no, you have never done wrong," came the cry.

"As God is our witness?"

"As God is our witness!"

"Now let me remind you of the story of our people and our God," said Samuel. He talked about Moses and Aaron and the escape from Egypt. He talked about the times the nation had worshiped other gods and about the disasters that had followed. He talked about the great leaders God had sent to rescue the nation – men such as Gideon and… and, well, Samuel himself.

"It's the dry season now," said Samuel. "I will show you that you sinned against God by asking for a king. I'm going to ask God to send rain."

Samuel prayed. The sky went dark and storm clouds billowed in. Thunder rolled and rumbled overhead.

"Don't be afraid," Samuel called out. "God has made you a promise and will never leave you. I will pray for you and I will teach you what is the good and right thing to do. Obey the Lord; serve the Lord faithfully and with all your heart."

It was a strange message for the kingmaker to give, and it signaled trouble ahead.

Dear God, May I learn what is good and right; may I be faithful in doing it.

*Dear God,
You want
obedience
more than
anything.*

Saul the warrior

ﻼ

KING SAUL BECAME famous as a warrior. He fought like a hero. He led his soldiers courageously. He defended his people fearlessly.

Yet Samuel, who had proclaimed him king, seemed grudging in his support. Saul felt he could not rely on the aging prophet for advice, and he began to decide for himself what to do and what not to do.

The relationship between the two grew more and more uneasy. Then Samuel brought a new message from God. "Go to war against our old enemies, the Amalekites," he told Saul. "Destroy everything they have. Do not keep any of their wealth for yourself."

The warrior king undertook a bold campaign and defeated the Amalekites completely. However, he did not follow the rest of Samuel's instructions: instead, he brought back the finest sheep and cattle.

When Samuel found out, he went to remonstrate with Saul.

"I hear mooing," he said to Saul sternly, "and bleating. Why is that?"

"I kept the best animals we captured," replied the king. There was doubt in his voice. "But only to offer to God."

Samuel scowled. "What do you think God prefers," he asked, "offerings or obedience? This is the end: God has rejected you as king."

He turned and left. It was a final parting.

David, son of Jesse

❧

SAMUEL SIGHED DEEPLY. Even though he knew God was speaking to him, he felt downhearted.

"Don't be sad," said God. "It's time to stop fretting about Saul. Go to Bethlehem, to the house of a man named Jesse. I have chosen one of his sons to be the next king."

"I can't do that!" replied Samuel. "Saul is still king. If he hears that I have chosen someone else to replace him, he will kill me."

"Simply say you are going to hold a religious ceremony for the people of Bethlehem," said God. "While you are there, I will show you who is to be the next king of Israel."

Samuel did as God said. Taking care to reassure the town elders that his visit held no sinister meaning, he nevertheless made quite sure that Jesse and all his family were properly included in the ceremonies. As they arrived, he saw a tall and handsome young man standing next to Jesse. "That must be the one," said Samuel to himself.

"Pay no attention to what the person looks like," said God. "Human beings judge one another by what they see on the outside. I look at the heart – the true person inside."

Samuel asked to meet all of Jesse's sons. One by one, he met not only the young man he had first seen but also his six brothers. They were all striking young men, but in his heart Samuel knew he had not yet found the one he was seeking. "I don't believe any of these is God's chosen one," he said to Jesse. "Have you no more sons?"

"There is still the youngest," replied Jesse, somewhat carelessly, "but he is just a boy; right now, he is out taking care of the sheep."

"I would like to meet him," said Samuel firmly, and Jesse sent for him. Even on the outside, David was impressive. He was strong and handsome, and his eyes sparkled. More than that, Samuel was convinced that David was the one whom God had chosen because of his character.

There, in front of his brothers, Samuel anointed him the future king of Israel.

*Dear God,
It is not what
I look like
that matters to
you, but who
I am.*

*Dear God,
Thank you for
music that
makes us
joyful.*

David the musician

KING SAUL WAS a troubled man. Looking after the kingdom of Israel gave him many things to worry about. He no longer had Samuel to advise him. Sometimes he fell into despair. Then even his waking hours felt like one long nightmare.

His servants wanted to help him. "Allow us to look for someone who can play the harp sweetly. The music will soothe you."

"Go ahead, find someone," replied Saul fretfully.

"I suggest David, son of Jesse, from Bethlehem," said one of his attendants. "He is a very good musician. He is also brave, handsome and a good soldier. God has truly blessed him."

Saul agreed, and he sent messengers to Jesse.

The father called for David, who was out looking after the sheep. "King Saul has asked you to go to help him," he said. "When you go, you must take these gifts from our farm."

David arrived at Saul's house with a goat, a donkey loaded with bread, and a leather bottle of wine.

Servants greeted him and led him to where Saul was. Then David began to play his harp.

The melody floated in the air like birdsong on a summer morning. Saul felt as if he had been set free from all the things that worried him.

From then on, whenever dark and troubling thoughts came to Saul, he would send for David and his music.

Goliath the Philistine

ONE DAY, THE Philistines launched yet another attack on the Israelites. King Saul lined up his army to fight them. Among the ranks were the eldest three of Jesse's sons. The people were as ready to do battle as they were ever going to be, and David was allowed to return to his father and his everyday work as a shepherd.

Saul's army gathered on a hilltop. They could see the Philistine army, which had lined up just across the valley. The tips of the soldiers' spears shone in the sunlight. The Israelites could see gleaming bronze and newly sharpened iron.

As they stood, trying to prepare themselves to fight the better-equipped Philistines, an enemy soldier strode out.

"Oh no," whispered the Israelite soldiers. "Look how tall he is. That must be their great fighter, Goliath. Look at his battle gear! Look at his spear and javelin!"

Goliath shouted across the valley. "Slaves of Saul!" he jeered. "Who dares to fight me? One-on-one combat – a fight to decide the whole war! Come on!"

There was no response. Goliath laughed mockingly before striding back to the Philistine ranks.There was not going to be any fighting that day.

The following morning, the armies once more made ready. Goliath came out again. He roared his challenge. He hurled insults. He went back to his fellow soldiers.

This went on for forty days. Back in Bethlehem, Jesse grew worried.

"David," he said to his youngest son. "Your brothers in the army will need more supplies. Take this food, and come back with news."

David set off cheerfully. He arrived just as the armies were getting into battle position. He ran to see what was happening, expecting a fight. Then Goliath came out, mocking and challenging. David watched in dismay as the Israelites began to run away.

Dear God, May I not be dismayed by mocking and insulting words.

101

David goes into battle

*Dear God,
May the tasks
I do every day
make me ready
to do greater
things.*

DAVID WAS SWEPT up in the crush of soldiers scrambling to safety. "Day after day we've had to put up with that taunting," explained the soldiers. "No one here thinks they can win… even though King Saul has promised a huge reward to anyone who kills Goliath."

"What reward?" asked David eagerly. "It's not right for that Philistine to get away with his boasts. Surely we have God fighting for us."

David's elder brother heard his bold talk. "Arrogant brat!" he said. "You've just come to watch the fighting."

David simply walked away from the rebuke. "What must I do to accept the challenge?" he asked everyone. Soon word reached Saul that someone had volunteered to fight the enemy, and he asked to see him.

"Oh," he said, when he saw David. "You're just a boy." He shook his head. "Don't go and kill yourself. Goliath is a professional soldier."

"Your Majesty," replied David, "I'm a shepherd boy. I have to protect my sheep from lions and bears. Sometimes I fight them with my bare hands. If God can save me from wild animals, then God can save me from this Philistine."

Saul was reluctant to let him go. After all, if the boy lost then the Philistines would declare victory. Then again, the Philistines were already the stronger side. Perhaps a battle of two champions would save the Israelites from worse disaster. "If you must, then at least wear my helmet and my battle coat," he said.

David let himself be dressed with leather and metal, but it was too heavy. "I'll go with what I'm used to," he said. He took his shepherd's stick and picked up five pebbles from a stream. Then, with his sling at the ready, he set off to meet Goliath.

David and Goliath

GOLIATH STRODE BOLDLY down the hill. Just one pace ahead walked his shield bearer. Behind, on the hilltop, his fellow soldiers watched eagerly. Goliath gripped his spear and squinted at the fighter who was coming toward him.

"Just a boy!" he sneered. "Almost too pretty to die." Then he roared, "What's that stick for, boy? Do you think I'm a dog? Do you think I'm going to bite you?"

David faced him squarely. "You've got a sword and spear and javelin," he said. "I trust in the God of my people. Today, everyone is going to see that God does not need swords or spears to save Israel."

Goliath strode forward again. David ran toward him. Quick as lightning, he reached into his bag, fitted a stone into his sling and whirled it at Goliath.

His aim was on target. Goliath fell. David took Goliath's own sword and cut off his head.

The Philistines recoiled in horror at the sight. The Israelite army was running forward, whooping with delight. The defeated Philistine army began to run.

When the rout was complete, David was proclaimed a hero! All the people of Israel adored him.

Dear God,
There are no
weapons in
the world
that can
defeat you.

*Dear God,
May I be loyal
to my friends
and brave
enough to
help them.*

David and Jonathan

ॐ

WHEN SAUL SAW how popular David was becoming, he grew jealous.

"My son Jonathan thinks the world of him," he said to himself. "And all the people do too. I must have him killed."

He kept sending David off to battle but the young man always returned victorious.

Saul held a meeting with Jonathan and his officials. "I'm going to kill David," he said. "He's too ambitious."

"No, Father!" argued Jonathan. "He is your best and most loyal soldier."

Saul frowned. He did not have the support he needed for an attempt on David's life. Isolated in his fear of the young rival, he hated David more every day. One day, when David was playing the harp to soothe him, Saul picked up a spear and hurled it at him.

David dodged the weapon and fled. He had no choice but to keep his whereabouts secret. Even so, he had complete trust in Jonathan's loyalty. Soon he found an opportunity to speak to him alone.

"Listen," he said to him. "Tomorrow is the New Moon Festival. Your father, the king, will notice I am missing. When he asks about me, you will know if he is still in a murderous mood."

"I'll come back here and shoot three arrows," agreed Jonathan. "If I tell my servant that the arrows have fallen close, then you can come back to Saul. If I say they have fallen farther away, then you must flee."

At the feast, Saul did indeed notice that David was missing. "What treachery is he plotting?" he growled.

"None!" replied Jonathan, innocently. "He told me he had to go to a family celebration, that's all."

"You mean you're still talking to him?" shouted Saul. "Listen, Jonathan! He's not your friend. He wants to be king after me – instead of you!"

Jonathan slipped away. He shot the arrows to give the warning. Then, when his servant had gone home, Jonathan and David hugged each other good-bye.

David and Saul

KING SAUL WAS a man obsessed. "We must get rid of David! We must get rid of David!" he urged his followers.

David had to live as an outlaw. It was not only the king's men he feared; he had to be careful not to anger the Philistines or any of the other people into whose territory he strayed.

Time passed, and gradually people came to join him. His family were among the first to show their loyalty. People with debts came to escape punishment. The poor came and offered to fight on his side: they hoped that David would become king and make the nation a fairer place to live. David's band of rebels became a force to be reckoned with.

Still Saul came hunting to kill his enemy. One night, when Saul and his men were close to hunting him down in the wilderness, Saul went into a cave to relieve himself. Little did he know that David and his men were hiding right at the back of the same cave.

"Now you can kill your enemy!" David's men whispered.

The young outlaw crept over… but all he did was slice a corner off Saul's cloak before retreating into the shadows.

Saul was starting on his way again when he heard a shout.

"Your Majesty!" called David. He dangled the piece of cloth like a flag. "I could have killed you just now. But I'm not the rebel you think I am. In the end, God will show you the truth."

Saul wept. In his heart, he knew David was right.

*Dear God,
May I not
be too angry
with those
who are angry
with me.*

105

9 April

❖

1 Samuel 25–31

Dear God,
May I never
be driven to
do something
that I know
is wrong.

Saul's defeat

❧

S AUL AND SAMUEL had not spoken in years; even so, news of the prophet's death made the king feel more alone than ever.

He was no longer a successful king. The Philistines were a constant threat. Other raiders came looting and killing. David and his rebel band sometimes sided with Saul's enemies.

Then Saul had an idea. It was the wrong thing to do – it was against God's laws and his own stated policy – but he was desperate.

He had heard of a woman in Endor who could summon up the dead. One dark night, Saul disguised himself and went to ask for her help.

The woman was suspicious, but at last she agreed to demonstrate her powers, and so she began her rituals. As she swayed and muttered, she suddenly understood. "You're King Saul!" she screamed. "You tricked me!"

"Don't be afraid," pleaded Saul. "Just tell me if you can see anyone from the realms of the dead. It's vital – for me, for the nation – for all of us."

"I see an old man in a cloak," she wailed, and Saul knew it was Samuel.

"Help me," he begged the prophet. "The country is torn apart by war. God does not speak to me. What shall I do?"

Samuel was stern. "You have disobeyed God," he said. "Tomorrow, the Philistines will defeat you and your sons. David will be the next king."

Samuel's words came true. By the next nightfall, the Philistines had killed Saul and Jonathan and many of the Israelite army.

David's city

Wᴴᴇɴ Dᴀᴠɪᴅ ʜᴇᴀʀᴅ the news that Saul and Jonathan were dead, he wept bitterly. The loyalty and friendship he had shown had been completely genuine. However, when the grieving was done, he was determined to establish himself as the next king.

His ambitions did not find a great deal of support. In fact, only the little tribe of Judah was ready to accept him. David made his home among them, in a town called Hebron.

Neither Saul's family nor the leaders of his army wanted to let go of power. Determinedly, they went to war against David. It was only after many years, when much blood had been shed, that all the tribes of Israel agreed that David was the best person to lead and defend them. He wanted to establish his rule clearly and decisively.

"Hebron is not the best place for me to rule all of Israel," said David to himself. "The hilltop fortress of Jebus is where I want to build a royal city. It is a notable landmark – it will be a fine symbol of my authority."

The Jebusites felt sure they were safe from attack: the hillside was steep and their city walls were strong. They had not reckoned with David – and all the cunning he had learned in his years as an outlaw.

David called his bravest fighting men together. "Who is bold enough to fight the Jebusites?" he asked. "Who is brave enough to take part in a daring attack?"

He explained his plan. Outside the city was a spring of water. It was possible to creep among the rocks into the hillside from which it came. There, the water formed an underground pool, which the Jebusites used as their water supply. A tunnel led up to the city itself.

David's men crept up the tunnel to capture the Jebusite fort. David's city was soon known as Jerusalem, and David set about building a royal palace there.

Dear God, May I try to bring quarrels to an end, not lengthen them.

A royal city

*Dear God,
May I learn
to treat what
is holy with
respect.*

DAVID BELIEVED WITH all his heart that his people were God's people. He wanted his royal city to be God's city.

"We are God's people because of the covenant God made with us long ago," he announced. "We must bring the covenant box to Jerusalem."

David and the people went to the place where it had been kept and loaded it onto an ox cart. Then, in a great procession, they began the journey to the city. Everyone danced and sang. Musicians played lively melodies on harps and lyres to a noisy rhythm of drums, rattles and cymbals.

Suddenly, the oxen stumbled. Someone reached out to steady the Box, forgetting how holy it was. He fell down dead.

At once the celebration stopped. David himself was afraid to bring the covenant box into the city. He took it to the house of a man named Obed Edom while he reflected on what to do next. Was the tragedy a warning? Should he change his plans?

In the three months that Obed Edom had the covenant box, he prospered. David was reassured. He organized a second procession. David himself led the covenant box into the city. He danced with delight. The people shouted for joy. Trumpets blared.

There in Jerusalem the Box was taken to a new tent of worship – a reminder of the tent that the Israelites had made for the Box in the time of Moses. The celebrations were exuberant and David was generous in providing gifts of food for everyone.

David's kindness

DAVID AND HIS armies won battle after battle. The nation's enemies were driven away. David had ample time to reflect on his success and he was thankful to God for all the blessings he enjoyed.

"I wonder, though," he said to his advisers, "if there is anyone left of Saul's family. I would like to show them special kindness, in memory of my dear friend Jonathan."

There was a servant of Saul's named Ziba, and he was sent to David.

"One of Jonathan's sons is still alive," said Ziba. "His name is Mephibosheth. He is crippled, but he has found a place in someone's household."

"Bring him to me," said David.

Mephibosheth, son of Jonathan and grandson of Saul, came to David and bowed low. What was the king thinking? Did he see him as a rival for the throne, in spite of his obvious frailties?

"Don't be afraid," said David. "I am simply going to give you the land that belonged to Saul. I am making Ziba and all his household your servants, just as they were servants to Saul. The land will provide for all of you.

"More than that, you will always be welcome as an honored guest at my table."

Dear God, May I remember to be kind even to those who were once my enemies.

109

*Dear God,
May I always
remember the
responsibilities
I have to
others.*

David and Bathsheba

THE USUAL TIME for kings to go to war was the spring. One particular year, David sent his armies to fight their enemies, but he himself stayed in Jerusalem.

Late one afternoon, he was strolling on his rooftop terrace. He could see into other people's houses… and he saw something that he found very enticing – a beautiful young woman was having a bath.

He soon realized that just having a good view of the scene was not enough for him.

"I want to know more about that woman," he whispered to a servant. "Send someone to find out who she is."

The reply came swiftly. The woman's name was Bathsheba. She was the wife of one of his most loyal soldiers, Uriah.

Desire for the woman made David reckless. He didn't want to think of loyalty or responsibility. He had decided he wanted to sleep with Bathsheba, and ordered that she be brought to him.

Not long after he had forced his attentions on her, Bathsheba sent David a message: she was pregnant, and the child could only be his.

"This is disaster," muttered David to himself. "If this news is leaked to anyone beyond my immediate circle, I will be in total disgrace. And then what would happen to my authority?"

Hurriedly, he made a plan. He ordered Uriah to come home – and Uriah was, as ever, perfectly willing to follow orders. "I'll stay in the palace, with the guards," he told the king. "I can't go and sleep with my wife. It's not right for a soldier to be distracted in this way in the middle of the fighting season."

Try as he might, David could not find a way to hide the fact that Bathsheba was pregnant and Uriah couldn't be the father.

In desperation, he ordered his commanders to send Uriah into the thick of battle… and then abandon him.

In spite of his strength and bravery, Uriah was killed. Bathsheba wept for him. David ordered her to come to the palace and become one of his wives.

Nathan's story

*Dear God,
If I do
something
wrong, help me
to confess it
and be sorry.*

THERE WAS A PROPHET in David's kingdom whose name was Nathan. God told him everything that had happened in the royal court. He knew in his heart that God was telling him to go to David.

"Listen," said the prophet to the king. "I have a story to tell. There were two men who lived in the same town. One was rich, and the other was poor. The rich man had many cattle and countless sheep. The poor man had just one little lamb.

"He really loved that lamb. It became a pet for his children. He fed it from a cup and cuddled it on his lap.

"Then, one day, a visitor arrived at the rich man's house. He knew he would have to give him a meal, but he didn't want to kill any of his own animals. Instead, he took the poor man's lamb and cooked it."

"That's terribly wrong!" cried David. "A serious injustice. Tell me – is this story true? That rich man deserves to die. He must repay the poor man four times over."

Nathan listened patiently as David gave his judgment. He paused. He looked the king straight in the eye.

"You are that man," he said. "God made you king. You had riches and many wives. But you stole Uriah's wife and had him killed. There will be punishment for this."

David's jaw dropped as the truth finally hit him, and his heart sank. He had betrayed the God whom he loved and trusted. "I have sinned," he wept.

*Dear God,
When I
confess the
wrong I have
done, make
me joyful.*

Sorrow and joy

WHEN DAVID SANG, his listeners always understood the deep feeling in the words. When David realized the grave wrong he had done, his song of sorrow was the most emotional of all.

*Be merciful to me, O God,
because of your great love.*

*Wash away all my evil,
make me clean from my sins.*

*I know that I have done wrong,
I have done wrong all my life.*

*You are right to condemn me.
I bow to your great judgment.*

*I am deeply sorry;
my sorrow breaks my heart.*

*Give me a new heart, O God,
one that is pure and loyal.*

*Lift me up; make me joyful,
and I will praise you.*

Bathsheba had already given birth to David's son, but the child who had been so wrongly conceived died young. David was deeply upset.

However, David's wife Bathsheba conceived and bore another son. David named this second child Solomon, and was delighted with him. Solomon was a bright and inquisitive boy; it seemed that God had blessed him with exceptional intelligence and wisdom.

Absalom's rebellion

❖

MEANWHILE, THE CHILDREN David had by other wives were growing up. Among them was Absalom. He was very handsome – and famous throughout the land for his long, dark hair.

He was also an angry young man. His half brother, Amnon, had seriously assaulted Absalom's sister and left her depressed. Since the attack, she had lived as a recluse in Absalom's house. Both Absalom and his father were furious at the crime, but David exacted no punishment. Absalom grew so angry that he took revenge himself – and killed the wrongdoer.

The whole affair left the royal household in utter turmoil. David was so distressed by Amnon's murder that he was slow to forgive Absalom. For three years the young man had to find refuge in another royal household. In that time, his loyalty to his father crumbled. Even when he was invited back to Jerusalem, he had little respect for the aging monarch.

As time passed, Absalom grew even more bitter and even more ambitious.

"I think I'd be a better king than my father," he said to himself. "I shall go and take my place at the city gates. People go there to have disputes settled by the king or one of his judges. I shall side with everyone who has a complaint, and then point out that the king has not sent a judge to help them. In that way, people will begin to look to me for leadership."

After some years, Absalom knew he had many followers. He left Jerusalem, declared himself king and gathered an army. Then he came back to claim the city.

David and his supporters fled.

Dear God, Listen to the cries for help of those whose families are in turmoil.

113

Dear God,
May I always
be determined
to resist
wickedness;
but may I
never become
brutal.

The war between father and son

❧

THE DAY CAME when the armies of Absalom and the armies of David lined up against each other. Before the battle, David spoke to his commanding officers, and all the troops heard what he said: "Whatever happens today, I don't want Absalom hurt. For my sake, don't harm him. That's an order."

All too soon, the fighting was under way, and the bloodshed was appalling. David's army got the upper hand and they chased Absalom's men as they tried to flee. Absalom himself jumped onto a mule and rode into the forest to escape.

As he crashed though the undergrowth, a group of David's men sprang an ambush. The mule bolted. Absalom's long hair caught in the branches of a tree – and held him there.

One of the soldiers raced to tell his commanding officer, Joab.

"Why didn't you kill the rebel?" shouted the officer. "I'd have given you a handsome reward – ten pieces of silver."

The man was shocked. "I wouldn't kill Absalom for a thousand pieces of silver," he replied. "We all heard the king's command. If I had disobeyed, you wouldn't have stood up for me!"

Joab spat dismissively. He swaggered off to the place where Absalom was trapped and smiled gloatingly. Then, with careful deliberation, he plunged three spears into Absalom's body. He nodded to the soldiers who stood nearby. "Finish him off, men," he said.

The news of Absalom's death broke David's heart. He wept for his son, as any father would. Even so, his tears made Joab angry.

"Stop this nonsense," he told David. "That boy of yours was a murderer and a rebel. We needed to take action against him – and it was costly to other families. He's not the only young man to have died in this affair. You should go out and publicly thank those who supported you," he said.

David recognized his duty. As he made his way back to Jerusalem, he tried to make friends with as many people as possible. His task now was to reunite the nation.

A song of thanksgiving

❧

KING DAVID, THE great warrior, defeated all his enemies. He knew that God had blessed him. He sang a song of victory – a song of thanksgiving.

The Lord is my protector,
my strong fortress.
God is my protection,
my shield, my defender.

Death threatened me on every side
like a stormy sea;
Destruction was rolling in
like the ocean tide.

I called to the Lord in my time of trouble.
In the holy temple, God heard my cry.

O Lord, you are faithful to those who are faithful to

You protect me,
you save me,
you give me victory.

O Lord, I will praise you.
Praise the Lord.

Dear God,
Be my shield
and my
defender.

115

*Dear God,
Surround me
with your
goodness
and love.*

The Lord is my shepherd

ॐ

MUSIC HAD ALWAYS been a joy for David. From being a shepherd boy who played music for the sheer joy of it, he was now able to command the talents of the nation's finest musicians to fill his court and his ceremonies of worship with melody and rhythm.

He loved composing his own songs and singing them. He wanted to create a new song – one that would help his people understand more about God's love – the God who had led them through times of war to times of peace. Then the memories of his boyhood gave him the idea he needed:

*The Lord is my shepherd; I have everything I need.
The Lord lets me rest in fields of green grass;
the Lord leads me to pools of fresh water.
The Lord gives me new strength, and leads me in the way I should go.*

*Even in times of darkness and trouble, I will not be afraid, O Lord.
You are always with me; you wield your shepherd's staff to protect me.*

*You prepare a feast for me, and welcome me as an honored guest.
My enemies watch in awe as you fill my cup to the brim.*

*I know that your goodness and love will be with me all my life
and your house will be my home as long as I live.*

A king to follow David

GOD HAD MADE David a great king. However, as the years went by, the man who had been fierce in battle grew weak and frail.

The prophet Nathan knew that the future of the kingdom needed to be made safe. He went to explain the whole situation to Bathsheba. "One of David's sons, Adonijah, is already plotting to put himself in power," he said. "If you and your son Solomon want to stay alive, you and I must act together."

Bathsheba readily agreed to his plan and soon she went to plead with David.

"Remember your promise," she said. "You said that our son Solomon would be the next king. Now I hear that Adonijah is claiming power. You must declare Solomon to be your chosen king and hold a ceremony at which the priests anoint him. Then everyone will know that he is the one you have chosen."

David saw the wisdom in her plan. He quickly arranged for Solomon to be declared king, and all the people came and bowed down to him.

Then David called Solomon to see him.

"It is time for me to die," he said. "Be confident and determined, and do what God tells you to do. Obey the laws that God gave us in the time of Moses. Take care to deal with our enemies and show mercy to those who have been our friends. Then you will prosper and our family will rule this kingdom forever."

Not long after, Solomon inherited David's kingdom. Without flinching, he got rid of Adonijah and his supporters. He was determined to rule supreme.

Dear God, Help me to achieve my ambitions without forgetting your laws.

Solomon's dream

*Dear God,
Give me the
wisdom to
understand the
difference
between good
and evil.*

W HEN SOLOMON BECAME king, there was no temple in Jerusalem. There were many different shrines in the city and the surrounding countryside, and different gods were worshiped at them.

Like his father, David, Solomon loved the God of his people. Like many of the people of Israel, he made offerings at various shrines.

On one occasion, Solomon went to make offerings at a famous shrine outside Jerusalem. In the night, he had a dream. The Lord, the God of Israel, spoke to him. "What would you like me to give you?" asked God.

Solomon thought for a moment before replying. "I am only young," he said, "and yet you have chosen me to rule your people. Make me wise, so I can rule them with justice. Help me to understand the difference between good and evil."

"You have asked for a good thing," replied God. "You did not ask for a long life, or great riches, or the death of your enemies. I will give you the wisdom you want, and also more wealth and honor than any other king. Keep my laws, and I will give you long life too."

When Solomon woke up, he went back to Jerusalem and made offerings to the Lord in front of the covenant box.

Solomon the judge

IT WAS THE KING'S duty to judge in difficult disputes. One day, two women came to see King Solomon.

"We want you to decide our quarrel," announced one, trying to sound calm.

"And give me back my baby – which this evil woman says is hers," interrupted the other.

"It's MY baby," wept the first. "I know it's terrible that you woke up to find yours dead. But that doesn't mean you can take my child and leave me with a corpse. I know the boy is mine."

"He's my darling baby boy," wailed the second. "Every mother knows her own child. Do you not care that you're breaking my heart?" Her voice rose to a shriek and tears rolled down her cheeks.

"THE BABY IS MINE!" cried the first.

And so the argument went on. Solomon looked from one to the other as they screamed and fought over who should keep the baby.

At last he spoke. "You each make the same case," he said, "with equal passion. So I shall decide equally." He whispered an order, and a guard came to him bearing a sword that had been filed to glittering sharpness.

"Cut the child in two," ordered Solomon. "Each woman can have half."

"NO! NO! NO!" One woman flung herself to the ground. "No. Give him to her. Do anything, but don't kill him."

The other woman stood still as a statue. "Go ahead with the judgment," she said.

Solomon raised his arm to stop the guard. "Give the baby to the first woman," he said. "She is the real mother."

When the people of Israel heard of this decision, they were all filled with respect for their king. They recognized that his wisdom could only come from God.

Dear God, Help me to know the difference between truth and lies.

1 Kings 4,
Proverbs 10, 12, 17,
Ecclesiastes 12

Dear God,
May I choose
to do the right
thing in every
detail of
my life.

Sayings of Solomon

KING SOLOMON WAS famous for his learning as well as his wisdom. He had been curious about everything since he was a boy, and through his growing-up years he had made careful observations of the natural world. People were astonished at how much he knew about trees and plants, animals and birds, reptiles and fish.

Like his father before him, he wrote beautiful songs. He wrote more than a thousand, including love songs that were full of tenderness.

He composed some 3000 proverbs – wise sayings to guide people in their everyday life, and many books were credited to him. Here are some proverbs which he may have written:

Good people are remembered as a blessing,
but the wicked will soon be forgotten.

Thoughtless words can wound as deeply as any sword,
but wisely spoken words can heal.

Being cheerful keeps you healthy.
It is slow death to be gloomy all the time.

Solomon's Temple

THERE WAS ONE thing in particular that Solomon wanted to achieve during his reign. It was to complete the project his father David had dreamed of: to build a temple that would be a fitting replacement for the tabernacle of old.

"My father, David, brought the covenant box to Jerusalem," he announced. "However, he was always busy with wars and fighting. He did not have time to build a temple to house it. Now that the nation is at peace, I want to build one: a permanent building where our nation can worship God."

It was clear to everyone how they should go about designing the Temple: it needed to follow the same design as the tabernacle. However, the materials used were to be more splendid by far. The building was made of stone and pine and cedar, and the whole of the inside was clad in pure gold. The innermost room was called the Most Holy Place: here, two golden statues of fantastical creatures stood with outstretched wings. They would shelter the covenant box itself. In the outer room, the tables and incense burners were all covered in gold. Five golden lampstands stood on either side, and their lamps would cast a flickering golden light for the priests as they performed the rituals of worship. Everything was designed to evoke the majesty and the holiness of God.

Dear God, May I stand in awe of your majesty and holiness.

121

*Dear God,
In your
home in
heaven, hear
my prayer.*

Solomon's prayer

WHEN EVERYTHING WAS ready, Solomon summoned all the leaders of the people of Israel to Jerusalem. In a great ceremony, the priests carried the covenant box to the Temple. Inside it were the two stone tablets that Moses had put there at Mount Sinai. Upon them were written the great laws – the ones the people had to follow in order to keep their side of the agreement with God.

When the rituals were complete, a cloud filled the Temple. It shone with the dazzling light of God.

Then, in front of all the people, Solomon raised his arms and prayed:

"Lord God of Israel, there is no god like you in heaven above or on earth below! You keep your covenant with your people and show them your love when they live in wholehearted obedience to you.

"But can you, O God, really live on earth? Not even all heaven is large enough to hold you, so how can this Temple that I have built be large enough?

"Listen to my prayer, and grant the requests I make to you today. Watch over this Temple day and night, this place where you have chosen to be worshiped. Hear me when I face this Temple and pray. Hear my prayers and the prayers of your people when they face this place and pray. In your home in heaven, hear us and forgive us."

The celebrations for the new Temple were both solemn and exuberant. There was feasting and festivity for seven days. The people gave thanks to God for the many blessings they enjoyed, and they praised their great king, Solomon.

When the noisy ceremonies were over, God came and spoke quietly to Solomon. "I have heard your prayer. If you continue to obey my laws faithfully, then I will protect the Temple for all time. But if you or your descendants turn away from me, then it will become a pile of ruins."

The visit of the queen of Sheba

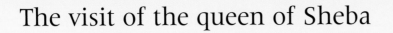

26 April

❖

1 Kings 7, 10

IN THE YEARS that Solomon was king, the land of Israel prospered. No one benefited more than Solomon himself. His own subjects paid taxes from the produce of their farms, while foreign merchants paid in gold to be allowed to do business within his territory. Defeated nations were forced into slavery and then put to work on his grand building projects.

Among these grand enterprises was Solomon's own palace. All the materials used were of the finest: stone from distant quarries, and cedar shipped from Lebanon. The staterooms were an architectural marvel: long, wide and high, and supported by rows upon rows of columns.

Solomon's throne was especially grand. It had six steps leading up to it, with a lion at each end of every step. At the back of the throne was the figure of a bull's head, and beside each arm was the figure of a lion. Nowhere in the world was there a throne like it.

People heard of Solomon's fame and came from far and wide to admire his kingdom. Every one of the celebrated visitors who came brought wonderful gifts. Among them was the queen of Sheba, who arrived in a great procession. She had many servants to wait on her. Her camels were laden with spices and jewels and gold. In spite of her own wealth, she was in awe of what she saw.

"I had heard you were both wealthy and wise," she said, "but what I see is even more impressive. Truly, your God has blessed you."

Dear God,
May I never
love money so
much that I
forget the needs
of others.

*Dear God,
May I never
allow others to
persuade me
to forget my
promises.*

The end of Solomon's reign

🐚

AT THE TIME of the Temple celebrations, Solomon was sincere in his devotion to God. However, as the years went by, he became distracted by all the demands of ruling a powerful kingdom, and he ceased obeying God's commandments. He turned his attention to enjoying the many luxuries that power and money could buy. He married many wives, and surrounded himself with hundreds of beautiful women. Some of them were foreign princesses, and he was happy to build shrines where they could worship their own gods.

He himself began to worship at the same shrines.

God was angry with Solomon. "You have broken your covenant with me," said God. "You have disobeyed my commands. For this reason, your family will not inherit your kingdom. Your son will rule in my holy city, Jerusalem, but only one tribe will be loyal to him."

Even while Solomon was still alive, the prophet Ahijah anointed one of Solomon's officials to be the future king. The young man's name was Jeroboam: he was hardworking and honest, and Solomon had promoted him to an important job in his government. When Solomon heard of the anointing, he tried to kill his young rival, but Jeroboam fled to Egypt. Solomon knew that there would be trouble when he died for his own son, Rehoboam.

Jeroboam and Rehoboam

❧

WHEN JEROBOAM HEARD that Solomon was dead, he came back from Egypt. The people of the northern tribes welcomed him as a hero. "We fear that Rehoboam will be as bad as his father," they said. "We no longer want to be taxed so heavily. We no longer want to be forced to work on the king's grand projects. Come with us when we go to talk to him."

So Jeroboam and the people of northern Israel went to plead with Rehoboam. "If you make life easier for us, we will be your loyal subjects," they announced.

Rehoboam asked them to give him three days to decide on his answer. He went to ask the old advisers who had served in his father's court. "Give them what they want," the old men warned him. "Then they will serve you."

"That's yesterday's advice," said the young king arrogantly. "I shall go and ask people my own age!"

Rehoboam's young advisers were indignant at what the older men had said. "Don't let the northern tribes think they can order you about," they warned. "Tell them this – if you thought my father was bad, expect worse from me. He beat you with a whip – I'll flog you with a horsewhip!"

Rehoboam went back to the northern tribes with his fighting talk. Crowds had gathered to hear what he had to say. They listened, grim faced.

"Down with David and his family," shouted someone. The crowds took up the chant. "Down with Rehoboam! Down with Rehoboam!"

"We want Jeroboam! Jeroboam for king!"

Rehoboam knew that they were ready to fight and to kill. He jumped into his chariot and escaped to Jerusalem. There, the tribe of Judah alone remained loyal to him. It was a tiny kingdom, but determined to survive.

Dear God,
May I never
fool myself
into believing
that your laws
can be treated
lightly.

The northern kingdom

❧

IN THE NORTHERN kingdom of Israel, Jeroboam grew afraid. "I need to defend my kingdom and keep it independent," he said to himself. "I can't afford to let my people go and worship at the Temple in Jerusalem. They might decide to declare their loyalty to Rehoboam, who rules there."

He decided to take matters into his own hands. He made two golden statues of bull calves, and placed one in a shrine at Bethel and the other at Dan. "These are our people's places of worship," he announced. "We will have our own shrines and our own priests."

The prophet Ahijah, who had anointed Jeroboam king, gave a stern warning. "God's laws forbid us to make metal statues to worship," he said. "You have led people astray. Your family will not inherit your kingdom."

The prophet's doom-laden words came true. After Jeroboam, a rival named Baasha seized power. Sadly, he was not faithful to God either, and his son was overthrown by another rival. One faithless king followed another. Within a few generations, the kingdom was ruled by a man named Ahab.

"I just refuse to be bound by all these nonsensical religious laws that date back to goodness knows when," he said to himself. "I need to build alliances with some of the powerful nations around, and that means accepting their traditions too."

To this end he married a foreign princess named Jezebel and started to worship her god, Baal.

"It would only be right to have a temple for Baal in my new capital city, Samaria," he told her, "and in it we can also have a statue of your goddess Asherah."

Jezebel was delighted. She employed hundreds of foreign prophets to organize the temple worship. Then she began to hunt down the prophets who served the God of Israel. Many were killed. It seemed as if there was hardly anyone left who was faithful to God.

The prophet Elijah

❧

A PROPHET NAMED ELIJAH came and stood boldly in front of King Ahab. "I serve the living God of Israel," he proclaimed. "I tell you that there will be no rain for the next two or three years."

Elijah knew that the king would blame him for the coming disaster so, having given his message, he fled to the wilderness. There, by a brook, on the far bank of the River Jordan, God took care of Elijah. Every morning and every evening, ravens brought him food. The brook provided water to drink.

When the brook dried up, God sent Elijah to a town not far away. There he met a widow who was gathering firewood. "Please give me some bread and some water," pleaded Elijah.

"I'm sorry," said the widow. "I have only a handful of flour and a drop of oil. I am collecting this wood so I can bake one last loaf. Then I and my poor son will starve."

"Don't worry," said Elijah. "Please make me a small loaf. You will find you still have enough to make your own bread. If you take care of me, you will have enough flour and oil for as long as this drought lasts."

Elijah's words came true: God provided for all three of them through the dry years. On one occasion, the boy fell ill and died, but God enabled Elijah to work a miracle and bring him back to life.

In this way, Elijah showed he was truly a man of God. Then the time came for him to go back to the king with a message from God.

*Dear God,
Thank you for
the miracles
by which you
take care
of us.*

127

Ahab and Elijah

*Dear God,
Protect those
who dare to go
on doing good
in dangerous
times.*

K ING AHAB WAS getting desperate. Around his home in Samaria, the earth was dry and bare. He called his servant Obadiah.

"Listen! You and I must go and look at every spring and every riverbed. They will be the only places where we can hope to find grazing for the animals. If we fail to find grass, we will have to kill the flocks."

Obadiah had not been searching for long when he met Elijah. He bowed low to the prophet. "Is it really you?" he asked in amazement.

"Yes it is," said Elijah, "and I want you to give a message to the king. Go and tell him that I am here."

"Don't make me do that," replied Obadiah fearfully. "Ahab is very angry about you. If I say you are here and then you go away, Ahab will kill me. I have already risked my life hiding faithful prophets from Queen Jezebel. I took them to secret caves and kept them supplied with food and water. Don't make me do something even more dangerous."

"I'll be waiting for Ahab," said Elijah grimly. "Go and announce that I want to see him."

Obadiah scurried off with the news. Soon after, Ahab came storming out to find the prophet he so despised.

"There you are!" he shouted. "The worst troublemaker in Israel."

"I'm not the troublemaker," replied Elijah. "You are. You disobey God and worship Baal. Now come to Mount Carmel with all the prophets of Baal, and we will see who is the true God of Israel."

The contest on Mount Carmel

Ahab accepted Elijah's challenge. He ordered all the people of Israel to come to watch the contest against the prophets of Jezebel's god.

Elijah addressed the crowd. "Today you must decide whom to worship," he cried. "Here are 450 prophets of Baal: they will sacrifice one bull. I am the only prophet of the God of Israel: I will sacrifice another. We will each pray for fire to burn the sacrifice. Whichever god answers by sending fire is the one to worship."

The prophets of Baal prepared their altar and their sacrifice. They prayed for fire as the sun rose high. They prayed in the noonday heat. As the afternoon wore on, their prayers grew louder and their ritual dancing wilder. No fire came.

"Now watch as I take my turn," announced Elijah. He went and repaired an old altar using twelve stones – one for each of the tribes of Israel. He dug a trench around it. He laid wood on the altar and the sacrifice on top. He ordered servants to bring water and pour it over everything – jar after jar of water, until it filled the trench.

Then he prayed: "O Lord, the God of Abraham, Isaac and Jacob, prove now that you are the God of Israel and that I am your prophet."

The fire came down from heaven. It burned the sacrifice, the wood and the stones. The earth around was scorched.

"The Lord is God!" cried the people.

"Then get rid of these false prophets!" ordered Elijah. The crowd turned on them at once.

Dear God,
May all the
world see the
power of your
goodness and
holiness.

Dear God,
When everything
around me is
going wrong,
may I hear the
quiet whisper
of your voice.

The voice of God

🐦

ONCE THE PROPHETS of Baal had been destroyed, Elijah and his servant went back to the top of Mount Carmel. They waited and they watched. After some time, the servant gave a sudden shout: "I can see a little cloud coming up from the sea."

"Right," said Elijah; "now you must go to King Ahab. Tell him to get in his chariot and ride home before the rain comes."

The storm blew in swiftly. Ahab raced home. He was glad to be in his palace as the drenching rain came hammering down. He sat inside and told his wife, Jezebel, of Elijah's victory over the prophets of Baal.

Jezebel was furious. Grimly she sat down to prepare a message to be delivered at once to Elijah.

"May the gods strike me dead if by this time tomorrow I don't do to you what you did to my prophets."

Elijah paled at the news. He fled for his life.

After a day in the wilderness he sat down in the shade of a tree. "It's all too hard – I wish I were dead," he groaned. Then he fell asleep, exhausted.

An angel woke him. "Come on, you need to eat, "said the angel gently. There, in front of Elijah, was a loaf of bread and a jar of water. The food and drink gave Elijah new strength and he was able to walk to the holy mountain in Sinai.

There, on the mountain where Moses had listened to God, Elijah waited. All at once, he found himself in a furious gale. Then there came an earthquake. Then flames shot into the sky. But God was not in the wind, nor in the earthquake, nor in the fire.

It was when everything fell still that Elijah heard the whisper of a voice. "Go back to Israel," it said, "and do what I ask of you."

Ahab's victory

KING AHAB SOON found that Elijah wasn't his only problem. King Benhadad of Syria launched a violent attack on Ahab's kingdom from the north. He sent messengers demanding total surrender, but King Ahab was not prepared to give in so easily.

"Go and tell King Benhadad that a real soldier does his boasting after a battle, not before it," he said. His words were a declaration of war.

A prophet arrived with words of encouragement. "Don't be afraid of that huge army," he said. "God will give you victory."

The Syrians laughed at the thought of battle with Ahab's small fighting force. They sat in their tents drinking merrily. Ahab's young soldiers seized the opportunity and attacked while their enemies were drunk. King Benhadad was forced to flee for his life.

"Don't be dismayed," his officials reassured him. "The gods of Israel are mountain gods, and so they had the advantage in the place where the battle was fought. We will certainly defeat them next year, when we fight on the plain."

The following spring, King Benhadad and the Syrians launched a second campaign.

A prophet came to Ahab. "Our God is not just a god of the mountains," said the prophet. "You will win, and everyone will know that the God of Israel is the Lord."

Once again, Ahab's army won a clear victory. The king was delighted. He was even more delighted when King Benhadad's officials came to see him. They were dressed in sackcloth and had ropes around their necks. "Our master, King Benhadad, pleads for mercy," they said.

"I'm glad he's alive!" said Ahab. "He's like a brother to me. I am eager to make a treaty with him."

When he had done so, he felt very confident of his wisdom. A prophet came and warned him: "You should not have let your enemy go free. You will pay with your life for this!"

Dear God,
You are the
Lord of the
mountains and
the plains,
and of all the
world.

Dear God,
May I
remember
your
commandment
never to tell
lies about
someone.

Naboth's vineyard

ↄ⃛

DESPITE THE PROPHET'S warning of trouble ahead, King Ahab's victory made him feel very sure of himself. He thought that he should be allowed to do whatever he wanted.

It so happened that there was a vineyard near his palace. It belonged to a man named Naboth. Ahab went to see him.

"Your vineyard would make a very convenient vegetable garden for me," said Ahab to Naboth. "I'll give you a better vineyard in exchange, or you can have the money instead."

"This is my family's property," replied Naboth. "It is simply not right that I should give up my inheritance."

Ahab stormed back to the palace and lay down in his room. He was furious. "No, I don't want anything to eat, and I don't want to talk to anyone," he shouted at the servants.

When his wife, Jezebel, found out the reason for his rage, she was as astonished as she was angry.

"You're the king, aren't you?" she said. "Cheer up. I'll make sure you get that vineyard."

Jezebel's plan was simple. She arranged for Naboth to be falsely accused of wrongdoing. He was declared guilty and stoned to death.

Then she went to Ahab. "Naboth is dead," she announced with evident glee. "The vineyard is yours."

Not long after, Elijah arrived at the vineyard to see Ahab.

"Ah, the enemy is back," sneered Ahab.

"You have done wrong," said Elijah severely. "You have led your people away from God, and God will bring disaster upon you. The kingdom will be taken from you. Your family will be destroyed."

Ahab's death

AHAB WAS DISMAYED at Elijah's rebuke. He tore his royal robes and put on sackcloth. His arrogance turned to humility.

"Because of his change of heart, I will not take the kingdom from him," said God to Elijah. "I will take it from his son after him."

Then, after a couple of years, the king remembered an injustice: the Syrians still held a place called Ramoth. "We must win it back," Ahab told his officials. "Perhaps Jehoshaphat, the king of Judah, will fight with us."

The two kings met, and 400 prophets were summoned to give their advice. "Attack Syria!" they agreed. "God will give you victory!"

King Jehoshaphat remained unsure. "Can't you find another prophet?" he asked. "I need to weigh the advice more carefully."

"Oh, there's one called Micaiah," said Ahab. "He always says exactly what I don't want to hear!"

"Call him," insisted Jehoshaphat.

Micaiah spoke fearlessly to Ahab. "I saw into the royal court of heaven," he said. "I heard God ask the angels how to deceive you so you would be killed at Ramoth. That is what must happen, and that is why the prophets have told you to attack."

"What fanciful nonsense!" sneered Ahab. "We'll go to war anyway." He leaned forward to murmur to Jehoshaphat, "You should fight in your royal robes. I will go in disguise."

Ahab hoped that his disguise would save him, but he was mistaken. By chance, a Syrian soldier shot an arrow that struck King Ahab between the joints of his armor. "Take me away from the fighting," he screamed to his charioteer.

Ahab remained propped up in his chariot while the battle raged. Neither side was strong enough to secure the victory. Evening came, and Ahab's life trickled away in streams of blood.

The soldiers were ordered to go back home.

Ahab's tumultuous reign was over.

Dear God, May I never put others in danger in order to keep myself safe.

Dear God,
May I remember
that it is a
serious mistake
to disrespect
your holiness
and goodness.

King Ahaziah

K ING AHAB'S SON, Ahaziah, had no respect for the God of Israel. Instead, he continued to worship Baal.

One day, he fell from the rooftop balcony of his palace and was seriously hurt.

"Send messengers to the city of Ekron," he pleaded. "Consult the god Baalzebub whom they worship there. I want to know if I will get better."

God sent Elijah to meet the messengers. "Why are you going to consult Baalzebub?" he asked. "Do you think there is no god in Israel? The Lord has this message for the king: 'You will die from your injuries.'"

The messengers went back to Ahaziah. They told him they had met a prophet and what he had said. Ahaziah was dismayed at their news. "What did the prophet look like?" he asked anxiously.

"He was wearing a cloak made of animals' skins and tied with a leather belt," they replied.

"That's Elijah!" exclaimed the king. "Send fifty soldiers to bring him here."

The soldiers went and found Elijah sitting on a hilltop. "Man of God, the king orders you to come down!" they shouted.

"If I am a man of God, then may fire come down from heaven and strike you dead!" replied Elijah.

At once the fire came down.

Another company of soldiers came, and the same thing happened to them.

The third company of soldiers pleaded for mercy. Elijah went with them to the king. "This is what God says," he told him. "You put your trust in Baalzebub. You acted as if there were no god in Israel. You will die."

Not long afterward, Ahaziah died, just as Elijah had warned. His brother Joram became king.

Elijah and Elisha

*Dear God,
May I catch
glimpses of
heaven.*

ELIJAH WAS GETTING old. Already, God had chosen Elisha to be his helper. He was younger, and it was he who would carry on the work of speaking God's message to the nation.

One day, Elijah set out with Elisha, knowing that the journey would be his last. Eventually they reached the River Jordan. Elijah took off his cloak, rolled it up, and struck the water with it. A path opened up through the river, and Elijah and Elisha crossed to the other side.

Elijah turned to speak to Elisha. "Tell me what you want me to do for you before I am taken away."

"Let me have a share of your power, so that I can take your place," replied Elisha.

"That is a difficult thing to give," sighed Elijah. "But if you see me as I am taken away, it is a sign that you will have a share of my power."

They continued to talk as they walked on. Suddenly, horses of fire galloped between them, pulling a chariot of fire. A strong wind whirled around, and Elisha saw Elijah being taken up into heaven.

"You were a father to me! You were the defender of Israel! And now you are gone!" cried Elisha.

He tore his cloak in sorrow. Then he picked up Elijah's cloak, which had fallen from him, and went back to the River Jordan. He rolled the cloak into a bundle and struck the water. A path opened up for him.

Waiting on the other side was a band of prophets.

"The power of Elijah is on Elisha," they cried.

From that day on, Elisha was able to work miracles.

Dear God,
Help me to
understand
that I can
trust in your
blessings.

King Joram

❧

KING JORAM OF ISRAEL was angry. "In the time of my father, King Ahab, the king of Moab knew his place," he raged. "He knew he had agreed to pay us taxes each year. Now he refuses to pay me. I will not let him get away with such impudence!"

King Joram got ready for war. He sent messengers to King Jehoshaphat of Judah, asking him to join him. Jehoshaphat agreed, and the two armies marched through the region of Edom. The king of Edom agreed to go to war on their side too.

After marching for seven days, they ran out of water. There was none left either for the soldiers or for the pack animals.

"We are done for!" said King Joram. "We cannot fight like this. The king of Moab has us at his mercy."

One of his soldiers spoke up: "Elisha is here. He was Elijah's helper."

"Elisha is a true prophet," said Jehoshaphat, and he sounded relieved. "We should go and ask his advice."

The three kings set off to meet the prophet, but Elisha did not look pleased to see them.

"Why should I help you?" he asked Joram. "Why don't you go and ask the prophets your father and mother consulted?"

"Because it is the Lord who has put us at the mercy of the king of Moab," replied Joram.

Elisha scowled. "I will only help you because I respect Jehoshaphat," he replied. "Bring me a musician."

As the musician played the harp, the power of God inspired Elisha.

"Dig ditches in this streambed," he said. "You won't see any rain, but the channel will be filled with water."

The next morning, water came flowing down. The Israelites were able to drink their fill. They were refreshed and ready for battle. When the Moabites attacked, the Israelites defeated them utterly.

Elisha and the poor widow

ONE DAY, A POOR woman went to visit Elisha. "Sir," she said, "my husband has died, and I am a widow. You know yourself that he was a prophet and very faithful to God. Even so, he owed some money, and I cannot pay the debt. The lender is a harsh man: he says he will take my two sons away and sell them as slaves."

"What do you have that is valuable?" Elisha asked her.

"Nothing," she replied, "unless you count a small jar of olive oil."

"Go to those who live near you," said Elisha, "and borrow as many empty jars as you can. Then go inside your house with your sons and shut the door. When you are alone, begin pouring oil from your jar into the borrowed ones. Set each one aside as soon as it is full."

The woman did as Elisha said. The oil did not run out until all the jars were full. Then the woman went back to Elisha to tell him what had happened.

"Sell the olive oil," said the prophet. "There will be enough to pay your debts and enough besides for you and your sons to live on."

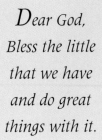

*Dear God,
Bless the little
that we have
and do great
things with it.*

137

*Dear God,
Even if we are
surrounded by
wealth, only
you are able to
give us what
we truly want.*

Elisha and the rich woman

ONE DAY, THE prophet Elisha went to a town called Shunem. A wealthy woman invited him to a meal.

"Come and visit us whenever you are in Shunem," she insisted.

Elisha was delighted by her generosity and went to have his meals at her house whenever he was in Shunem.

"I feel it is a real privilege to know such a holy man," said the rich woman to her husband. "I would like us to build an extra room in our house – one that we can always keep ready for him."

They did so, and Elisha was very grateful.

He asked his servant, Gehazi, to find out if there was anything he could do in return, but it seemed that the woman had everything she wanted.

"She says she is happy enough; but I believe she is sad that she does not have a son," Gehazi told Elijah. "Her husband is an old man now."

Elisha called the woman. "This time next year, you will have a son," he promised.

His words came true. The woman had a baby boy and she took great delight in watching him grow up in her loving care.

One day, when the young man was helping with the harvest, he started to feel unwell. "My head hurts," he cried.

The servants rushed to carry him home, but he was so unwell, he died in his mother's arms. Stricken with grief, she laid him on the bed in Elisha's room.

She asked for servants to bring her a donkey and set off to find Elisha. When the prophet heard the bad news, he sent his servant Gehazi hurrying on ahead to see if he could help. The servant's efforts were in vain: the boy gave no sign of being alive.

Then Elisha came to the house. He said prayers. He clasped the cold, still body. Little by little, the young man revived. Elisha called the mother and gave her back her son. Nothing could have made her happier.

Naaman, the Syrian

❧

THE PEOPLE OF ISRAEL and the people of Syria were deadly enemies. Sometimes the kings led their armies against each other. Sometimes there were raids along the border. In one raid, a little Israelite girl was taken as a slave.

She became a servant in the house of Naaman, the commander of the Syrian army. One day, she noticed that her mistress, Naaman's wife, was very upset.

"My husband is very ill," wept the woman. "He has a dreadful skin disease. I'm afraid he might die!"

"Oh dear," said the little servant girl. "I wish he could go to the prophet who is famous in Israel. He would be able to cure him, I'm sure."

The girl was so confident about the miraculous powers of the prophet that eventually Naaman was told about him. Desperate for a cure, Naaman asked the king for permission to go and find the famous man.

"Of course you can go," said the king. "I will give you a letter to explain why you are in Israel."

Soon, Naaman arrived at the court of the king of Israel. He brought money and gifts of fine clothing to give as payment for being cured. He handed over his royal letter.

The king of Israel was dismayed at what he read. " 'This letter will introduce my officer Naaman. I want you to cure him of his disease.' How I am meant to do that?" he exclaimed. "It's a trick! The man's trying to start a quarrel with me. Then we'll have war all over again."

Dear God, May I be confident of your power to help and to heal.

139

Naaman and Elisha

*Dear God,
Your blessings
cannot be
bought.*

Wᴴᴇɴ Eʟɪsʜᴀ ʜᴇᴀʀᴅ of Naaman's visit, he sent a message to the king of Israel: "Send the man to me. I will show him that there is a prophet in Israel."

Naaman arrived by chariot at Elisha's house. The prophet sent a servant out to him with the message: "Go and wash seven times in the River Jordan, and you will be cured."

Naaman was furious and drove off angrily. "I thought he would at least come out and say a prayer and wave his hand over me like a proper holy man," he complained. "If bathing in a river was meant to be the cure, I'd choose one in Syria – they're all better than any river in Israel."

Naaman's servants spoke soothingly. "If he'd asked you to do something hard, you'd have done it," they said. "Why not try what he says?"

Grudgingly, Naaman did so. To his amazement, his skin healed perfectly.

"We must hurry back and give the prophet the gifts he so richly deserves," he announced to his servants.

Elisha shook his head when the gifts were presented.

"I won't accept them," he said. "I do what I do in the name of the God of Israel."

"Then let me take back a load of earth to Syria," pleaded Naaman. "Now that I know there is no god except the God of Israel, the soil will be a little piece of the land of Israel, where I can offer my worship."

The wicked servant

Elisha's servant, Gehazi, watched the wealthy soldier drive away. "Why did my master let him go without paying?" he asked himself. "It's not right. I'm going to follow him and demand some kind of reward."

When Naaman saw the man chasing him, he stopped his chariot.

"Is something wrong?" he asked.

"No," said Gehazi, "but two prophets have just arrived at my master's house. He would like you to give each of them some silver and two sets of clothing."

"Of course!" said Naaman. "I'll give him that and more besides!"

The servant took the goods and went home feeling very pleased with himself.

Elisha called him. "Where have you been?" he asked.

"Oh, nowhere, sir," replied the servant.

Elisha simply looked at him. Then he spoke. "I know exactly where you've been and what you've done," he said. "This is no time to accept gifts! You will suffer the same disease that Naaman had!"

The servant looked at his skin and shuddered. He could see already the telltale signs.

Dear God, May I never lie and cheat in order to gain an advantage.

*Dear God,
Open my eyes
to see the many
ways in which
you take care
of me.*

A ring of fire

THE WAR BETWEEN Syria and Israel rumbled on for many years.

In one campaign, the king of Syria tried to ambush the king of Israel. However, it seemed that the Israelites always got to know of his plans, and he was not successful.

"Someone must be a spy!" he thundered to his officers. "I demand to know which of you it is!"

"It's not us," they declared. "It's that prophet Elisha. He's a famous seer, and that's how he knows your plans and is able to protect his king."

"Then I will capture him," said the king of Syria, and he glowered menacingly.

He sent his army off in search of Elisha. It was not long before they had surrounded the town where he was staying.

"Master!" cried Elisha's servant. "We're doomed! We're going to die. Whatever shall we do?"

"Don't be afraid," said Elisha calmly. "There are more on our side than on theirs." Calmly he prayed to God. Suddenly, the servant had a vision: he saw a ring of horses and chariots of fire protecting Elisha.

When the Syrians attacked, Elisha prayed again: "O God, make the soldiers blind," he said.

The prayer was answered immediately. The soldiers began blundering about helplessly. Elisha went to offer help. "I will lead you to the place you are looking for," he said.

He led them to Samaria, the city of the king of Israel. Then he prayed that they would see again. The enemy soldiers blinked as their world turned bright… and then they saw. They were surrounded by the enemy.

"Splendid!" exclaimed the king. "Shall I have them put to death?"

"No!" replied Elisha. "You would not have killed these men if you had captured them in the fighting. Give them a feast and let them go."

A dreadful siege

❧

S OME TIME LATER, King Benhadad of Syria came and laid siege to the city of Samaria. The Israelites who were trapped inside grew desperate for food. The few wretched morsels that they had were being traded for huge sums of money. It was even whispered that some of the meat in the cooking pots was human flesh.

The sufferings of his people made the king of Israel angry beyond measure.

"Get rid of Elisha!" he ordered. "It's his fault that God is not helping us. I want him beheaded. Go get him right now."

Elisha knew what the king was planning. He was ready for the king's messenger. "God says this," he told the man. "By tomorrow, the people in Samaria will be able to buy all the food they want."

It seemed impossible; but events took a curious turn when four men in Samaria decided to sneak away to the Syrians to beg for mercy.

Under cover of darkness, they crept into the enemy camp. "There's no one here," whispered one. "They've just gone."

"But they've left everything… look… horses and chariots… that stack of chests and whatever's inside."

"Look… glorious food, and plenty to drink as well!"

With a shout of glee they began to feast and enjoy themselves.

"Oh," said one suddenly, "we mustn't be found out as traitors. We have to be the ones to tell the people in the city what a chance they've got."

They hurried back with the news. Soon soldiers were sent to find the Syrians, but they had simply fled. It seemed that God had caused them to hear a noise that sounded like a huge army advancing on them. Even the king of Israel was finally convinced of his people's surprise victory. Elisha's words had come true.

Far away in Syria, King Benhadad was overthrown by a rival named Hazael.

Dear God, May I trust that your love and goodness will overcome every difficulty.

*Dear God,
You choose the
time for waiting
and the time
for action.*

The future king

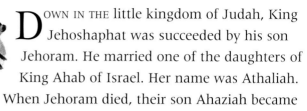

Down in the little kingdom of Judah, King Jehoshaphat was succeeded by his son Jehoram. He married one of the daughters of King Ahab of Israel. Her name was Athaliah. When Jehoram died, their son Ahaziah became king in Judah. Like his grandfather Jehoshaphat, Ahaziah helped King Joram of Israel fight against Syria. They were glad of the kinship between them, and the alliance that made them stronger in war. However, neither of them had much respect for the God of their people.

In one battle, King Joram was badly wounded. While he was out of action, the prophet Elisha seized the chance to act. "Listen," he said to a younger prophet. "Go and find the army officer named Jehu. Anoint him with olive oil and explain the meaning of the ceremony."

The young prophet obeyed. "God says this," he announced to Jehu. "You will be the new king of Israel. You will overthrow Joram. In this way Ahab's wicked family and the murderous Jezebel will be punished."

When Jehu's fellow officers heard the news, they all cheered. They blew trumpets and shouted, "Jehu is king!"

At once Jehu began his campaign to get rid of Joram. He drove his chariot toward Jezreel, where Joram was recovering from his wounds. Ahaziah was there with him.

On the watchtower, a guard saw Jehu driving like a madman toward the city. The king sent messengers to find out why he was coming – but to his dismay, the messengers stayed with Jehu.

Joram was alarmed. "I shall go and meet him myself," he said. "I need to know why he's coming." He and Ahaziah rode out, each in his own chariot.

In the field that had belonged to Naboth, the kings came face to face with the daring young soldier. The horses snorted as they stamped to a standstill. The confrontation was about to begin.

Jehu's rebellion

KING JORAM AND King Ahaziah looked fiercely at Jehu.
"Are you coming in peace?" called Joram.

"How can there be peace while your mother Jezebel still worships false gods and indulges in witchcraft!" cried Jehu.

"Treason!" shrieked Joram. He turned his chariot and fled.

Jehu fitted an arrow to his bow. It whistled through the air and lodged in Joram's back. The king slumped down dead.

"Bury him out here," Jehu ordered his fellow soldiers. "I've got the other one to deal with."

Jehu turned to see Ahaziah driving his chariot away at top speed. "After him!" Jehu called to his men. They raced off and managed to wound him.

"I can keep going," gasped Ahaziah to his men. "Surely we can make it back to Judah. We don't have to be victims of Israel's military uprising."

He struggled on as long as he could, but he only survived long enough to reach the city of Megiddo. There he breathed his last.

His officials took his body to Jerusalem, where he was buried.

Dear God, May I never forget that a life of wrongdoing brings its own punishment.

145

Jezebel

*Dear God,
May I live my
life so well
that I earn
people's respect,
not their
hatred.*

JEHU SET OFF to find Jezebel. By the time he reached the city of Jezreel, she had heard the news of his rebellion. Her blood ran cold in her veins and she felt a mixture of dread and defiance. Her son, the king, was dead. Was there anything she could do to avert disaster? It seemed unlikely… no… impossible.

Even so, she was proud to be a king's daughter. She deserved to look regal in her final hour. She put on eye makeup and arranged her hair. Then she went and stood at a palace window above the street.

Jehu drove through the gate. "Murderer!" she cried. "Why are you here?"

Jehu looked up and shouted, "Who is on my side? Throw her down!"

Jezebel's own officials pushed her out through the window. She tumbled to her death in the street below.

Jehu drove his chariot over her and went to claim the palace. He didn't hurry to tell his servants to go and collect Jezebel's body. By the time he did, there were only a few bones left. Dogs had taken the rest.

King Jehu

JEHU SET ABOUT making himself the king of Israel. His methods were grim and determined.

First of all he wrote to the rulers of the city of Samaria, who were looking after seventy members of Ahab's family. "Bring me their heads in a basket," Jehu demanded. The rulers hurried to obey, fearful for their own lives as this strict new king began his reign. Their terrifying gift was left by the city gate, a grisly warning of the ruthlessness with which the new king would act.

Jehu then left Jezreel to go to Samaria. On the way he met some of Ahaziah's family. They said they were on their way to pay their respects to the children of Queen Jezebel, and at once he knew they were his enemies. Immediately he had them executed. Then he tracked down all the rest of Ahab's relatives and had them put to death.

Next, Jehu called together all the people of Samaria. "King Ahab served the god Baal a little," he announced, "but I will serve him more. Priests, prophets and ordinary people – everyone who worships Baal must come together for a day of worship. I will lead the ceremony."

It was a trick. Jehu made sure that only those who wanted to declare themselves loyal to Baal went into the temple. Then he sent armed men to surround the building. At his sign, they moved in to kill them. He had the temple of Baal torn apart. Its most holy place was turned into a public toilet.

The situation was far from perfect. Jehu himself was not completely faithful to the God of Israel. He did exactly what Jeroboam had done when Israel first broke from Judah: he set up shrines with golden bull statues in Bethel and Dan. Even so, it was through him that Elijah's warnings to Ahab all came true. Ahab's family was totally wiped out.

20 May

❖

2 Kings 10

*Dear God,
Though I
respect those in
authority, may
I respect you
far more.*

Queen Athaliah of Judah

*Dear God,
Make me
willing to take
risks for the
sake of what
is good
and right.*

Down in the kingdom of Judah, news of Ahaziah's death reached his mother, Athaliah.

"Kill the royal family," she ordered her soldiers. "I will be queen here."

Ahaziah's son Joash was only a baby. His aunt Jehosheba rushed to save him. "Hurry," she she said to the woman who was nursing him. "There is a room in the Temple where we can hide the boy. The priests will help us."

For six years Jehosheba hid Joash in the Temple buildings. When the little prince was seven, the priest Jehoiada held a secret meeting with the palace guard. He told them of his plan: "We will act on the sabbath. When the time comes for the changing of the guard, both the soldiers going off duty and the soldiers coming on duty must play their part. Some need to be ready to hold off any trouble from Athaliah at the palace. Others must defend the Temple, where I will proclaim Joash the rightful king of Judah."

On the chosen day, everything went as planned. The crowds outside the Temple clapped and cheered: "Long live the king! Long live the king!"

Athaliah heard the shouting and sound of trumpets. "Treason!" she shrieked. "Treason!"

No one came to help her. The murderess suffered the same violent death as her many victims.

The boy king, Joash

A̶T THE TEMPLE, Jehoiada spoke to the people. "The time has come," he said, "for us to renew the covenant our people made with God: we must declare ourselves to be the Lord's people again, as we were in the time of Moses."

The people all agreed, eager for their nation to have a new start.

"There must also be a covenant between the king and the people," announced Jehoiada. "We must agree to serve the king."

The people all agreed; they recognized the importance of strong rule in a world that was so often torn apart by war and faithlessness.

Joash proved to be a good and able king. He followed Jehoiada's advice and was faithful to God.

One day, Joash summoned the Temple priests. "The Temple is in need of repair," he said. "Collect money from the people when they come to offer sacrifices. Use that money to pay for the work."

The priests collected lots of money, but nothing was done to the building. Joash called Jehoiada and the other priests a second time.

"Why is the Temple still in the same state?" he asked. "You must not keep the money you collect. Whatever the people give, you must hand it over so the work can be done."

The priests knew they had to obey. Jehoiada set up a proper collecting box in the Temple for the people's offerings. Every time it was full, it was counted to see exactly how much had been given. The money was used to pay carpenters, builders and stonemasons.

Little by little, the Temple was restored… just as the people's obedience to God was restored.

Throughout his life, Joash did all he could to defend the Temple, keeping the Syrian king Hazael at bay and encouraging his people to be faithful in worship.

22 May

❖

2 Kings 11–12

*Dear God,
If I ever turn
away from you,
make me
obedient again.*

Dear God,
Make me bold
to fight evil
and injustice.

Israel at war

🐌

WITHIN THE NORTHERN kingdom of Israel, King Jehu was feared and respected. However, King Hazael of Syria was confident that his armies were strong. They captured a good deal of Jehu's kingdom.

Jehu's son and then his grandson, Jehoash, succeeded him as king. Neither of them were faithful to God, and they both suffered defeats at the hand of King Hazael.

Then Jehoash heard more bad news: the prophet Elisha was very ill. Jehoash decided to visit him before he died.

"Bring a bow and some arrows," said Elisha. Jehoash did so. Elisha placed his hands on the king's hands and then told him to go to a window that looked toward Syria.

"Shoot an arrow," said Elisha.

Jehoash did so. As it flew, Elisha said, "You are God's arrow. You will defeat the Syrians."

Then Elisha told the king to take the rest of the arrows and hit the ground with them. He did so three times, then stopped.

"What a disaster!" said Elisha angrily. "Now you will defeat them only three times. If you had been willing to make five or six strikes, you would have won completely."

Even though Jehoash was not as determined as Elisha had hoped, God did not want Israel to be destroyed. Indeed, when Hazael died and his son, Benhadad, came to the throne, Jehoash won back some of the land that had been taken. His son, another Jeroboam, won even more. For a time, Israel prospered.

The warnings of the prophet Amos

ONE DAY, A SHEPHERD named Amos journeyed from his home in Judah to the kingdom of Israel.

He was astonished at all he saw – there was luxury beyond anything he had imagined! The rich people had built themselves beautiful mansions. Many had one for summer and another for winter. Inside the houses, the furnishings were luxurious. The tables were piled high with delicious food. Wealthy people enjoyed lavish parties at which wine flowed in abundance.

But turn a corner, and what did Amos see? Poverty far worse than he had feared! The rich did not even try to help the poor people. Oh, they might lend them money – but if the poor could not repay, the rich would sell them as slaves.

Amos was angry. "Listen to what God says!" he said. "You are glad when God punishes your enemies for all their wickedness. Now God is going to punish you for yours.

"You have forgotten God's holy laws. Our God is the God of heaven and earth, the God of sea and sky. God doesn't want your noisy religious ceremonies – God wants you to live in a way that is good and fair and right.

"Listen to me! God showed me a vision. God was standing next to a wall, holding a plumb line to check that the wall was built straight. God said, 'Look, Amos. My people are like a wall that is out of line. I am going to punish them. They will be taken away from their land into exile. Their kingdom will be left in ruins.'"

Amos paused. Suddenly he felt more sad than angry. Then he knew that God was telling him to say one more thing.

"One day, God will repair those ruins. One day, all of God's people will return to the land. They will have food and wine to share, and they will live in peace."

Dear God, May those who are loyal to you always have food and wine to share, and may they live in peace.

*Dear God,
Help me to
accept what
you have to
say to me.*

The story of the prophet Jonah

🐋

I N THOSE DAYS of long ago, the kings of Israel fought many wars against Syria. Then, worse news came: another nation was threatening to make all the world its empire. Its name was Assyria, and it lay many miles north. Its capital city, Nineveh, was famous for its wickedness. If any place deserved God's punishment, it was, surely, Nineveh.

The story of the prophet Jonah was also a story about Nineveh.

It all began when God spoke to Jonah:

"You are my prophet, Jonah, and the people of Nineveh are very wicked. You must go to warn them that I do not like their wickedness."

Jonah was not happy. In fact, he was furious.

"I will not go," he muttered to himself. "The people of Nineveh are our worst enemies. They truly are wicked and they deserve to be punished."

He shut out what God had said and began packing a bundle of belongings. Then he hurried on his way. The road east would take him to Nineveh; Jonah headed west.

The westward road led to the seaport of Joppa. At the dock Jonah saw a ship that was about to sail to Spain. He paid for his journey and climbed on board.

Soon after, the sailors hauled up the bright square sail and a steady breeze carried the boat out to sea. Jonah sat in the front of the boat and watched as the sun set. Then he went below for a good night's sleep.

The storm at sea

IN THE NIGHT, as Jonah slept soundly in the safety of the boat, the breeze began to blow more strongly. Out on the deck, the crew hurried to lower the sail before they lost control. The wind was getting fiercer, and fiercer still. It whipped the sea into great waves that lifted high above the mast and then came crashing down.

"Lighten the boat! Throw the cargo overboard," shouted the captain.

"May the gods of my people save us!" cried one of the sailors.

"And the gods of my people too," prayed another.

"There's more cargo down here," the captain called out from the hold. "Let's get it out – oh, it's that passenger." He grabbed Jonah and shook him. "WAKE UP AND START PRAYING TO YOUR GOD!" he cried.

Just then, all the crew came tumbling below decks for safety. They huddled together and began to murmur, "Someone wicked has brought this storm down on us. It's no ordinary storm: it's a punishment from heaven. Who's to blame? Who's the villain on this boat?"

They cast lots to find out, and the answer was beyond doubt: the guilt lay with Jonah.

"It's true," wailed Jonah. "The storm is all because of me. I'm a Hebrew, and I worship the God who made land and sea. I'm running away from God." He buried his head in his hands.

"Why on earth did you do that?" wailed the sailors. "What can we do?"

"Throw me overboard," moaned Jonah. "Then the storm will stop."

The sailors did not want to do that. Instead, they began rowing as hard as they could for land. But the storm was too much for them, and in the end they had to give in.

"O God, don't punish us for taking this man's life," they cried, as they hurled Jonah into the sea. Then, to their amazement, the sea grew calm.

26 May

❖

Jonah 1

*Dear God,
Help me to live
my life so I am
never ashamed
to declare
what I
have done.*

153

Rescued from the deep

*Dear God,
When I
stubbornly
refuse to do
what is right,
please bring
me to my
senses.*

JONAH SWIRLED DOWN in the deep, green water. He could not hold his breath much longer. Soon it would all be over and –

GULP.

God had sent along a great fish who came and swallowed him.

Deep inside the belly of the fish, Jonah took several deep breaths. He hardly knew whether to scream or to laugh. In the end, he began to pray.

"O Lord my God, I thought I was about to die. I was sinking so deep. The water pressed me down and the seaweed was wrapped around me; but from the bottom of the ocean you heard my prayer, and you have saved me. I will worship you with thanks and praise."

God heard Jonah's prayer, and God whispered to the fish. It swam through the waves and took Jonah to shore. Then it opened its mouth and spewed him up onto the beach.

Jonah lay in a heap on the sand.

"Get up, Jonah," said God. "Go to Nineveh. Give the people my message."

This time Jonah hurried to do as he was told.

A grim warning

JONAH COULD NOT resist a contemptuous sniff before he began to preach. It was God's idea to warn these detestable people. He might as well take his chance to scare them.

"Listen to this," he cried out to the people of Nineveh. "In forty days your city will be destroyed – reduced to rubble, razed to the ground, ruined."

"Listen to that prophet," they began to whisper. "He's very serious."

"Do you think his message is really a warning from God?"

"It could be. Well, you have to agree, we're not exactly religious as that man would understand it, are we?"

Unbelievable as it may seem, the people decided to change their ways. They went without food and wore rough, scratchy sackcloth to show how sorry they were for all the bad things they had done. The king heard the news and gave an order: "Everyone must turn away from wicked deeds. Everyone must pray to God, that God will be kind to us and forgive us," he said.

Dear God, May I take notice of your warnings.

155

*Dear God,
Thank you for
your unfailing
love and
forgiveness.*

The moral of the story

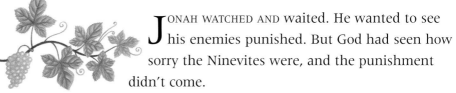

JONAH WATCHED AND waited. He wanted to see his enemies punished. But God had seen how sorry the Ninevites were, and the punishment didn't come.

"I knew you'd do this, God," Jonah sulked. "I knew it from the beginning. You're always patient and kind, always ready to let people off the punishment they deserve."

He hunched his shoulders and trudged out to a place outside the city.

On a hill overlooking Nineveh, Jonah built a little shelter. He sat in it and glowered. He was still hoping to see God's anger turn on the city. He was eager to see his enemies destroyed. But while they lived, he felt so miserable that he simply wanted to die. And anyway, the sun was unbearably hot.

Then God made a plant grow up right by Jonah's shelter. Its big leaves cast a cool shade over him. "Oh, that's rather nice," said Jonah. "What a pleasant surprise." For a few hours, he felt quite content.

But the next day, a little worm came and chewed the stem. The plant wilted. It drooped and died. The sun beat down, hotter than ever.

"Oh, my lovely plant!" moaned Jonah. "It wasn't much to ask, was it? Just a little something to make life bearable. Really, truly, I might as well die, the way things are."

"Oh dear," said God. "Are you very sad about your plant? Even though it came and went in a day?"

"Yes I am!" snapped Jonah.

"Sad about a plant," said God, "even though you did nothing to make it grow."

"It's a tragedy," sobbed Jonah.

"Well," said God gently, "perhaps you'll understand why I care so much about the people of Nineveh and all the animals they keep there too."

Hosea: a prophet for Israel

HOSEA WAS PERPLEXED. Everything seemed to be going wrong. He believed God had called him to be a prophet. He believed God had wanted him to marry Gomer. Now she was being an unfaithful wife. He believed with all his heart that God wanted him to be faithful to her. What did it all mean?

Little by little, he began to understand. Just as he felt the pain of being abandoned by his faithless wife, so God felt the pain of being abandoned by his faithless people in the troubled kingdom of Israel. His insight gave him inspiration, and he began to preach.

"Listen, people of Israel!" he called. "There is no love in this land, no faithfulness. No one obeys God. People commit all kinds of crimes.

"You have turned away from your true God. You worship idols that are nothing more than sticks of wood or hideous chunks of silver and gold.

"You have forgotten that God rescued our people from slavery in Egypt. You have forgotten how much God has provided for us. You will be destroyed in war. You think you are strong, but you will be blown away like smoke from a chimney.

"Come back to God! Ask God to forgive you! Then God will be our God once again. He will take care of us and our nation will flourish like a well-watered garden."

Dear God, May we work with you to transform this world into a well-watered garden.

Isaiah: a prophet for Judah

*Dear God,
You are holy,
and yet you
welcome us
as friends.*

IN THE LITTLE kingdom of Judah, King Joash had tried to help people worship the God of Israel. His son Amaziah and his grandson Uzziah after him were also faithful to God, but not so the people they ruled.

In the year that King Uzziah died, a man named Isaiah had a vision.

"I saw the Lord," said Isaiah. "He was sitting on a high throne, and his flowing robe filled the Temple. Around him were winged creatures that shone like blazing fire. They were calling to each other:

> *Holy! Holy! Holy!*
> *The Lord almighty is holy.*
> *God's glory fills the world.*

"Then I said to myself, 'I am doomed! Everything I say is sinful. I live among people who say sinful things. Yet I am looking at God.'

"Then one of the creatures flew down, holding a burning coal in a pair of tongs. The creature touched my lips with the coal and said, 'Your guilt has gone; your sins are forgiven.'

"Then I heard God speaking: 'Whom shall I send? Who will be our messenger?'

"I answered, 'I will go. Send me.'

"God told me to be a prophet, sometimes warning of trouble and war, at other times proclaiming God's promises."

The coming king

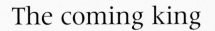

THE PROMISES GOD made through Isaiah were good news indeed for a nation that was so often at war:

The people who walked in darkness have seen a great light.
They were sad: God has made them happy –
as happy as those who bring the harvest safely home.

A child has been born! He will be our king.
He will be called "Wonderful Counselor," "Mighty God,"
"Eternal Father," "Prince of Peace."
He will be a king from David's royal family.
His kingdom will always be at peace….

Wolves and sheep will live together, and leopards will lie down with goats;
calves and lion cubs will feed together,
and little children will take care of them.
There will be nothing harmful in this new kingdom.

Dear God,
May all the nations of the world be able to gather their harvest crops in peace.

The attack on Jerusalem

ISAIAH SPOKE OF justice and peace. He knew that God's love and protection would not fail.

The people, however, were not convinced.

"The prophets may say lovely things," they agreed, "but it would be foolish to trust in the God of Israel completely. We've just had two kings who were faithful to God, but that doesn't seem to have made our nation safe. Surely it can't do any harm to worship other gods as well? After all, we are only choosing the ones that have been revered in this land for generations. Maybe they will hear our prayers more clearly. Maybe they have more power here than our God."

The king after King Uzziah's son Jotham was Ahaz; he thought in exactly this way and did not trust in the God of Israel. Like the people, he liked to worship all the pagan gods.

It did him no good. The king of Israel plotted with the king of Syria. Together they made war on Judah. Soon they had fought their way to the city of Jerusalem. They came and camped around the walls, ready to capture the city. Ahaz was desperate.

He sent messages to plead for help from another foreign ruler: Tiglath-Pileser, the emperor of Assyria.

"There'll be a price to pay for any help I give," the emperor told Ahaz.

Ahaz was well aware of that. He sent gold and silver from the Temple to show how eager he was to benefit his rescuer.

In order to impress Tiglath-Pileser further, Ahaz pushed aside the altar in the Temple that was dedicated to his own God. Instead he built a new altar and went on to worship the gods of Assyria.

Tiglath-Pileser agreed to help. In all the world, there was no army as terrifying as his. His fighting men swept down on the armies of Syria and Israel and crushed them.

The prophet Micah predicts disaster

꙳

I N A LITTLE TOWN in Judah lived a man named Micah. He was dismayed that his people were not faithful to their own God.

"Listen to what God has to say!" he cried. "Disaster is coming, and all because you have turned away from God. I hear jackals howling, and I want to howl with misery. I hear ostriches wailing, and I want to join in their wailing. You are going to be defeated… utterly defeated. Weep for yourselves, weep for your children."

The people refused to listen. "Don't preach at us," they said. "We know that God is kind to those who do right."

"You don't do what is right!" railed Micah. "You're all trying to make yourselves richer. You make the poor poorer. You don't care about justice. All you care about is having enough alcohol to get drunk on!

"You are going to be defeated and destroyed. Jerusalem will be left in ruins. The people will be scattered. Listen everyone, listen, listen."

No one was listening. He did not know what else God could tell him to say; but then God gave him a new message to proclaim.

"In spite of your faithlessness, one day, God will bring the people home. They will show the world that God is God. People from every nation will come to worship in the Temple. God will put an end to fighting. Warrior nations will beat their swords into plows, and their spears into pruning knives. Everyone will live in peace in their own vineyards and under their own fig trees. This is God's promise.

"One day, a new king will be born in Bethlehem. He will rule with all the majesty of God. Everyone in the world will respect him. He will bring us peace."

Dear God, May nations lay aside their weapons and seek instead to provide enough food for everyone.

Israel is destroyed

༜

*Dear God,
Whenever I
feel that my
dreams are
shattered,
leave me a
ray of hope.*

THE WONDERFUL NEW kingdom that God promised remained a distant dream for Micah. All around him, in the kingdom of Judah, neither King Ahaz nor the people had any intention of changing their ways and renewing their faithfulness to God.

It was no comfort to him that in the northern kingdom of Israel, things were even worse. Since the time of Jeroboam, there had been one faithless king after another. The people, too, had chosen to forget the stories of how their own God had taken care of them in days gone by. Instead, they turned to other gods – the storm god Baal and the goddess Asherah. They had built shrines to them everywhere – in every town and every village; on all the hilltops and under shady trees.

God had sent prophets to warn them, but the people hadn't listened. "We dare not trust just one God in these dangerous times," they had whispered. "We must try to have all the gods on our side. We will even sacrifice our own children if we must."

In spite of their zeal in worship, the gods offered no protection. The new king of Assyria, Shalmaneser, made war against Israel and was triumphant. Then he demanded a yearly payment from the defeated nation. When the king of Israel refused to pay, Shalmaneser and his armies invaded. He forced the people of Israel to leave their homes and live in other parts of the empire. He sent other defeated nations to occupy their land.

The national dream was shattered. The ancient stories of the people's ancestors seemed meaningless. Had God not promised Abraham that the land would be his home? Had Moses not led them back to that land after years of slavery? Had Joshua not fought to make the land their home? And what of David, who had established a strong and unified kingdom?

The only remnant of the dream was the tiny kingdom of Judah with its defiant capital city, Jerusalem.

King Hezekiah

❦

KING AHAZ OF JUDAH had a son, Hezekiah. When he was growing up, he learned the stories of his people, including those of the nation's great king, David. When he became king, these stories still inspired him.

"I want to follow David's example," he said to himself. "I shall be brave in war and faithful to God."

At once he began to make changes. "No one in Judah is to worship other gods," he announced. "We have a Temple to our own God in Jerusalem. That is the place where everyone should come. Today I am giving orders for all other shrines to be torn down."

For a while, everything went well. Then the Assyrians swept down on the little kingdom. The emperor Sennacherib commanded huge armies. The soldiers were well trained, well supplied and well equipped. Their powerful flame throwers could hurl fire and chaos into any walled city, however strongly it was defended. Their powerful siege machines could hammer at the gates. One by one, the little walled cities of Judah fell.

Hezekiah was afraid. He knew that the Assyrians would soon reach Jerusalem. He sent a message to Sennacherib. "Please stop your attack," it read. "I will pay whatever you want."

Sennacherib laughed at the offer of terms. Did the tiny nation of Judah think they could buy him off? "I'll have a large quantity of gold," he said to himself, "and an even larger quantity of silver." He ordered a messenger to return to Hezekiah with his demands.

The silver was gathered from the palace treasury and the Temple treasury. Finding enough gold was more difficult. It had to be stripped from the doors of the Temple. Hezekiah could only hope that it would be enough.

Sennacherib simply took note that the peace offering had arrived. "Now is the time to take Jerusalem," he announced.

Dear God,
Make me wise
to the ways of
wicked people,
so that I am
not deceived
by them.

Dear God,
May I be
resolute even
when danger
threatens.

The siege of Jerusalem

HEZEKIAH WATCHED IN dismay. The Assyrian army camped outside Jerusalem was huge. Sennacherib had sent three of his highest officials to lead the campaign. They demanded to see the king.

"I shall choose three of my officials to meet those scoundrels from the emperor," declared Hezekiah. "We are not beaten. We will not give in."

The Assyrian officials laughed at Hezekiah's envoys. "You've got nothing to bargain with," they said. "Your God isn't going to help you. You haven't got an army of any size. The fact is, your God wants us to destroy your nation and all its wickedness."

The envoys looked nervously over their shoulders toward the city. "You may speak your own language," they said. "We understand it. We'd rather you didn't speak our language – the people on the city walls might hear."

"Ha!" One of the Assyrians gave a brief and mocking laugh. "They need to hear this." He began to shout.

"Listen, all of you in Jerusalem. The emperor of Assyria has a message. Give in without a fight. Then you can live here until we resettle you somewhere else in the empire. It will be a good place. You'll prosper there."

The watchers on the city walls stood still and silent. The envoys turned on their heels and marched back to the king.

Hezekiah's prayer

HEZEKIAH WAS IN despair. "Whatever shall I do?" he cried. He ripped his royal robes and put on sackcloth to show his misery.

"Go," he said to one of his officials. "Tell the prophet Isaiah what has happened. Ask him to pray for our people."

Isaiah sent a message back to the king. "Don't let the Assyrians frighten you. God is greater than the emperor and will make him go back to his own country."

It was hard to believe. The emperor had been angered by Hezekiah's bold response and was moving ever closer to attack Jerusalem. He wrote a final letter to try to force Hezekiah to surrender.

"You are foolish to trust in your God. Haven't you heard what happens to those whom I decide to destroy? Remember all those famous nations of days gone by? Where are they now? What happened to their gods?"

Hezekiah went to the Temple.

"O God of Israel," he prayed. "You are king of the universe. You are the one who made earth and sky. Sennacherib has destroyed the gods of other nations – the gods that were only bits of stone and wood. Please rescue us, so that all the other nations will know that you are God."

Hezekiah also asked Isaiah for advice and the prophet spoke encouragingly. "The Assyrians will not shoot a single arrow against Jerusalem," he said. "God will defend the city."

That very night, a disaster struck the Assyrian camp. In the morning, nearly 200,000 soldiers had died. Sennacherib led his army back to Nineveh. Not long after, two of his sons assassinated him.

Dear God, May I learn from the stories of long ago of the great things you can do.

❖

2 Kings 21,
Zephaniah 1–3

*Dear God,
May I learn
to be wise
while I am
growing up.*

The boy king, Josiah

❧

GOD TOOK CARE of King Hezekiah, and Hezekiah in turn remained faithful to God all his life.

Then his son Manasseh became king.

"I'm fascinated by other religions," he said to his advisers. "I'd like to revive them. I'm going to have all the old places of worship rebuilt."

He set about the task with great enthusiasm. He restarted the worship of Baal and Asherah. He built altars to other gods inside the Temple. He put his trust in fortune-tellers and magicians. He even sacrificed his own son.

Many prophets spoke out against his actions. "God says this: 'You have made this nation more wicked than ever before. I will punish Jerusalem. I will abandon my people,'" they cried.

Manasseh had no time for them. "Superstitious nonsense!" he exclaimed. "I have ruled successfully for many years. I still have a son to carry on after me. Everything is fine the way it is."

Manasseh's son Amon did inherit the kingdom. He continued to worship other gods. Like his father, he paid no attention to God's laws.

One day, his own officials assassinated him. The people of Judah made Amon's son king in his place. The boy was only eight years old. His name was Josiah.

The book of the Law

❧

WHILE THE YOUNG king was growing up, a prophet named Zephaniah began to preach his message.

"Shameless nation! Jerusalem is doomed because of your wickedness! Turn back to God! Obey God's commands. Perhaps you will escape punishment on the day of God's anger."

Unlike his father and grandfather, Josiah did pay attention. He wanted to be a good and faithful king.

One day, King Josiah sent the court secretary to the high priest Hilkiah.

"Find out how much money he has collected from the people who come to worship at the Temple," he said. "Tell him to give it to the men in charge of keeping the building in good repair. They are honest, and they can pay all the tradespeople they need."

The court secretary delivered his message and came back to the king. "Everything to do with the money is in order," he said. "But while I was there, Hilkiah gave me this. It's the book of the Law. It's been lost for very many years and he's only just found it. Listen."

When Josiah heard the Law read aloud, he was dismayed. "Our people haven't obeyed these laws for generations," he exclaimed. "What shall we do? Is there a prophet who can help me?"

Josiah's officials went to a prophet named Huldah, whose husband worked at the Temple.

"Tell the king this," she said. "God is going to punish Jerusalem and all its people. They have rejected God too many times. Yet, because the king has repented, disaster will not come in his lifetime. He will die in peace."

When Josiah heard this, he summoned all the leaders of the people together. They went to the Temple, along with the priests and the prophets. There, the whole book of the Law was read aloud.

"Today," said Josiah, "we will make a new covenant with God. God will be our God; we will obey God's laws."

❖

2 Kings 22–23,
Zephaniah 1–3

*Dear God,
May I read your
laws faithfully.
May I remember
them. May I
obey them.*

Dear God,
I will obey
your Law.
May you
count me as
one of your
holy people.

A Passover festival

K EEPING GOD'S LAWS is the most important thing for us to do,"
announced Josiah. "However, we must also worship God in the
right way."

The Temple and the city were full of idols and altars to other gods.
Josiah had them destroyed. Then he went to other places in Judah and
got rid of all the places of worship that were dedicated to other gods.

"The time has come," said Josiah, "to celebrate the most important
festival of our people. We must celebrate the Passover to show we
remember the covenant God made with us in the time of Moses. All the
instructions for the festival are in the book of the Law. We will follow
them faithfully."

There had never been a Passover like it since the time of the judges.
There was a great procession to the Temple: first came the singers, then
young women playing tambourines, and then the musicians. They sang a
Passover psalm:

When the people of Israel left Egypt,
Judah became God's holy people.

The Red Sea saw them and fled away;
the River Jordan waited to let them walk through.

And why did these wonders happen on earth?
Because of our God, the Lord of heaven.

Praising God

THE SOUND OF SINGING echoed through Jerusalem. No other king in the history of the nation was as devoted as Josiah to obeying God's laws.

Praise the Lord!
Praise him, all his angels,
all his heavenly armies.
Praise him, sun and moon;
praise him, shining stars.

Let them all praise the name of the Lord!
He commanded, and they were created;
they were fixed in their places forever,
and they cannot disobey.

Praise the Lord from the earth,
sea monsters and all ocean depths;
lightning and hail, snow and clouds,
strong winds that obey his command.

Praise him, hills and mountains,
fruit trees and forests;
all animals, tame and wild, reptiles and birds.

Praise him, kings and all peoples,
princes and all other rulers;
young women and young men,
old people and children too.

Let them all praise the name of the Lord!
His name is greater than all others;
his glory is above earth and heaven.
He made his nation strong,
so that all his people praise him –
the people of Israel, so dear to him.

Dear God,
May all the world praise you in the way it should.

*Dear God,
We cannot
control all the
things that
happen to us,
but we can set
our hearts on
doing good.*

Jeremiah's desperate warnings

ﻬ

WAR WAS NEVER far away from the little kingdom of Judah. Good King Josiah himself was killed in battle when he tried to stop the Egyptian army from advancing. His son, then his grandson, ruled after him, but they had to pay the victorious king of Egypt large amounts of gold and silver in return for peace.

Although the people of Judah feared further attacks from Egypt to the south of their territory, the greater threat was from the north. There, the nations had fought among themselves and the armies of Babylon had showed themselves mightier than those of Assyria. Now the rulers of Babylon wanted to command a vast empire.

A prophet named Jeremiah tried to warn the people.

"Listen to what God says," he cried. "People are coming from the north: a mighty nation is getting ready for war. They have bows and swords at the ready. When they ride to war, it sounds like the roar of the ocean. They are coming to Jerusalem.

"Put on sackcloth! Roll in ashes! Weep for your wickedness."

Jeremiah went and stood in the Temple gate.

"Change the way you are living," he pleaded with the people. "It's not good enough just to have a Temple. Be fair to one another. Stop taking advantage of those who are weak – people from other countries, people who have little or no money. Be faithful to God in every way. Don't think you're safe just because you come to the Temple. God will not defend it if you do not obey God's laws."

Neither the people of Judah nor their kings paid any attention to Jeremiah. They forgot about God. They forgot about justice. They simply struggled to survive as a nation.

Then, in the time when Josiah's great-grandson Jehoiachin was king, King Nebuchadnezzar and the armies of Babylon invaded Judah. They removed Jehoiachin from power, stripped the land of its treasures, and forced thousands of its finest citizens to go and work in other parts of the empire.

Jeremiah and the well

❧

JEHOIACHIN'S UNCLE, ZEDEKIAH, was left to rule the little that remained of the population.

"If there's one thing I don't need," he told his officials, "it's that defeatist prophet going around with his message of doom and gloom. I gather he's trying to tell people that we might as well give in to the Babylonians. I'm going to keep him under house arrest in the palace."

The king's officials were only too happy to do all they could to keep Jeremiah quiet, but he was not easily silenced. Zedekiah gave his permission for stronger measures to be taken against the prophet.

Zedekiah's officials went to seize Jeremiah. They threw him down a well in the palace courtyard. There was no water in it, only mud. Jeremiah sank into the slime. He was brokenhearted at the way his own people had refused to listen to him. He was in deep despair that they no longer heeded God.

The only person to have compassion on Jeremiah was a foreign slave. He talked to the king and was granted his permission to rescue Jeremiah. He took a few helpers with him and passed a rope down to the prophet. Together they managed to pull him up into the sunlight.

After that, the prophet was kept in the palace courtyard.

13 June

❖

Jeremiah 27, 37, 38, 2 Kings 24–25

*Dear God,
Open my eyes
to the goodness
and kindness
of those whom
I counted as
outsiders.*

*Dear God,
Show your love
to those who
face utter
defeat.*

The destruction of Jerusalem

KING ZEDEKIAH HAD never given up hope of defying the Babylonians. However, it became clear that they were determined to crush any hint of rebellion. King Zedekiah desperately longed for a message from God, and he had to turn to his old enemy, Jeremiah, to ask for help.

"This is what God says," replied Jeremiah. "The nation is doomed because its people have been wicked for so many years. Now is the time to surrender to the Babylonians. If you do, you will live. The city will not be burned down. If you resist, the enemy will show no mercy."

It was not what Zedekiah wanted to hear – he desperately wanted to free the nation from foreign rule. But his boldness was misplaced. King Nebuchadnezzar and his armies moved in to attack with overwhelming force. Jerusalem, the city that had been the nation's pride and joy, was captured.

Zedekiah tried to escape through the palace garden, but the Babylonians hunted him down and took him prisoner.

Meanwhile, in Jerusalem, the destruction was terrible. The palace was set afire and the houses and the city walls were torn down.

Then the Babylonians set about destroying the Temple. Everything that was made of bronze – including the great pillars at the entrance – was broken into pieces and taken away to Babylon. Everything that was used in the worship of God was plundered. The beautiful golden box that dwelled in the holy of holies – the precious covenant box – was never seen again. Finally, the attackers set fire to the main building.

The high priest was led away to live in exile in Babylon along with many others. Most of the people of Judah were forced to live in a foreign land. Jeremiah himself was treated kindly by the victors, but nothing could protect him from the crushing blow of his people's defeat.

Lamenting the disaster

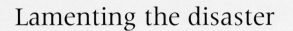

JERUSALEM LAY IN ruins. The smell of charred wood mingled with the rising stench of rotting flesh. A poet sang his lament.

How lonely lies Jerusalem, once so full of people!
Once honored by the world, she is now like a widow;
The noblest of cities has fallen into slavery.

Judah's people are helpless slaves, forced away from home.
They live in other lands, with no place to call their own –
Surrounded by enemies, with no way to escape.

The Lord rejected his altar and deserted his holy Temple;
He allowed the enemy to tear down its walls.
They shouted in victory where once we had worshiped in joy.

The thought of my pain, my homelessness, is bitter poison;
I think of it constantly and my spirit is depressed.
Yet hope returns when I remember this one thing:

The Lord's unfailing love and mercy still continue,
Fresh as the morning, as sure as the sunrise.
The Lord is all I have, and so I put my hope in him.

Dear God,
Your love and
mercy bring hope
in the midst
of disaster as
surely as the
morning sun
chases away
the darkness.

173

*Dear God,
May I see a
glimpse of
your glory.*

Ezekiel's vision

🐋

EZEKIEL HAD ONCE been a priest. He was among the first group of people to be taken from Judah to Babylon, and he lived with them by the River Chebar. One day, he saw a storm approaching. Lightning flashed from a huge cloud, and the sky around it was glowing. Then, from where the lightning was flashing, he saw something that shone like bronze.

As he gazed, he saw the most amazing vision: heavenly creatures, a sapphire throne and, on the throne, a human figure shining like bronze in the middle of a fire. The whole vision shone with a bright light and shimmered with all the colors of the rainbow. It was the dazzling light of God's presence.

Ezekiel fell to the ground. Then he heard a voice. "Mortal man, stand up. I want you to speak to the people on my behalf. They will not always listen, but you are to go on speaking the words I will give you."

Ezekiel was eager to obey God. He did his best to explain to others what God was telling him, but they did not seem to care. They seemed to think of him and his strange visions as little more than entertainment.

Ezekiel knew in his heart that his home country of Judah was going to be crushed and defeated. When the awful news came that Jerusalem had been laid waste, he was devastated. However, from that moment on, God gave him messages of hope. In spite of the disaster, God's love had not failed.

The good shepherd

THE PROPHET EZEKIEL cried out to all the people who had been leading citizens in Judah. "Listen to this!" he called. "Listen to what God has to say!

"You were meant to take care of the people in the way that a shepherd takes care of a flock of sheep. But you just exploited people. You made yourselves rich. You didn't care for those who were sick or weak or whose lives were in turmoil. Now look at the consequences! Our people are scattered in different places all over the world.

"God has rejected you – but God will come to take care of the people, like a good shepherd. God will bring them back to their own land – back to the mountains and the streams and the green pastures.

"God will look for those who are lost. God will heal those who are sick or wounded.

"God will give them a king – a king like David – to be their leader.

"God will bless them. God will set them free. God will give them a safe place to call their home. God will provide them with all they need.

"Listen, everyone! Listen to what God is saying: 'You are my people, my sheep, the flock that I feed; I am your God.'"

Dear God,
Please give me
a safe place
I can call my
home.

175

The valley of bones

*Dear God,
Wherever hopes
and dreams
are dead, may
you bring life.*

ONE DAY, EZEKIEL felt that God had come very close to him. Then, by a miracle, it seemed that God transported him to another place.

He was standing in a valley. Everywhere God showed him, there were many bones – human bones. They were completely dry, and there was no trace of flesh to be seen.

"Mortal man," asked God, "do you think these bones can live again?"

"I don't know," the prophet replied. "Only you know that."

"I want you to prophesy to them," said God. "Tell them to listen to God's word. Tell them that I am going to breathe new life into them. Then you will truly know that I am God."

Ezekiel did as he was told. Then he heard a rattling sound. He saw the most awesome sight. The bones were moving – they were joining together, and turning back into lifeless bodies.

"Now speak to the wind," said God. "Say that God commands it to blow life into these bodies."

The wind obeyed. The bodies stood up. There were enough people to make an army.

"Now go and tell the people of Israel what you have seen," said God. "I am going to bring their dead to life. I am going to take them back to their own land. Then they will know that I am God."

Ezekiel hurried to tell his message. He wanted to give the people hope that the days of exile would one day come to an end.

Far from home

❧

THE EXILES FROM Judah were overawed by the city of Babylon. The Babylonians had their own gods, and there were temples and shrines to them everywhere.

However, there was nothing that could take the place of their beloved Temple. The best the people could do was to meet together and read from the books of the Law and writings of the prophets. That way they could encourage one another to be faithful to God.

One day they met on the banks of the great river that ran through the city. They sat on the ground among the willow trees that bent low over the water and chanted a sorrowful prayer.

> *As a deer longs for a stream of cool water,*
> *so I long for you, O God.*
> *I thirst for you, the living God;*
> *when can I go and worship in your presence?*

Some Babylonians were strolling by. "Oh, you're the Jews, from Judah!" they exclaimed. "Please sing us one of your songs. We've heard you used to have lively music at your Temple. We'd love to hear some of it."

The Jewish exiles bowed their heads. "We don't feel like singing any of those lively songs," said someone, and he hung up his harp on a willow branch. "We just want to remember how Jerusalem used to be. Before we were your captives. When we were happy."

The Babylonians moved on, chattering about other things.

"I could wish for all kinds of dreadful things to happen to the Babylonians," said the man with the harp. "Surely their wicked empire can't last forever." Then they continued with the prayer:

> *Why am I so sad?*
> *Why am I so troubled?*
> *I will put my hope in God,*
> *and once again I will praise him,*
> *my savior and my God.*

*Dear God,
There is no place on earth where you cannot be found.*

*Dear God,
You give me
wisdom and
strength. You
answer my
prayers.*

In the court of King Nebuchadnezzar

FROM THE TIME of the fall of Jerusalem, the Jews felt themselves to be at the mercy of more powerful nations. To give themselves hope, they told stories about God's care for them. The stories about the Jews in the court of King Nebuchadnezzar provided memorable reminders of God's power, God's love and the wisdom of being faithful in prayer and worship.

So it was, the stories said, that when Nebuchadnezzar attacked Jerusalem, it was God who allowed him to raid the Temple and to take prisoners. Nebuchadnezzar chose handsome and intelligent young people who would be able to work in his government. Among them were four brave men: Daniel, Shadrach, Meshach and Abednego.

One day King Nebuchadnezzar had a dream. He called for his magicians and fortune-tellers and demanded that they explain its meaning.

"Tell us your dream," they said, "and we will explain it to you."

"No," said the king. "I've decided that would be far too easy. You must tell me the dream as well. If you can do that I will trust your answer and give you a great reward too."

"But your request is impossible!" exclaimed the magicians and the fortune-tellers. "Only a god could know what was in your dream."

King Nebuchadnezzar was furious. He turned to his bodyguard. "Round up all my advisers," he ordered. "Execute the lot of them and destroy their property as well."

When Daniel, Shadrach, Meshach and Abednego heard the dreadful news, Daniel went to find out why such a harsh order had been given. He came back to his friends. "Let us pray," he said. "Perhaps God will give us the insight we need to explain the mystery of the dream."

When they had finished praying, Daniel asked to see the king.

King Nebuchadnezzar's dream

❧

Oﾍe of the king's bodyguards led Daniel to see Nebuchadnezzar himself. "I bring you one of the Jewish exiles," he announced. "He says he will tell you about your dream."

"Indeed I will," said Daniel calmly. "There is a God in heaven who can reveal mysteries. I prayed to God, and God showed me that you dreamed of what will happen in the future.

"Your Majesty, you dreamed of a huge statue. Its head was finest gold, its chest and arms were silver, its waist and hips were bronze and its legs were iron. The feet of the statue were iron and clay together.

"As you were looking at it, a huge stone broke away from a cliff even though no one had touched it. It smashed the feet of iron and clay. The statue fell. It crumbled into dust and the dust was blown away by the wind. The stone that had destroyed the statue grew into a mountain and it covered all the earth.

"Your Majesty, this is what the dream means. The statue is all the empires of the world. Your own great empire is the head of gold. Other empires will come after yours… though none will be as great as yours.

"Then the God of heaven will come and smash those empires. They will vanish completely. God will establish a kingdom that will last forever."

As King Nebuchadnezzar listened, his eyes revealed his astonishment. He was clearly impressed with Daniel. "I will give the order for offerings to be made to your God," he said. "I will give you a job in the heart of my government."

"I have three friends who helped me in my prayers," said Daniel.

"I'll give them excellent jobs too," said the king.

Dear God, May your kingdom come. May it last forever.

Dear God,
May I
remember your
commandment
to worship
you alone.

Shadrach, Meshach and Abednego

KING NEBUCHADNEZZAR WANTED everyone in his empire to worship the gods of Babylon, as he did himself. That was why he gave this order:

"Make a statue – bigger than any other statue in the whole world. Set it up on the wide plain outside the city. Then I want all the officials in my empire to come to a great ceremony of dedication: the princes, the governors, the lieutenant-governors, the commissioners, the treasurers, the judges, the magistrates – everyone who is anyone must be there."

The king's command was obeyed with scrupulous efficiency. On the appointed day, the officials of the empire came and stood in front of the glittering new statue. A herald made the announcement:

"People of all nations, all races, all languages: listen. First you will hear the sound of trumpets. Then you will hear the sound of oboes, lyres, zithers and harps, and then all the other instruments will join in. When the music starts, you are to bow down to the glorious golden statue that the mighty and majestic King Nebuchadnezzar has made. Anyone who does not bow down and worship will be apprehended, arrested and ultimately annihilated in a blazing, fiery furnace."

The music played. The people all bowed down.

"Excellent," said Nebuchadnezzar to himself. "My plan has been a complete success."

"Your Majesty, Your Majesty!" A group of Babylonian officials hurried to speak to the king. "Those Jews you promoted to a high rank – Shadrach, Meshach and Abednego – they did not bow down. They defied your orders. They do not respect your god."

Nebuchadnezzar flew into a rage. "Bring them to me!" he cried.

The fiery furnace

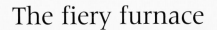

SHADRACH, MESHACH AND ABEDNEGO came and stood before the king. "Answer me directly," he snarled. "Did you or did you not bow down to my golden statue? If you did not, you will be thrown into a fiery furnace. No god will be able to save you."

"We're not going to make excuses," replied the three. "We didn't bow to the golden statue. If God wants to save us from the furnace, then God will. Whatever happens, we will never bow down to that lump of metal."

Nebuchadnezzar was furious. "Make the furnace seven times hotter," he ordered. "Tie these men up. Throw them in."

The furnace was made so hot that the soldiers who hurled the men into it were burned. Nebuchadnezzar watched with grim pleasure.

Suddenly he leaped to his feet. "What's this?" he cried. "We tied up three men and threw them into the flames. Why do I see four men? Why are they walking around? Why does the fourth one look like an angel?"

He rushed to the door of the furnace. "Shadrach! Meshach! Abednego! You worship the greatest God of all. Come out!"

The three men walked free. They were completely unharmed.

"Praise the God of Shadrach, Meshach and Abednego," said Nebuchadnezzar. "They were faithful to their God, and their God saved them. I now forbid anyone from any nation, any race or any language to say anything against their God."

Then Nebuchadnezzar promoted the three young men to even higher positions in his empire.

Dear God,
Look after me,
for I seek to
be faithful
to you.

*Dear God,
May all the
people of the
world discover
the truth that
should guide
them.*

Belshazzar's feast

NOT LONG AFTER Nebuchadnezzar's reign, a king named Belshazzar came to the throne.

One night, he gave a great feast. As the evening wore on and the drink flowed, the mood grew more and more festive.

All at once, Belshazzar thought of an idea to make the celebration even merrier. "Bring out those wonderful gold and silver cups," he said, "the ones Nebuchadnezzar took from the Temple in Jerusalem. We shall drink from them to our own gods."

As he and his guests drank yet more wine in this disrespectful fashion, a disembodied human hand appeared in the shimmering lamplight. It started to write on the wall.

Belshazzar began to shake with fear. "Bring my advisers – the magicians and wizards and astrologers," he babbled. "I will give power and riches to anyone who can read the message and interpret its meaning."

The king's wise men came, but none of them could interpret the message.

Then the queen mother hurried to the feasting hall. "Your Majesty! Do you not know about the wisest man of all? Nebuchadnezzar made him the chief among the advisers. His name is Daniel."

Daniel was summoned immediately and ushered to the king, who promised gifts and a position of great authority. "I don't want any reward from you," Daniel said. "Nebuchadnezzar learned to fear the living God, whom I worship. You have shown no respect. Here is the message: it has three words.

"*Mene* means number: the days of your kingdom are numbered.

"*Tekel* means weight: your value has been weighed and it is not enough.

"*Parsin* means division: your empire will be divided up and given to the Medes and Persians."

Belshazzar heaped rewards upon Daniel, but his gratitude did not save him. That same night, Belshazzar was killed, and Darius the Mede seized power.

Darius the Mede

❧

DARIUS CHOSE GOVERNORS to help him rule the empire. He chose Daniel and two others to supervise all the other governors and the king's own interests.

Daniel was so good at his job that, within a short time, the king was thinking of putting him in charge of everything.

The other governors and supervisors were jealous. "How can we get rid of Daniel?" they asked one another. "He's so good at what he does. The only chance we've got of finding fault with him is through something to do with his religion."

As they talked, they had an idea. They went to see the king.

"May Your Majesty live forever," they said. "We, the governors of your empire, have agreed on a plan to make sure that everyone is loyal to you. For thirty days, no one is to ask for anything from any god or human except you. Anyone who disobeys must be thrown into a pit of lions.

"So issue the order and make it a law of the Medes and Persians – one that cannot be changed."

"I will indeed," said Darius. "Pass me the order, and I will sign it with my seal."

When Daniel heard about the new law, he went home. He went upstairs to the room that faced Jerusalem. There, he knelt down and prayed, just as he had always done.

Daniel's enemies were watching. They hurried to the king.

"Your Majesty! Do you remember your law… the law to prove your subjects' loyalty?"

"Oh yes," replied the king. "A very strict law that cannot be changed. What of it? What happened?"

"O king," they said, "Daniel is not obeying the law. He continues to pray to his god three times a day. O king, by your own law, he must be thrown to the lions."

Dear God, May I be diligent and careful in everything, as if I were doing it for you.

183

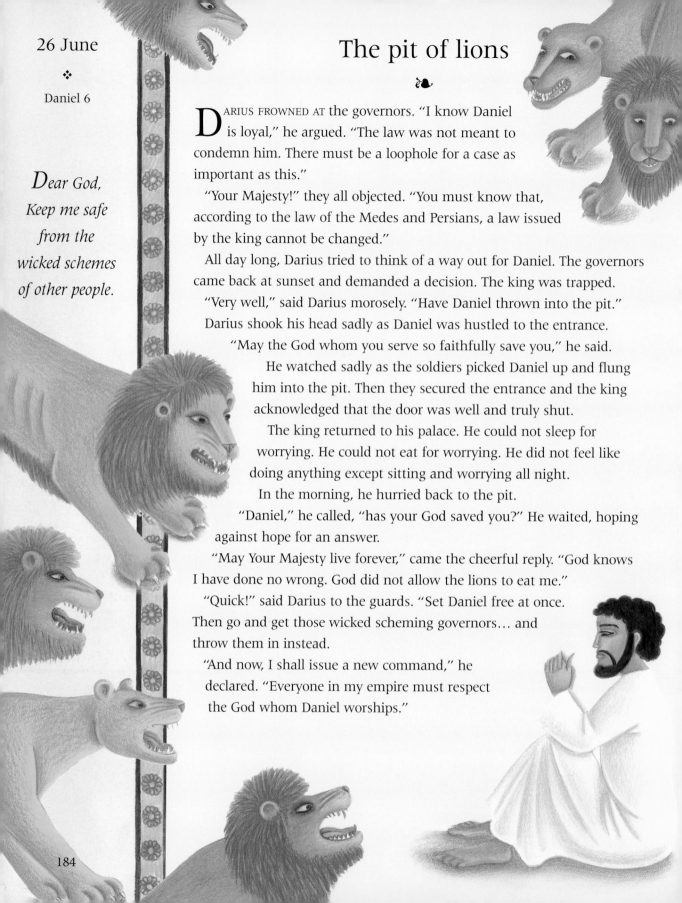

The pit of lions

*Dear God,
Keep me safe
from the
wicked schemes
of other people.*

Darius frowned at the governors. "I know Daniel is loyal," he argued. "The law was not meant to condemn him. There must be a loophole for a case as important as this."

"Your Majesty!" they all objected. "You must know that, according to the law of the Medes and Persians, a law issued by the king cannot be changed."

All day long, Darius tried to think of a way out for Daniel. The governors came back at sunset and demanded a decision. The king was trapped.

"Very well," said Darius morosely. "Have Daniel thrown into the pit."

Darius shook his head sadly as Daniel was hustled to the entrance.

"May the God whom you serve so faithfully save you," he said.

He watched sadly as the soldiers picked Daniel up and flung him into the pit. Then they secured the entrance and the king acknowledged that the door was well and truly shut.

The king returned to his palace. He could not sleep for worrying. He could not eat for worrying. He did not feel like doing anything except sitting and worrying all night.

In the morning, he hurried back to the pit.

"Daniel," he called, "has your God saved you?" He waited, hoping against hope for an answer.

"May Your Majesty live forever," came the cheerful reply. "God knows I have done no wrong. God did not allow the lions to eat me."

"Quick!" said Darius to the guards. "Set Daniel free at once. Then go and get those wicked scheming governors… and throw them in instead.

"And now, I shall issue a new command," he declared. "Everyone in my empire must respect the God whom Daniel worships."

The story of Job

I<small>N SPITE OF</small> the stories about Daniel and his friends, everyday life for the Jews in Babylon was often difficult.

When they met together, they talked about the many problems they faced. Why do so many bad things happen? They wanted to know.

"Listen again to the story of Job," said a wise man. "Perhaps it will help us to understand."

"Once upon a time, in the land of Uz, lived a man named Job. He had everything he could want to enjoy the good life: a large and happy family, vast flocks of sheep, huge herds of cattle, and more camels and donkeys than any of his neighbors – oh, and an army of servants to help him look after everything. He was the richest man in all the lands of the East.

"More than that, he was a good man. He was careful not to do anything wrong and he was careful to make offerings to God for any wrongdoing that anyone in his family might have unintentionally committed.

"One day, that terrible chief of wickedness, the evil Satan, came roaming the earth. He was on his way to a meeting with God and all the angels.

"'Did you see Job while you were visiting the earth?' asked God. 'There is no one on earth as good and faithful as him. He worships me and does nothing evil.'

"'Humph,' said Satan, who had no respect for God at all. 'You bless him, he thanks you. It's easy to be good if you've got everything. Now, if he were to lose all his blessings, he wouldn't be nearly so grateful. He'd curse and swear at you.'

"'We'll see,' replied God. 'You can take everything he has. Just don't harm Job himself.'

"At that, Satan left, eager to do mischief."

*Dear God,
When you give
good things,
may I learn
to praise you.
When you take
them away, may
I learn to
praise you.*

Disaster strikes Job

ের

JOB KNEW NOTHING of the conversation between God and Satan. Then, one day, a servant came running.

"'Master! We were plowing with your oxen. Your donkeys were nearby. Raiders came and stole your animals. They killed the servants. Only I survived. Everything has been taken!'

"Before he had finished speaking, another servant came and said, 'Master! Lightning struck your sheep and your shepherds. Only I survived. Everything has been destroyed.'

"As he was speaking, another servant came and said, 'Master! Your children were feasting together. A storm swept them all away. Only I survived. Everything has been taken.'

"Job flung himself on the ground and wept for grief. Then he stood up and spoke solemnly. 'God has given. God has taken away. Praise the Lord.'

"Up in heaven, God and Satan met again. 'Well,' said God, 'Job is still as faithful as ever, isn't he?'

"'Nonsense!' replied Satan. 'He's just happy to be alive. Let me hurt his body and then you'll hear him curse you.'

"'All right,' said God. 'Only you mustn't kill him.'

"Satan gave Job a terrible skin disease. His sores tormented him and made him feel very depressed. He went and sat by a garbage dump.

"His wife came to give him a piece of her mind. 'Silly old fool!' she said. 'You're too religious for your own good. Why don't you just curse God and die?'

"'No,' said Job. 'We welcome the good things God gives us. We can't complain if we get trouble.'"

Job's three friends

JOB CONTINUED TO suffer, but not once did he complain against God. Then three of his friends heard of his troubles: Eliphaz, Bildad and Zophar. They came to see him and wept to see their old friend in such a dreadful state. They sat on the ground with him for seven days and seven nights and none of them said a word.

"At last Job broke the silence. 'I wish to God I'd never been born,' he said. 'At least then I wouldn't have all this misery. All my worst nightmares have come true.'

"Eliphaz broke in. 'Come on, my old friend. You have to face the truth. No one is good enough for God. Be glad that God is correcting you for your failings.'

"'If I had done wrong, I would accept that,' replied Job. 'But you are talking nonsense. Do you think I don't know right from wrong?'

"Bildad shook his head. 'God always does what is right. Maybe it was your children who did something wrong! God will never abandon those who are truly faithful.'

"'I've heard all that before,' retorted Job. 'I am completely innocent, but God is doing nothing to help. I wish I'd never been born. I wish I were dead.'

"'Nonsense, nonsense, nonsense,' interrupted Zophar. 'God is wiser than you. God is greater than you. Get your thinking straight again and turn back to God.'

"'Oh, stop standing up for God!' said Job angrily. 'I'm only a human being and I've been as good as a person can be. I only want God to let me enjoy what's left of my life. There isn't going to be anything for me to enjoy when I'm dead.'"

Dear God, May I not criticize those in need, but support them through their pain.

Dear God, Make me wise enough not to question your wisdom.

The end of the argument

❧

JOB ARGUED AND argued with Eliphaz, Bildad and Zophar.

"'Bad things don't happen to good people,' they insisted.

"'I am a good person and bad things have happened to me,' replied Job.

"'You can't be good enough.'

"'But I know I am.'

"'Listen carefully, dear Job. Listen to what we have to say about God. It's terribly important that you correct your understanding of our Maker.'

"The four men argued and argued… and still they went on arguing.

"In the end, a passerby named Elihu decided it was time to join in.

"'You old men are making me angry. I'm only young, but I can see that you're all talking nonsense. You three haven't proved that Job has done bad things. Job, you're not taking God seriously. God is the creator. No one tells God what to do. Look – just look at the sky. It's dazzlingly bright! And where is that wind blowing from? The glory of God should fill us all with awe.'

"Then a great storm broke, and God finally spoke to Job.

"'Were you there when the world was made?' asked God. 'When the universe exploded into being? Have you ever made the sun rise? Have you explored the sea? Can you command the rain to fall or make the strong winds blow? Can you teach the hawk to fly? Does the eagle ask you how to build its nest? You can't do any of these things… yet you dare to challenge me.'

"Job bowed his head.

"'I'm ashamed. I'm sorry,' said Job."

Learning God's Law

T HE TEACHER WHO had told the story paused. "That can't be the end!" exclaimed the children.

"No it isn't," said the teacher. "The three friends had to say sorry to God for telling Job things that weren't true. God gave Job more blessings than ever before – more sheep, more cattle, more camels, more donkeys and a whole new family. He lived to see his grandchildren and his great grandchildren. It's a story with a happy ending."

"What must we do to be wise?" asked a boy.

The teacher wagged a finger. "You must all learn God's laws and you must obey them," he replied. "Now, there's a psalm about the Law I want you all to learn. It's very long, but it's divided into different parts: one for every letter of the alphabet. The first one begins like this:

> *Happy are those who live good lives,*
> *who obey God's laws,*
> *who follow God's commands.*
> *They never do wrong;*
> *they walk in the right paths...*

"Is that the first part?" sighed the boy.

"About half of it," said the teacher. "And there are twenty-two parts in all."

All the children gasped. Learning a psalm as long as that was going to take some effort.

"It is the most worthwhile thing you can ever do," said the teacher. "We are not in Jerusalem, we do not have the Temple, but by learning to love the Law and by obeying it, we can truly worship God."

Then the old teacher got up and walked to the window. "There's the road," he said. "It could be the beginning of our homeward journey. One day, I'm sure, God will enable us to return to Jerusalem."

Dear God,
May I put effort
into the things
that are
worthwhile.

Dear God,
May I
remember that
justice does not
depend on
shouting and
loud speeches.

Dreaming of home

MANY OF THE JEWS in Babylon dreamed of going home. Among them were prophets, who could perceive God's plans for the nation.

"Listen, you people of Israel," wrote one. "I made you, I will save you. Your troubles may seem like deep, swirling water, but they will not drown you. Your troubles may seem like a wall of fire, but they will not burn you. I am the Lord your God, the Holy One of Israel. I will bring my people home from east and west, from all over the world.

"You remember how I rescued you in days of old – how I led you through the sea. Do not cling to the past. Watch for the new thing I am going to do. I am going to make a path through the wilderness. I will make streams flow there. Your children and your children's children will live in a rich and fertile land.

"One by one, everybody in the world will come to join you. 'I belong to God,' they will say. Everyone in the whole world will be my beloved people.

"Listen! I will send my servant, whom I have strengthened by my spirit. He will not shout or make loud speeches. Quietly, gently, he will bring justice to all the world."

The homecoming

❧

T HE GREAT EMPIRE of Babylon that held the people captive was never completely secure. Rival nations struggled to take their share of power. At length, Cyrus of Persia became the ruler of the whole empire. He issued a new command:

"The God of heaven has made me the supreme ruler of the world. That great and mighty God wants me to build a Temple in Jerusalem. It is the city of the Jews, and they must do the building. If any Jewish people in the empire need help to pay for the journey home, their neighbors are to give it. They must also supply gifts to be offered to God in the Temple."

Cyrus himself handed back to the Jews the gold and silver cups that had been taken from the Temple when it was destroyed.

Soon, long lines of exiles began wending their way back home. Many walked, though a few rode donkeys or mules, and there were camels to carry the heaviest loads. Weary but joyful, they reached Jerusalem.

As soon as they could, the people built an altar in their ruined city. Morning and evening they made offerings to God there.

They sang a psalm:

> I call to you, Lord; help me now!
> Listen to me when I call to you.
> Receive my prayer as incense,
> my uplifted hands as an evening sacrifice.

3 July

❖

Ezra 1, 3,
Psalm 141

*Dear God,
My gift to you
is a prayer
from the heart.*

191

*Dear God,
I want to
learn to love
truth and
peace.*

A new power struggle

❧

THE JEWS WERE delighted to be back in Judah. "Now we can truly be God's people again," they said.

However, in all the upheavals of empire building, other people had been resettled in the land. They were naturally suspicious of the Jews who had come back to make their home there. They grew even more worried when the Jews began to rebuild their Temple.

"Those Jews will treat us like outsiders in our own home," they said to one another. "Perhaps if we join in the rebuilding, they will accept us."

The Jewish leaders did not want their help. "The emperor said that our nation must do the work," they said.

The other people were angry at the response. "How dare they act so arrogantly!" they raged. "Let's write to the emperor to complain. Let's tell him just how rebellious the Jews are. Let's warn him that it would be a big mistake to let them rebuild their city."

Their campaign was successful. For several years, no work was done on the Temple.

Then two prophets began to speak out. "What right do you think you have to live in well-built houses while the Temple lies in ruins?" cried Haggai. "Can't you see what is happening? Your harvests are poor, your vineyards bear little fruit, you can barely afford the clothing you need. All this is because God has sent a drought. There will be no rain, no blessing and no prosperity until the Temple is restored."

"Don't be afraid!" said Zechariah. "God wants our people to set an example of justice and peace. When we do that, all the nations of the world will want to worship in Jerusalem. That is the way we can truly be God's people."

The second Temple

❧

THE JEWS WERE encouraged by what the prophets said. They appealed to the new emperor, Darius, to let them complete the Temple. At last, and only after a long search, Darius found the order that Cyrus had written. He agreed to their request.

At once, work began again in earnest. The builders and the craftworkers were full of enthusiasm and did the finest work they could. However, there was not much money to spend on materials, and the second Temple was not nearly as splendid as Solomon's.

"Don't be discouraged," said Haggai. "The time will come when everyone in the world will worship God. Then we shall be able to use all the gold and silver in the world."

"This is a time to rejoice," said Zechariah. "God has told me that a new king is coming to our nation. He will come in triumph – and yet he will be a humble king. Look! I can almost see him now, riding to Jerusalem on a donkey. It is a sure sign that he is coming to bring peace to all the world."

At last, the Temple was ready. There was a great ceremony of dedication. Once again, the people celebrated Passover. Together they sang a psalm:

When the Lord brought us back to Jerusalem, it was like a dream!
How we laughed, how we sang for joy!
The other nations all said, "The Lord has done great things for them."
Indeed, the Lord has done great things for us, and we are glad.

Dear God,
Your many
blessings make
us laugh and
sing for joy.

King Xerxes' banquet

Dear God,
May I
understand
that money
can buy both
good things
and
bad things.

FROM HIS ROYAL throne in Persia's capital city of Susa, King Xerxes ruled a vast empire. One day, he decided to organize a huge celebration to show off his wealth. It began with a banquet for all his officials and nobles and army generals. When that was done, he gave a banquet for all the people of Susa, rich and poor alike.

"Who would have dreamed of such a day?" they wondered. "Here we are, walking on a courtyard that shines like jewels!"

The intricate patterns of paving stones – white marble and red feldspar, shining mother-of-pearl and blue turquoise – seemed to belong more in heaven than on earth. The people drank from gold cups which servants refilled time and again.

King Xerxes was enjoying the drinking himself. On the seventh day of the banquet, when he was more than a little merry, he sent for his wife, Queen Vashti. She was inside the palace giving a banquet for the women.

"I want everyone to see how lovely she is," he roared drunkenly.

Queen Vashti was not amused. "Tell the king that I will not comply with this rude and drunken request," she said to the messenger.

The king was furious at her. "I won't allow this!" he said to his advisers. "I give a banquet to show everyone my power and wealth, and my wife makes a fool of me."

"Then make a new law, " said the advisers, "stating that in your empire husbands are in charge of their households. After that seek out the most beautiful young women in the empire and choose a new wife."

"Excellent!" said the king.

Esther and Mordecai

❧

IN THE CITY of Susa lived a Jew named Mordecai. He had been among the captives taken from Jerusalem in the time of King Jehoiachin. He looked after a young cousin as if she were his daughter. Her name was Esther.

The king's officials noticed Mordecai's relative when they were searching for the most beautiful women in the empire. They chose her to be among those who were taken to the palace to be paraded in front of the king.

"A word of advice, my dear," whispered her cousin Mordecai. "Don't tell anyone you're Jewish."

Once in the harem, Esther and the other girls were given beauty treatments for a whole year. Mordecai spent time every day walking up and down in front of the harem courtyard in order to glean news of how she was doing. He was anxious for her future, most of all on the day when she was taken to the king.

In truth, no one should have been surprised at the outcome. King Xerxes chose the beautiful Esther to be his new queen and proclaimed a public holiday of celebration.

Meanwhile, Mordecai had been given a job as a palace administrator. One day, he heard of a plot against the king. He told Esther, and she told Xerxes himself. He gave orders for the traitors to be hanged.

"This has been a sordid affair," Xerxes growled, "but it is an important part of our history. I want it properly written up for the official records."

And that was that. Some time later, the king chose a new prime minister. His name was Haman. The king ordered all his officials to show Haman respect.

Mordecai refused. "I'm not going to bow and kneel to him!" he snorted. "I'm a Jew. I don't bow to a foreign official."

Haman was furious at Mordecai's stubborn attitude. "Your Majesty," he said to the king, "there is a whole race of rebels in the empire. I think you should make a law that will enable us to… exterminate them."

"Whatever you advise," agreed the king.

Dear God, May I be brave to declare where my loyalties lie.

195

*Dear God,
May I know
when it is time
for me to act
boldly and
bravely.*

Haman's plot

HAMAN MOVED SWIFTLY to carry out his plot against the Jews. At once he sent messengers to every part of the empire. His proclamation was brutal: on the thirteenth day of the month of Adar, all Jews were to be slaughtered and their belongings taken.

Mordecai wept at the news. "This is a disaster!" he said. "Haman wants to be rid of an entire people – my people!" He put on sackcloth and ashes to show his grief. There was anguish like his in every Jewish home throughout the empire, along with much weeping and wailing.

Esther's servants whispered the news to her. She sent a secret message to Mordecai and he sent a reply. "You must go and plead with the king for your people. You are our only hope."

She read his plea with tears in her eyes. "I can't just go!" she said. "Anyone who goes to see the king without being summoned is put to death – well, unless the king holds out his scepter as a sign of forgiveness. The king hasn't summoned me for a month." She sent another message explaining all this to Mordecai.

In return, he sent a warning. "You won't be safe just because you are queen. You're still Jewish. You have to think of your people. Maybe it was for a time like this that you were made queen."

Esther thought long and hard about his words. Perhaps her cousin was right. Perhaps it was her duty to take the risk. Either way, it seemed that she would not have much longer to live. She sent a final message:

"Please ask all the Jews in Susa to fast and pray for me for three days. I will fast and pray as well. Then I will go to the king, even though it is against the law to go without being summoned. If I must die, then I will die."

Esther and the king

❧

FOR THREE DAYS, Esther fasted and prayed. Then she put on her royal robes and went to the entrance to the throne room. She stood there facing the king. Their eyes met. Esther willed herself to stay calm. Would he welcome her? Would he order her execution? She hardly dared breathe.

The king eyed her thoughtfully. His new queen – Esther. He hadn't had time to spend with her for ever so long. And what had she come for? He was intrigued.

Slowly he held out his gold scepter.

It was the sign Esther needed. She sighed with relief as she came nearer.

"Tell me what you want," said the king. "I promise you shall have it."

"If it pleases Your Majesty," said Esther, "I would like you and Haman to come to a banquet tonight."

"I shall be delighted," he said.

Esther's dinner party for the two men was a great success. At the end, the king asked Esther again what she wanted.

Esther lowered her eyes respectfully. "Please come to another banquet tomorrow," she said. "Then I shall tell you."

I wonder what Esther wants, thought Haman happily. It must be something to do with me and the king. She must think me very important to invite me a second time!

As he trotted out of the palace he saw Mordecai. The two men looked at each other. Mordecai did not get up or even nod in respect.

"Insolent Jew!" muttered Haman, when he arrived home. "The king and queen adore me, and there's that nasty little foreigner treating me like dirt."

"Use your authority to have a gallows built," said his wife. "Hang the scoundrel."

Dear God, May I learn gentle ways of persuading people to do right.

*Dear God,
May good
deeds be
rewarded.*

Changing fortunes

KING XERXES ALSO felt happy as he left Esther's dinner party. The only trouble was, he couldn't get to sleep.

"Bring out some of the imperial history books," he said to his servants. "I'd like someone to read to me."

He listened thoughtfully as he heard again the account of a serious plot against his life. "That Mordecai, the one who foiled the plot –" he asked, "how did we reward him?"

"We didn't do anything, Your Majesty," his servants replied.

"Find me an official at once," said the king.

The servants found Haman. He was hurrying to Xerxes to ask for Mordecai to be hanged and was delighted that the king wanted to see him.

"There is someone I want to honor very highly," said Xerxes to Haman. "What do you suggest?"

Haman was thrilled at what he heard. It must be me! I can name my own reward, he thought. "Your Majesty," he said, smiling broadly, "I think you should give that man royal robes to wear. Have one of your own horses dressed in finery for a parade. Then let the man ride though the streets, with a nobleman going ahead to proclaim his greatness."

"Excellent," said the king. "Now go and do all that for Mordecai the Jew. He's sitting at the palace entrance."

Esther's triumph

HAMAN HAD NEVER had such a bad day. "You can't begin to imagine the shame of it!" he said to his wife. "I had to go all over the city telling everyone how much the king values Mordecai," he moaned to his friends. "And you already know what I think of that meddling Jew. I felt so humiliated."

"Oh dear," they replied. "You're losing power to him. You'll never win now."

Haman tried not to let their pessimism get him down. After all, there was still Esther's banquet to attend. It cheered him up to imagine what part he might have to play in the queen's mystery scheme.

At the dinner party, the time came for her to make her request. "Please, Your Majesty," she said, "my people are under threat. An enemy wants them exterminated."

"That's an outrage!" said the king. "Who is this enemy?"

Esther paused for just a moment and then looked directly at her husband, the king, as she spoke the name.

"Haman."

"Haman? The man who's wheedled his way into my trust?" The king stormed out of the room to think about what he had just heard. Haman pleaded with Esther. "Save me, save me!" he said, flinging himself onto the couch where she was reclining. "Please, please, Esther, I am your devoted –"

"WHAT DO YOU THINK YOU'RE DOING WITH MY WIFE!" shouted the king from the doorway. Two slaves grabbed Haman. "This man built a gallows on which to hang Mordecai," said one.

"Hang Haman on them instead," said the king.

After that, the king agreed that the Jews should be able to defend themselves from their enemies on the day that had been set for their extermination. Mordecai sent letters to the Jews throughout the empire encouraging them to celebrate their victory. The festival, called Purim, has been celebrated ever since.

Dear God, Save the people you love from their enemies.

*Dear God,
May people
who have power
and influence
help to bring
about the
things that
you want.*

Nehemiah

THE JEWS WERE able to thrive throughout the Persian empire. Indeed, it was only a minority of them who had returned to Judah and Jerusalem. In the time of King Artaxerxes, one devout Jew was working in the royal palace in Susa. His name was Nehemiah and he was the king's wine steward.

One day, when he was at work, the king noticed that Nehemiah was looking gloomy. "Is there any reason why you are sad?" he asked.

Nehemiah was startled. "I'm sorry, Your Majesty," he said. "I have just heard news about the Jews who have gone back to Jerusalem. There are constant squabbles between them and the other peoples who live in the region, and our once-glorious city has still not been rebuilt. The walls are in the same state as when the city was burned down."

"What do you want to do about it?" asked the king.

Nehemiah had already said long prayers to God about Jerusalem. Now he said a short, silent prayer before answering.

"If Your Majesty would allow it, I would like to go to my homeland and help rebuild Jerusalem."

"Then you shall go!" said the king. Artaxerxes gave Nehemiah all the help he needed to make the journey safely. Nehemiah arrived in Jerusalem and began to assess the situation. One night, with just a few companions, he rode a donkey around the walls to see what repairs were needed. He could tell there was a long job ahead of him.

Rebuilding the walls

❧

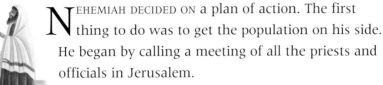

NEHEMIAH DECIDED ON a plan of action. The first thing to do was to get the population on his side. He began by calling a meeting of all the priests and officials in Jerusalem.

"We must rebuild the city walls," he said. "It will be a clear message to our troublesome neighbors to leave us alone. God has answered my prayers in letting me come here. God has given me the support of the emperor himself."

Nehemiah's confidence made everyone enthusiastic. They organized themselves into family and community groups that would each build a section of the city walls. It was such hard work that they made up a song to help keep them going:

There's so much rubble to take away,
How can we build the wall today?

The non-Jews who lived nearby were dismayed by their enthusiasm and by the progress they were making. They plotted together to attack Jerusalem, but the Jews were determined not to give in. Instead, they prayed to God to protect them.

"An attack could come at any time," said Nehemiah, "so we need to be ready for that. Half of the workers must build while the others stand guard, fully armed. I want someone with me at all times ready to sound the bugle if we see trouble. If you hear it, gather around. I am confident that God will fight with us."

The work went on from morning until evening, day after day. Each night, the people stayed on the alert, ready to jump up and defend the city if needed. The walls grew higher and higher.

Nehemiah knew that he himself was a target for his people's enemies. "Make me strong, God," he prayed. "Don't let my enemies defeat me."

Dear God, Please make me strong to complete whatever you want me to do.

Dear God,
May we share
food and drink
with those who
do not have
enough.

Ezra reads the Law

NEHEMIAH WAS TIRELESS in organizing the rebuilding of Jerusalem. When, at last, the walls were complete, the Jewish people had a city to be proud of, a city where they could build their homes and be safe.

Nehemiah stayed on as governor of Judah. It was an important job, but he refused to make himself rich. Instead, he made everyone agree to treat poor people fairly. Every day, he prayed faithfully to God.

The next project was to make the Temple the holy place that it deserved to be. A Jewish priest named Ezra arrived from Babylonia with a crowd of priests, musicians, guards and workmen and he took charge of re-establishing the worship there, following all the customs of days gone by.

Ezra was also a scholar: he understood more than anyone about the laws God had given to Moses. He called all the people to a huge open-air meeting in the city. There, from a wooden platform, he read the Law to them in Hebrew. He had helpers standing by to give a translation into Aramaic, the language everyone now spoke.

When the people heard the laws, they began to weep. "We have failed to obey our God," they cried. "Whatever shall we do?"

"Don't be upset," he answered. "This is a holy day. Go home and have a feast. Share your food and wine with anyone who doesn't have enough. The joy that God gives you will make you strong."

A great festival

❧

ALL THE PEOPLE in Jerusalem were eager to relearn the traditions of their people. Ezra dedicated himself to teaching them about God's Law and how to keep it faithfully.

As they studied their holy books, they rediscovered God's commands about the festival of Shelters. Once a year, everyone was supposed to build a little shelter and sleep out in it for the week of the festival: in this way, they would be reminded of how God had sheltered the people in the time of Moses, as they journeyed from Egypt to their new land.

They agreed to revive the tradition at once. The people brought branches of pine, olive, myrtle and palm and made little huts throughout the city: on the flat roofs of their houses, in their courtyards and in two of the public squares. Every day for seven days the Law was read aloud.

After the festival came the time for the people to confess their sins. A prayer was said, reminding them of the long history of their people, and of how God had taken care of them since the time of Abraham.

"Time and again we have failed to obey your laws," they prayed. "We are sorry. We promise now to keep your holy laws."

Ezra and Nehemiah both wanted the best for their people. They wanted everyone to live good and holy lives.

*Dear God,
May our
festivals be
both joyful
and holy.*

And now I give you a new commandment: love one another.

If you have love for one another, then everyone will know

that you are my disciples.

Words of Jesus from John 13:34–35

THE NEW TESTAMENT

Dear God,
Make me ready
to believe the
messages you
give me.

Zechariah

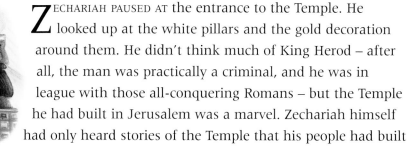

ZECHARIAH PAUSED AT the entrance to the Temple. He looked up at the white pillars and the gold decoration around them. He didn't think much of King Herod – after all, the man was practically a criminal, and he was in league with those all-conquering Romans – but the Temple he had built in Jerusalem was a marvel. Zechariah himself had only heard stories of the Temple that his people had built when they returned from exile. In those days, there had not been enough money to create anything splendid; but this new building was one of which the Jewish people could be proud.

Zechariah hurried inside. He was a priest and it was his turn to burn the incense on the altar in the inner room while the people outside prayed to God. He set about the task and watched with awe and reverence as the sweet-smelling smoke curled into the air.

Something caught his attention: what could he see to the right of the altar? Surely it couldn't be…

"Don't be afraid," said the angel. "God has heard your prayer. Your wife will have a son. You are to name him John. He will be a prophet and will bring many people back to faith in God."

Zechariah simply shook his head. "How shall I know if this is so?" he said. "I am old, and so is my wife, Elizabeth."

"I am Gabriel," said the angel. "I have brought you this message directly from God, and you have not believed it. For this, you will be unable to speak until the child is born."

The angel vanished. Zechariah stood there for – he didn't know how long – and then he stumbled outside.

Those who had come to worship were still there, wondering why he had taken so long. He tried to explain but he couldn't speak. He gestured at them to try to explain but it did good.

The time came for him to return home to his wife, Elizabeth. Zechariah had plenty of time to wonder what the vision had meant.

Then one day, Elizabeth came hurrying to greet him. "I'm pregnant," she exclaimed. "Can you believe it!"

Mary and the angel

🐌

Nazareth was only a small town: a huddle of flat-roofed houses nestled on a hilltop in Galilee. It had never been famous for anything.

One day, God told the angel Gabriel to visit a young woman who lived there. Her name was Mary, and she was soon to be married to a man named Joseph.

"Peace be with you," said the angel. "God is with you and has blessed you."

Mary looked up and trembled with fear. Who was this visitor who was speaking to her? What did the words mean?

"Don't be afraid," said the angel. "God has chosen you to be the mother of a baby boy. You will name him Jesus. He will be known as the Son of the Most High God. He will be your people's king, and his kingdom will last forever."

Mary shook her head. "That's impossible," she said. "I'm a virgin. I know I can't be going to have a baby." She looked directly at Gabriel.

The angel held her gaze. "It is God's power that will make all this come true," said Gabriel. "Remember the news about your relative Elizabeth. Everyone thought she was too old to have a baby, but she is now six months pregnant. There is nothing God cannot do."

Mary lowered her eyes. "I am ready to do what God wants," she said. "If what you say is true, then I accept it."

All at once she was alone. She could hardly believe what had just happened.

Dear God,
May I always
be ready to
do what you
want.

Mary and Elizabeth

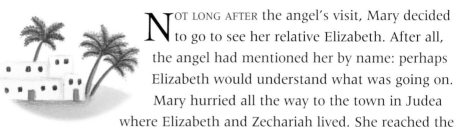

Not long after the angel's visit, Mary decided to go to see her relative Elizabeth. After all, the angel had mentioned her by name: perhaps Elizabeth would understand what was going on. Mary hurried all the way to the town in Judea where Elizabeth and Zechariah lived. She reached the entrance to the house and called out, "Hello! Is anyone home? It's Mary, from Nazareth."

Elizabeth clutched her middle. The baby was kicking inside her. Suddenly she knew exactly why Mary had come and what she was going to say.

"Mary!" she cried. "God has blessed you more than any woman in the world. God has blessed the baby you are going to have. I feel so privileged that you have come to tell me first. The baby inside me is jumping for joy too. It's all because of your deep trust in God."

Mary felt happier than ever.

"From my heart, I praise the Lord," she sang.

God has blessed me, God has made me happy.
Our God is coming to help our people.
God's promises are all coming true.

The two woman laughed and sang together. Then they agreed that Mary should stay awhile as they had so much going on in both their lives.

Soon after Mary went home, it was time for Elizabeth to have her baby. Everyone was surprised that she wanted to call him John. "Why not Zechariah, like his father?" they asked.

Zechariah asked for something to write with. "His name is John," he wrote. At once, he was able to speak again, and he began to praise God. "I know for sure that God's promises to help our people are all coming true," he said.

Joseph

JOSEPH HAD ALWAYS tried to do the right thing: he was, quite simply, a decent and honest person. When he had first heard that his bride-to-be was pregnant, he had been both dismayed and perplexed.

"What is the right thing to do now?" he had asked himself. "I can't marry Mary; but I don't want everyone gossiping about her."

He could not sleep for worrying. At last he had decided. "I shall break off the engagement quietly," he had told himself. "That way, Mary and her family will have a chance to sort themselves out as best they can; when the gossip dies down, I'll just have to make a new future for myself."

The more he had thought about it, the more that had seemed like a good plan. He hadn't felt happy, for he had still felt very committed to Mary, but he would have to let time heal his pain about that. He had lain down and fallen asleep.

That night, in a dream, an angel had appeared to him.

"Joseph: don't be afraid to marry Mary. Everything is part of God's plan. She will have a son who will save people from their sins. You are to call him 'Jesus.'"

When Joseph woke up, the message was still ringing through his head, and he made a new plan. "I shall marry Mary and take good care of her and her child, whatever the cost."

Dear God, When I don't know which way to go, speak to me and help me make the right choice.

209

The baby in the manger

*Dear God,
May I
recognize the
Son of God.*

THE LAND OF the Jews was part of the Roman empire. Around this time the emperor, Augustus, issued a new law: everyone had to take part in a census. He wanted to know exactly how many people he ruled so he could calculate how much they could pay in taxes.

It was a huge task: everyone had to go to their hometown to put their names on an official list. Mary was soon to be married, so she and her future husband had to put their names down together. Joseph could trace his family back to the nation's great king David – and that meant they had to travel from Nazareth in Galilee to Bethlehem in Judea.

All over the empire, people were on the move for the same reason. When Mary and Joseph reached Bethlehem, there were no rooms where they could stay.

"My baby will be born soon," said Mary anxiously. "We must find somewhere to lie down for the night."

The only place they could find was a shelter for farm animals. It gave them a roof over their heads, but not much else.

There, Mary's baby boy was born. She wrapped him in swaddling clothes and laid him in the manger as tenderly as if it were the finest cradle. She smiled at his sleeping face. On this, his first night on earth, her child was as good as homeless. Would the angel's words really come true? Would people really call him the Son of the Most High God?

The shepherds on the hillside

OUT ON THE hillsides nearby, some shepherds were keeping watch through the hours of darkness. They needed to be ready at all times to keep their sheep from harm. They were used to the ordinary perils of the night: a thief, a sly fox, a lion prowling in the shadows.

Oh! But what was that? A sheet of lightning? But no, the light was strong and steady, and in its midst stood someone who shone like gold.

"Do not be afraid," said the angel – for that is what it was. "I come with good news – news to make the whole world joyful. A new king has been born in Bethlehem: the promised one, the messiah, the Christ.

"Listen – I want you to know that I am telling the truth. You can go and find the baby. He is wrapped in swaddling clothes and lying in a manger."

All at once, a multitude of angels appeared.

"Glory to God in heaven," they sang. "Peace on earth."

For a moment, heaven and earth were cradled in the same pure, clear light. Then the night sky went dark and all the angels vanished.

The shepherds waited, stock-still with amazement. "Well," said one slowly. "Were we dreaming? Shall we go to Bethlehem?"

They hurried off up the hill and searched the streets. Soon they found Mary and Joseph and the baby just as the angel had said. Mary listened carefully to their news. She wanted to remember every detail of this miraculous night.

Dear God, May I recognize angels. May I see heaven on earth.

*Dear God,
May I see your
goodness with
my own eyes.*

In the Temple

AMONG THE JEWISH people, it was the custom to have a naming ceremony a week after a baby was born. Mary and Joseph gave their child the name the angel had said: Jesus.

Not long after, Mary and Joseph went to the Temple in Jerusalem for another ceremony. This one was to dedicate their baby to God.

While they were there an old man named Simeon came up to them. Mary let him hold baby Jesus. Simeon's aged face creased into wrinkles as he smiled at the newborn. He felt strangely happy and he knew why.

"I can die happy now," he said. "With my own eyes I have seen the one God has sent to rescue us – the one who will bring a blessing to all the world."

He looked up at Mary. "There will be hard times ahead," he warned. "You must be ready for heartbreak over the things that will happen to your son."

An elderly woman named Anna came over to see the baby. "What an adorable baby," she began. Then she smiled such a joyful smile that her face no longer looked old. "Thanks be to God," she said. "I am sure this is the child God promised to send our people. This is the best news in all the world. I must go and tell everyone that God is going to do great things for us – as great as the miracles our people saw in days of old. Oh, there's someone I must tell over there."

As the old woman hurried away, Mary took her baby back from Simeon and hugged Jesus close.

The star in the east

❧

Around the time of Jesus' birth, a new star appeared in the night sky.

Some astronomers who saw it were thrilled.

"What a discovery!" they said to each other. "What a truly momentous sign!

"All our learning tells us that it can only mean one thing: a king has been born among the Jewish people.

"And a great king he must be for his coming to be told so spectacularly in the heavens above."

The men set out to find the newborn king. "It is almost certain that he will be in Jerusalem," they said to each other. "That is the great city of the Jewish people."

When they got there, they began asking for directions. "Where is the baby born to be king of the Jews?" No one had any idea, but soon the news of their inquiries began to spread. It spread as far as the palace, and to King Herod himself.

He summoned the priests and teachers who advised him on things to do with religion. "All this talk about a king and a sign in the heavens," he said. "I'm wondering if it's linked to what the scriptures say about a king, a messiah. Do the writings also tell us anything useful... such as where he will be born?"

"Indeed they do!" came the reply. "Listen to what the prophet Micah said:

"Bethlehem... from you will come a leader who will guide my people –"

"Excellent!" said Herod. He called for one of his officers. "I'll meet those astronomers privately," he said. "Have them brought here."

In a secret meeting at the dead of night, Herod told the astronomers to go to Bethlehem.

"It is only right that you wise and learned people find this wonderful child," he said flatteringly, "but I need to know about him too." He leaned forward. "You will come back and tell me where to find him, won't you?"

*Dear God,
May I learn
to see the signs
you give the
world.*

The three gifts

*Dear God,
Show me what
gift I can
offer you in
worship.*

THE LEARNED ASTRONOMERS journeyed on from Jerusalem.
"Look!" said one of them. "The star is shining right over the road to Bethlehem. Truly, everything is working together to bless our journey."

And indeed the star led them all the way to one particular house.

They went inside and, to their joy, they found Mary and Jesus.

The astronomers knelt down to worship the little boy. Then they brought out their gifts: gold, frankincense and myrrh.

They rested before setting out on the journey home and, as they lay dreaming, they all came to think the same thing. "It would be most unwise to go back to Herod," they agreed.

"From what I've been hearing, we were lucky not to have more trouble from him when we met him," said one. "Apparently he can be ruthless when angry – his rivals have a habit of going missing."

They chose a different road – one that went well clear of Jerusalem. The night after they had gone, Joseph had a dream too. Once again an angel spoke to him: "Get up now! Take the child and his mother and escape to Egypt. King Herod is looking for the newborn king. He wants to kill him."

The little family fled in the night. It was not until Jesus was a young boy that they dared return to their own country, and to Nazareth.

The Passover in Jerusalem

IT WAS THE DREAM of every Jew to be in Jerusalem for the Passover festival. Jesus' parents went every year, along with many people from Nazareth.

When Jesus was twelve years old, he was allowed to go too. The days of celebration felt like a joyful holiday, but all too soon, it was time to go home.

Jesus' parents were swept along in the tide of people going back north to Galilee. As the day wore on, they began to wonder where Jesus was.

"He could be anywhere!" they said.

They began asking among their friends and relatives. "Have you seen Jesus? Can you think where he might be?"

No one had seen him. "Oh dear," said Mary, her eyes filling with tears. "He must be somewhere between here and Jerusalem. Or maybe he stayed in the city – or maybe something terrible has happened to him and…"

"We'll go back at once!" her husband said. "There has to be an explanation. There's no need to panic yet."

For three days the couple searched. They went back to Jerusalem and asked everywhere if anyone had seen Jesus. No one could help them.

Helpless and despairing, they decided to search the Temple, dodging through the crowds to look in every corner.

Then they saw him: Jesus was just sitting with a group of rabbis. They were talking about the scriptures and how to understand them. The older men looked impressed at the things the boy was saying.

"Jesus! Why have you done this to us!" Mary said, panic in her voice. "We have been terribly worried."

Jesus looked astonished. "Why did you have to look for me? Didn't you know that I had to be in my Father's house?"

His answer did not make any sense to them. "Just be sensible and come home with us now!" they said.

Jesus went obediently, and grew up a good son.

*Dear God,
Help me to
be obedient to
those who
love me.*

*Dear God,
May each day
be a new
beginning.*

John the Baptist

JESUS AND HIS relative John both grew into honest young men. From the time John was able to make up his own mind, he knew in his heart that God was calling him to be a prophet.

One day, he went off to the wilderness in Judea. He dressed in rough brown cloth woven from camel's hair, with a leather belt tied around his waist – the rough, simple type of clothing that prophets of days gone by had chosen. He ate only the food he could gather for himself – locusts and wild honey.

He began to preach to passersby, and the message he gave was clear and inspiring. Soon the news began to spread that it was worth a trip to see him. People came from Jerusalem and the country round about to hear what he had to say.

"Turn away from your sins," he cried. "God will forgive you. Remember the words of the prophets of old, and make yourselves ready for God to come among us.

"Don't think it is enough to be descended from Abraham. That's not what makes you one of God's people. What matters is that you live as God wants, by God's standards of goodness and righteousness and holiness."

Many people were touched by what he said but they wanted to know more. "What must we actually do?" they asked.

"Share your belongings with those in need," John replied. "You, tax collectors – stop cheating people. Only take what is legal. And as for you soldiers – act fairly. Don't bully people into giving you money. You have your pay."

Those who accepted John's challenge asked to be baptized in the River Jordan. It was a sign of a new beginning.

Jesus is baptized

*Dear God,
May your
Holy Spirit
make me truly
your child.*

JOHN'S PREACHING WAS bold and outspoken. He declared what was right and wrong without hesitation. He even dared to criticize the king of Galilee, whose name was Herod. People began to wonder if he might be the man to lead the Jewish people to freedom: they began to ask themselves if he was God's messiah. The number of John's followers and supporters was growing steadily, and among them were those who were prepared to fight for their people's freedom.

John knew what to tell them all.

"Listen to what I've been saying: I'm telling you to get yourselves ready for the messiah," he said. "All I do is baptize you with water. There's someone much greater than me whom God will send. I'm not fit even to be his servant and untie his sandals. He will baptize you with God's Holy Spirit."

Around that time, Jesus arrived from Nazareth in Galilee and asked John to baptize him.

The preacher was puzzled at his cousin's humility. He shook his head at the request. "Surely it should be you who baptizes me," he replied.

"God would want it this way for now," said Jesus.

John shrugged. "I suppose you know what you're doing," he said, and he led Jesus down to the water.

He baptized him by holding him for a moment beneath the eddying water of the River Jordan, and then lifted him up into the clear air. As he did so, he saw something like a dove fluttering down from the sky. It came and settled on Jesus' head. At once, John knew that this was a sign of God's Holy Spirit. It was telling him that Jesus was truly God's chosen one.

Dear God,
Help me learn
the scriptures,
so I will know
how to do
what is right.

Temptation in the wilderness

❦

AFTER JESUS WAS baptized, he went out into the wilderness to spend time alone.

He stayed there for forty days, and in that time he ate nothing. By the end, he was desperately hungry. Then he heard the devil whispering.

"If you are God's Son, order this stone to turn into bread."

"No," said Jesus. "The scripture says, 'Human beings cannot live on bread alone.'"

The thought that the devil had put in his mind vanished like a forgotten dream.

Not long after, as Jesus gazed at the dusty landscape, he thought he saw something shimmering in the heat. "Look," whispered the devil. "Here are all the kingdoms of the world. They're mine; but I could give them to you… if you worship me."

Jesus stood up. "The scripture says, 'Worship the Lord your God and serve only him,'" he said aloud. At once, the kingdoms vanished.

Jesus knew in his heart that his mission was to lead people to God: the God whom his people worshiped at the Temple.

"Yes," came the whisper. "Imagine yourself standing on the highest point of the Temple. Are you really God's Son? you wonder. What will make people believe your claim? You could throw yourself down. Remember the scriptures: 'God will order the angels to take good care of you. They will hold you up in their hands.'"

Jesus shook his head. "The scripture says, 'Do not put the Lord your God to the test,'" he said firmly.

The devil fled: Jesus could not be tempted away from what God was calling him to do.

Jesus begins to preach

❧

JESUS LEFT THE wilderness and went back to Galilee. He began preaching in the synagogues. Everyone began to talk about what a fine young teacher he was.

On one occasion, he went back home to Nazareth and to the synagogue there. He was asked to read the scripture passage for the day, which came from the book of the prophet Isaiah.

Jesus unrolled the scroll. He found the place and began to read.

> *The Spirit of the Lord is upon me,*
> *because he has chosen me to bring good news to the poor.*
> *He has sent me to proclaim liberty to the captives*
> *and recovery of sight to the blind;*
> *to set free the oppressed*
> *and announce that the time has come*
> *when the Lord will save his people.*

Then Jesus rolled up the scroll and handed it back. He sat down. Everyone was looking at him, wondering if he was going to offer some comment on the passage, as was the custom.

"This passage has come true today," he said, "as you heard it being read."

The people were astonished and began to whisper. "What do you think this means? He's only the son of Joseph, isn't he?"

Jesus sighed. "I'm sure you're wondering if I'm going to do the sort of things you've heard I did in Capernaum. It's not far away – but far enough. The people there believe me. No prophet is ever welcome in his hometown. Think of Elisha: in his day, there were many sick people in Israel, but the only person he cured of a dreaded skin disease was a foreigner, Naaman, the Syrian."

Suddenly, everyone was angry. The elders hustled Jesus out of the synagogue. Younger men dragged him out of the town.

"Let's throw him off a cliff," they shouted. "Who does he think he is?"

Somehow Jesus managed to slip away. He would never be welcome in Nazareth again.

29 July

❖

Luke 4
(quoting Isaiah
61:1–2)

*Dear God,
May I be ready
to respect the
wisdom of
those who are
close to me.*

*Dear God,
Thank you for
your power
to heal.*

Jesus in Peter's house

JESUS HURRIED TO Capernaum, on the shore of Lake Galilee. The people in the synagogue there were amazed by the things he said and did. On the day Jesus arrived, there was a man in the synagogue who could not control the things he said and did – some evil power seemed to be in charge of him. He began screaming:

"What do you want with us, Jesus of Nazareth? Are you here to destroy us? I know who you are – you're God's holy messenger."

"Be quiet," said Jesus – but it was the evil he was addressing. "Leave that man alone."

At that, the man fell down. When he stood up, he was in his right mind.

Jesus left the synagogue and went home with one of his friends, who was a fisherman.

"Excuse the mess," said Simon, as he showed Jesus into the house. "My mother-in-law is sick and we've got behind with the chores." He shrugged sadly. "In fact, I'm not sure she's going to survive the fever she has."

Jesus asked to see her. He went to the old woman's bedside. She moaned fitfully as the visitor took her hand. "Listen to me, fever," said Jesus. "Leave her alone!"

The woman sagged back into the bedclothes. Then she blinked and sat up. "Who are you – oh! A guest of my son-in-law. I'm so sorry I wasn't at the door to welcome you. Give me a moment and I'll make you a meal."

"But mother…" began her daughter.

"I feel fine," said the older woman, and she stood up and smoothed out the creases in the clothes she was wearing. "I shall get to the kitchen at once and I'll have everything ready in no time."

It was not the first time Jesus had healed someone. News of his miracles was spreading through the town. At sunset, all kinds of people arrived at the house, bringing with them friends and relatives who were unwell. Jesus healed them all.

Jesus and the fishermen

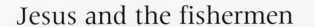

ONE DAY, JESUS was preaching on the shore of Lake Galilee. His message was simple: "Here is good news! You can turn away from your sins! You can make yourselves ready for God's kingdom." Crowds came to listen to what he had to say.

"We can hardly see," said those at the back. "Let's squeeze forward."

Soon everyone was beginning to push and shove. Jesus was dismayed. What could he do?

Then he saw the two boats on the beach. One belonged to his friend Simon. He and his fishing partners were nearby, washing the nets.

Jesus climbed aboard and asked Simon to push the boat farther into the water. Now everyone could see him as he continued preaching.

When Jesus had finished, he spoke to Simon again. "Take this boat into deeper water and let your nets down for a catch."

"It's not worth it," said Simon. "We fished all night and caught nothing." Jesus simply raised his eyebrows.

"Oh, if you like, I'll do what you say," said Simon. "You'll soon see."

But when the men let down their nets as Jesus said, they caught so many fish that they struggled to land them.

Suddenly Simon felt afraid. Now he knew for sure there was something special about Jesus. "Don't be afraid," said Jesus. "From now on, you will be helping me to catch people."

On that day, four of the fishermen left their boats and their nets to follow Jesus: Simon and his brother Andrew, and James and his brother John.

*Dear God,
Make me ready
to follow Jesus.*

*Dear God,
Thank you for
the healing
power of
forgiveness.*

The hole in the roof

❧

JESUS' MIRACLES BECAME the talk of Galilee. Suddenly, the religious leaders were curious to find out more about him. Someone offered his house as a place where they could meet together. When the day came, as many of them as could crowded in.

There were lots of other people who wanted to see Jesus that day. Among them were four men whose friend could not walk. They came to the house carrying the crippled man by using his sleeping mat as a stretcher. They were hoping that Jesus might heal him.

Then they saw the crowd spilling out of the doorway. "It's no use," they agreed. "We'll never get in that way."

"That bird on the roof is closer to him than we're going to get," said one.

"The roof!" said another. "Come on! We'll break in through the roof."

They all hurried up the steps, laughing at their own cleverness. Then they scrabbled away at the roof surface.

Inside the room, someone nudged his neighbor. "Workmen," he said. "They'd better be careful or they'll send the ceiling crashing onto Jesus. Whoa! Here it comes!"

In a sudden shower of dust, the four men broke a hole and lowered their friend down on his stretcher, right in front of Jesus.

Jesus looked up and saw the friends on the roof. He saw their hopeful expressions and their complete faith in him. He looked down at the crippled man at his feet. "Your sins are forgiven, my friend," he said.

The religious leaders exchanged looks. How dare Jesus say that! Only God could forgive sins. Jesus was well aware of their discontent.

"It's easy to say, 'Your sins are forgiven,'" he said. "It's harder to say, 'Get up and walk.' I want you to know I have power to do both. So –" and here he turned to the man "– get up, pick up your bed and walk."

At once the man did so. "Praise God!" he cried. He hurried away, leaving everyone stunned with amazement.

Matthew the tax collector

❧

THE RELIGIOUS LEADERS were increasingly uneasy about Jesus. "He seems to think he is above the Law," they grumbled. "How dare he call himself a teacher if he doesn't obey the fundamentals of our faith?"

"Indeed," continued one. "As a Pharisee, I am appalled at the way he disregards the little details in our Law that make all the difference between holy and unholy living."

Jesus knew only too well how critical and suspicious they were, but refused to be cowed. In fact, it was around this time that Jesus called a tax collector named Matthew to be one of his disciples.

Matthew was delighted. "We must celebrate!" he announced. "Jesus – I'm going to invite you to a big feast. Many of my tax collector friends are coming. It should be lots of fun – with lots of food and lots of drink. They're a thirsty bunch.'

The party went ahead, and soon the Pharisees found out about it and that Jesus had gone to it. It wasn't long before they came to complain. "How dare you let people think you're a teacher of the Law – a rabbi. How dare you eat and drink with people like tax collectors – the Law calls them outcasts. They work for the Romans, which is bad enough; nearly all of them are cheats. They don't care at all about being holy."

Jesus smiled. "People who are well don't go to a doctor, only those who are sick. I haven't come to tell respectable people to change their ways. My message is for outcasts."

Dear God, May I never pretend to be holier than others.

Dear God,
Be part of our
celebrations and
bless them.

The wedding in Cana

ON ONE OCCASION, Jesus and his disciples were invited to a wedding. It was being held in the town of Cana, not far from Nazareth in Galilee, and Jesus' mother was there too.

Everyone was enjoying the music and the dancing, the eating and the drinking. When the festivities were at their height, Mary came hurrying to talk to her son. "The host has run out of wine!" she whispered. She looked at him pleadingly: "It would be an utter disgrace for him not to have provided enough for his guests. You can't let that happen!"

"Mother, you mustn't tell me what to do," said Jesus. "It's not the right time yet."

Mary shot him a glance. It was the one she had used when he was growing up, to remind him that what she had said was what she wanted done. Then she went and whispered to the servants, "If my son Jesus tells you to do something, just do it, won't you?"

Shortly after, Jesus went over to the servants. "See these six stone water jars?" he said. "I'd like you to fill them to the brim with water."

The servants hurried to do so.

"Now take a cupful and ask the man in charge of the feast to taste it."

They did so, and the man took a sip. "Very good!" he said. He called the bridegroom. "I'm impressed. Most people serve the best wine first and have something cheaper for when people are somewhat inebriated. You have saved the best wine until now."

The music started up again. If anything, the party was livelier and more joyful than before.

Nicodemus

əð

THERE WAS A TIME when Jesus went to Jerusalem for the Passover festival. He performed many miracles there and these demonstrations of his power and authority meant that people began to believe in him. The Pharisees remained sternly critical of everything Jesus did and said – but one, named Nicodemus, was curious to know more about his message. One night, he visited Jesus so he could ask him questions.

"Rabbi," said Nicodemus to Jesus, "it is clear that you have been sent by God. There is no other way anyone could work miracles."

"I will tell you the truth," replied Jesus. "No one can see God's kingdom unless they are born again."

Nicodemus laughed. "How can that happen? How can that be?" he exclaimed.

"The first time a person is born it is to human parents," said Jesus. "A person can also be born of the Spirit."

Nicodemus shook his head in disbelief.

Jesus said, "I'm surprised that a great teacher like you doesn't understand. I want to make things clear. If you don't believe me when I tell you about the things of this world, how will you believe me when I tell you about the things of heaven?

"Listen carefully: God loved the world so much that he gave his only Son to save it. God's Son has come from heaven itself and can explain everything about God's kingdom. Everyone who believes in him will be born again: they will have eternal life. God will not judge them: they have seen the light.

"The people who do evil things don't want to come to the light: they are afraid that their wrongdoing will be discovered. The people who do what is good and right welcome the light: they know that it will show they are obedient to God."

*Dear God,
Thank you for
your love for
the world.*

Dear God,
May I recognize
the right time
for fasting
and the right
time for
celebration.

The old and the new

JOHN THE BAPTIST and Jesus were both preachers, and both had attracted many followers. However, in many ways they were very different.

John had made his home in the wilderness and had lived a very frugal life there. His disciples often chose to follow his example and go without food too. When they fasted, they spent long hours in prayer.

Jesus, on the other hand, seemed always to have an invitation: to stay at someone's house, to come to a feast. His disciples seemed to enjoy all the eating and drinking too.

"Why don't your disciples fast in the way that John's disciples do?" some people asked Jesus.

"Do people at a wedding wave the food aside?" replied Jesus. "While the bridegroom is there with them, they know it's time to celebrate with a feast. When the day comes that the bridegroom is no longer with them, then they will fast."

"Listen!" he said. "If you have an old coat with a hole in it, do you tear a piece off a new coat to patch it? Of course you don't! You will have ruined the new coat, and the new patch will shrink and pull a bigger hole in the old.

"If you have new wine, do you put it into old wineskins? Of course not! The new wine will burst the skins and you will have neither wine nor wineskins left.

"Then again, people who are used to drinking old wine don't like the new. 'The old is better,' they say."

Everyone had to agree that Jesus' preaching was something new; but some wondered if John was angry to have a rival. They went to inquire.

"I have already said that I am not the messiah," said John, "and the messiah must become more important than I am."

The woman by the well

As the number of Jesus' followers continued to grow, the Pharisees in and around Jerusalem became more and more hostile. In order to avoid conflict, Jesus headed back to Galilee. His route took him through the region known as Samaria. Many Jews looked down on the Samaritans – they despised them for having different religious traditions.

When he reached the town called Sychar, Jesus sent his disciples on to buy food. He himself sat down by a well.

It was noon. A woman came to draw water.

"Can you give me a drink?" asked Jesus.

The woman glared at him. "You're a Jew," she said. "Your religious rules forbid you and me to use the same cup."

"If you knew who I am and what God can give you, you would ask me for a drink," replied Jesus. "Then you would never be thirsty again. You would have the water of eternal life."

The woman was puzzled. She began to ask more questions. As the conversation progressed, she grew afraid. Jesus seemed to know all about her and the history of her stormy relationships.

"Oh," she said sarcastically. "So you're a prophet. Well, answer this then: does God mind that we Samaritans have our place of worship here? You Jews seem to think that Jerusalem is the only place to worship God."

Jesus shrugged. "That old argument will soon be over," he said. "God is Spirit, and people can only worship God by the power of the Spirit."

The woman frowned and looked at Jesus with sudden curiosity. "I know that the messiah will come and explain everything one day," she said.

Jesus paused before replying. "I am he," he said. The woman was astonished. She hurried to tell everyone in her community. Soon a crowd of Samaritans had gathered to listen; then they, too, believed in Jesus.

Dear God,
Break down
the barriers of
prejudice.

Dear God,
May I be ready
to do good seven
days a week.

Jesus and the sabbath

❧

WHENEVER THE PHARISEES met together, they always seemed to end up talking about Jesus. His preaching challenged the beliefs they held so dearly. In addition, it was quite obvious that he was becoming very popular. They were jealous and angry about the influence he was gaining.

"I saw him and his disciples break the sabbath," said one Pharisee to his friends. "They were walking through a cornfield and they picked heads of corn, rubbed them in their hands and ate the grain."

"That's dreadful," the friends agreed. "Harvesting, threshing and winnowing. All forbidden activities on the sabbath."

"It got worse," said the first man. "I challenged him about it. He quoted the story of when King David and his men ate the bread that had been offered to God, the bread that only the priests should eat. He said that the sabbath was made for people, not the other way around."

"Well, I saw something similar but worse," commented another. "Jesus was actually in the synagogue one sabbath and a man with a paralyzed hand was there too. He called the man to the front and asked us all a question about the Law: what kind of work was allowed on the sabbath – to help or to harm? Then, to underline his point, he told the man to lift his arm, and at once the man could use his hand. People may say it's a miracle, but I say that's medical work."

"The whole Jesus movement is getting quite out of control!" spluttered another, suddenly very angry. "How can we stop the man? He's undermining all the things we try to do to make our people God's people. He's confusing people about the laws. Who does he think he is? The messiah?"

"We'll have to do something," they agreed. The problem was – what could they do that would silence Jesus?

Disciples, followers and family

❧

ONE EVENING, JESUS and some of his disciples went to a quiet place among the hills. Jesus went off alone and spent the night praying to God. In the morning, he returned to his disciples.

"Today I am going to choose twelve of you to be my apostles: the ones I will send out to spread my message." He chose the four fishermen – Simon (whom he renamed Peter) and his brother Andrew, James and his brother John. He also chose Philip, Bartholomew, Matthew, Thomas, James and Judas. Then there was another Simon, who had the nickname "the Patriot" because he also supported a group of freedom fighters. Finally there was Judas Iscariot, who later became a traitor.

A number of women, too, were utterly devoted to Jesus because he had healed them. One of these was Mary from the village of Magdala – everyone called her Mary Magdalene. Another was Joanna, who was married to an important government official. Then there were Susanna and a number of wealthy women who used their own money to fund the Jesus movement.

One day, Jesus' mother and several other members of the family came to see Jesus. However, they couldn't even get near the house because there was such a huge crowd.

Someone pushed their way through and told Jesus that his relatives were waiting outside. Jesus simply continued speaking to the crowd.

"Who is my mother? Who is my family?" he asked his listeners. "I will tell you. It is all those who hear the word of God and obey it."

Dear God, May I dedicate myself and all that I have to do your work.

Joy to the WORLD

229

Dear God,
I want to be
one of your
children.

Who is truly blessed?

🕊

ONE DAY, JESUS looked at the crowd of people who were his friends and followers.

"Those of you who know that you don't understand about God should count yourselves blessed: the kingdom of heaven belongs to you.

"Those of you who are in sorrow should count yourselves blessed: God will comfort you.

"Those of you who are humble should count yourselves blessed: you will receive all the blessings God has promised.

"Those of you who want nothing more than to live as God wants should count yourselves blessed: God will give you your heart's desire.

"Those of you who are merciful to others should count yourselves blessed: God will be merciful to you.

"Those of you who are pure in heart should count yourselves blessed: you will see God!

"Those of you who work for peace should count yourselves blessed: you will be called God's children.

"Those of you who are persecuted because you live as God wants should count yourselves blessed: the kingdom of heaven belongs to you.

"As for those of you who are insulted and rejected and told you are evil because you follow me – you should dance for joy. There will be a great reward for you in heaven. Through all our long history, that is how our people have treated true prophets."

Making a difference

🐚

JESUS WANTED TO encourage his followers. He knew they could make a huge difference in the world. He knew they must.

"You, my followers, are to the human race what salt is to food. If salt loses its saltiness, there's no point using it. People throw it out and trample on it.

"You, my followers, are like light for the whole world. No one lights a lamp only to hide it under a bowl. They put it on a lampstand so that its light fills the whole house. You must let your light shine: people need to see the good things you do so they will praise your Father in heaven."

Jesus wanted his followers to live good and holy lives. However, he knew that the teachers of the Law were suspicious about his teaching. He needed to make his opinion about the Law quite clear.

"I haven't come to do away with the Law of Moses or the teachings of the prophets. I have come to make their teachings come true. You must obey the Law faithfully and teach it to others. You will only be part of God's kingdom if you are more faithful than the teachers of the Law and the Pharisees in doing what God wants."

Dear God, Make me faithful to do what you want.

PEACE ON EARTH

Dear God,
May I seek
to be perfect.

More than keeping the Law

🐚

JESUS' LISTENERS WERE puzzled at what Jesus said about the Law. The Pharisees were very strict about keeping the laws down to the finest detail. How could anyone do better?

Jesus explained.

"The Law says that you should not murder. I say, you should not even be angry. Don't try to worship God if you have a quarrel with someone. Go and make peace with them first.

"The Law says that people should be faithful in marriage. I say, just imagining having an affair with someone is wrong. Turn away from temptation. Divorce is not meant to be an easy way out.

"The Law says you should not break a promise you have made to God. I say, don't swear in the name of anything that God has made. Simply say 'yes' or 'no' to show what you mean to do.

"The Law says you can take fair revenge: an eye for an eye, a tooth for a tooth. I say, don't take revenge at all. If someone slaps you on the right cheek, turn to let them slap the other. If someone sues you, let them have more. If one of the occupying troops makes you carry his pack one Roman mile, go a second mile as well.

"It used to be said, 'Love your friends, hate your enemies.' I say, love your enemies. Pray for the people who try to hurt you. In this way, you will become the true children of your Father in heaven.

"You must be perfect, just as God is perfect."

The prayer Jesus taught

❧

JESUS WAS EAGER for his followers to be devoted to God. Nevertheless, he warned them that true devotion was quite different from making everyone notice just how religious you were.

"Some people make a big show of their faith," he said. "They simply want to be admired by others. Well, if that's what they want, then that is all the reward they'll get. God isn't impressed at all.

"So, if you give to someone in need, do it in such a way that not even your closest friend knows. God will reward the good you do in private.

"When you pray, don't stand up in a place of worship or on a street corner where everyone will notice you. Go to your room, close the door, and pray in private.

"Don't use a lot of meaningless words in your prayers. God already knows what you need. Simply say this:

Our Father in heaven:
may your holy name be honored;
may your kingdom come;
may your will be done on earth as it is in heaven.
Give us today the food we need.
Forgive us the wrongs we have done,
as we forgive the wrongs that others have done to us.
Do not bring us to hard testing,
but keep us safe from the Evil One.

"If you forgive other people the wrong things they have done, God will forgive you. If you don't forgive, you will not be forgiven the wrong things you have done."

Dear God,
May your
kingdom come.

*Dear God,
May I set my
heart and
mind on
serving you.*

The lure of money

ﻝﺍ

JESUS WARNED HIS followers about being too fond of money and all it can buy.

"Don't store up riches for yourselves here on earth. Metal will go rusty, moths will eat the finest fabrics, robbers will look for ways to steal from you. Instead, do the things that will make you rich in heaven. Then your whole life will be focused on the things that last forever.

"You know that life is hard for anyone who works for two bosses. They can't serve both of them equally. In the same way, no one can serve both God and money.

"You, my followers, should not spend your lives fretting about food and drink and what clothes to wear. Isn't life worth more than food? Isn't the body worth more than clothes?

"Look at the birds! They don't sow seeds, they don't gather a harvest, they don't have stores of food in barns; yet God still looks after them. Don't you think you are worth more to God than the birds? Do you really think you can live longer by worrying about it?

"Look at the flowers! They don't work to make clothes for themselves. Yet God makes them beautiful for that brief moment of blooming. Their petals are far more wonderful than any of the royal robes King Solomon wore. If God takes care of the flowers, can't you also believe that God will take care of you?

"So don't worry about the future. The pagans are bothered about these material things, but you don't have to be. Set your hearts and minds on doing the things that God wants, and God will take care of all you need."

The parable of the wealthy man

❧

As Jesus was teaching, a man in the crowd called out to him. "You're on the side of justice. My brother won't share the property our father left us when he died. Come and tell him to divide it up properly!"

"I don't have any right to do that," said Jesus. "However, there's one thing I can tell you – and everyone who is listening.

"Don't long for money. Your worth is not measured by what you own.

"Listen: there was once a rich man whose land produced excellent crops. He should have been happy, but in fact his success left him tormented with worry. 'I haven't enough room to store them,' he said to himself. 'What can I do? It's all so difficult.'

"Then he had an idea: 'I know! I'll pull down the old barns and have bigger ones put up in their place. I'll be able to store all my grain and everything else I own. Then I'll be happy. I'll be able to take life easy. "Eat, drink and be merry": that will be my motto.'

"Then God spoke to him: 'You foolish man! You're going to die tonight. You wanted to keep everything for yourself. Who's going to get their hands on it now?'

"This story is a warning: it shows you what it will be like for those who pile up riches for themselves but are not rich in God's sight."

14 August

❖

Luke 12

Dear God, May I do the things that are valuable to you.

235

The parable of the two builders

ð

Dear God,
May I learn
and do what
is good and
right.

JESUS LOOKED SHARPLY at his crowd of listeners. Some were cheering. Some were shouting: "Jesus is our Lord! Jesus is our Lord!"

"Why do you call me, 'Lord, Lord?'" cried Jesus. "You don't actually do what I tell you!"

There was a sudden hush.

"Imagine a man who wants to build a house," said Jesus. "He works hard and digs the foundations on solid ground. Then, when the winds blow and the rains come and the river floods, his house survives.

"You are like that person if you not only listen to my words but also obey them.

"But who are you like if you listen to my words and don't obey them?

"I will tell you. You are like a man who builds his house without laying a proper foundation. When the winds blow and the rains come and the river floods, his house collapses… with the most enormous crash!"

The Roman officer and his servant

As soon as Jesus arrived back in Capernaum, he was greeted by a group of men who were highly respected in the community.

"Jesus, we have an urgent request," they said. "We have been sent to you by one of the Roman officers who is based in our town. He's a Gentile and one of the occupying troops, but he loves our people. Indeed, he recently funded the building of our synagogue. Now he needs your help."

They went on to explain. One of the officer's most loyal servants was dying. He wanted Jesus to heal him of his sickness.

Jesus hurried toward the man's house. On the way, some of the officer's friends came to speak to him. "Sir, we have a message for you. Our friend says this: 'Please do not bother to come to my house. I am not worthy to meet you. I myself am used to giving orders to get things done. I believe that, if you just give the order, my servant will be healed.'"

Jesus turned to the crowd. "Did you hear that?" he asked. "This Roman soldier has more faith than I have seen among any of my own people."

The messengers looked at him inquiringly. "Shall we just go back then?" they asked. Jesus nodded his agreement, and the men hurried on their way.

When they reached the house, they found their master smiling and laughing. "My servant is well again!" he cried. "It's a miracle! A real miracle!"

Dear God, May I learn to respect the faith of those people who are foreign to me.

*Dear God,
Comfort those
who are in
prison, and be
with them to
the end of
their troubles.*

John the Baptist in prison

JOHN THE BAPTIST had begun his work as a preacher before Jesus took up a similar calling. Even though Jesus had become the more popular, John had continued to urge people to live good and holy lives. He had also been outspoken in criticizing the local ruler, King Herod of Galilee. The time came when King Herod lost patience.

"Go and arrest him," he ordered his soldiers. "I made the decision to marry my brother's wife. That's my business, and I don't want some self-styled prophet bad-mouthing me to his followers. I want him thrown into jail, as that's the only way of keeping him quiet."

Alone in prison, John the Baptist had plenty of time to think – plenty of time to feel gloomy. Was Jesus really God's chosen one? Had he been right in ever thinking as much? He arranged for some of his followers to find out.

The friends delivered the message: "Are you the one John said was going to come, or should we expect someone else?"

At the time, Jesus was surrounded by adoring crowds. Many had come to him with incurable diseases: they had been healed. Others had been taken to him because inner demons were driving them mad: they were now in their right mind. A few had been blind: they could now see.

Jesus spoke to the messengers: "Go back to John and tell him about all these miracles. Tell him that the Good News is being preached to the poor."

John had that much to comfort him on the day the executioner came to his cell. "I'm afraid you're part of the celebrations at the king's birthday party," he said. "Herod's stepdaughter did some wild dance to entertain the guests. Herod got so carried away with it he said she could have anything she wanted. I gather she and her mother – that wife you disapprove of – have requested to have your head on a plate."

John was duly executed and his message was silenced. However, Jesus' message was proclaimed more and more widely.

The woman who washed Jesus' feet

IN ONE TOWN where Jesus went, a Pharisee named Simon invited Jesus to a meal. As they were eating, a woman crept into the room. People who saw her began whispering. She was well known for her disreputable life. What was she doing here?

The woman knelt at Jesus' feet, weeping. Her tears ran over his feet and she dried them with her hair. She had brought a jar of expensive perfume, which she poured all over Jesus' feet.

The Pharisee was shocked. "If this man were a prophet he wouldn't let a woman like her touch him!" he said to himself.

Jesus knew what he was thinking. "Simon," he said. "Listen to this story. There were two people who each owed money. One owed the moneylender 500 silver coins, the other fifty. Neither of them could pay, so the moneylender let them both off. Which one do you think was more grateful?"

"The one who was let off the bigger debt," replied the Pharisee.

"That's right," said Jesus. "When I came into this house, you didn't even give me a bowl of water so I could wash my feet. She has lavished care on me with love and kindness because her many sins are forgiven. People who think they have few sins are not going to show nearly as much love: they don't think they have much to be forgiven for."

"What are you talking about?" complained some of the other guests. "Who is this, who goes around forgiving sins?"

Jesus simply turned and spoke to the woman. "Your faith has saved you. Go in peace."

*Dear God,
Help me always
to remember
that I need
your forgiveness
as much as
anyone.*

Dear God,
May I not only
listen but also
understand.

The parable of the sower

JESUS TOLD THIS parable to the crowds who gathered to listen to him. "One day, a man went to sow grain. He walked up and down the plowed earth, flinging handfuls of seed from his basket.

"Some of the seeds fell on the path by the side of the field. The passersby could not help but trample on them. Wild birds came swooping down to snatch what they could, eager and hungry.

"Some of the seeds fell on rocky ground, where the soil was thin and crumbly. There they sprouted, but their roots soon had nowhere to go except along the barely covered rock. The sun beat down and dried the soil up. The seedlings shriveled and died.

"Some of the seeds fell among thornbushes. There, in the shade, the seeds germinated and their shoots began to show; but the wild plants grew much more strongly and quickly choked them.

"Fortunately some of the seeds fell on the good soil that had been prepared for them. Their roots grew deep into the earth and their leaves reached up to the sun. When harvest time came, the plants that had each grown from a single seed produced as much as a hundred grains."

Jesus smiled and looked quietly at the sea of faces – everyone watching, wondering.

"That's the end of the story," said Jesus. "You all listened. I wonder if you understood what it means?"

The meaning of the parable

❧

WHEN JESUS HAD finished talking to the crowds, the disciples gathered around with their questions.

"What did that story about the sower mean?" they wanted to know.

Jesus smiled. "The reason I tell parables is to sort those who are able to understand about God's kingdom from those who are not.

"Listen: the seed is the word of God. The seeds that fall on the path stand for those who hear its message; but the devil comes and snatches away their understanding so they are not saved.

"The seeds that fall on the rocky ground stand for those who hear the message and are full of enthusiasm. However, the message does not really take root in their heart. When times are hard, they give up on their faith.

"The seeds that fall among thornbushes stand for those who hear the message and would like to live by it. However, all the everyday things of life leave no room for their faith. Nothing comes of what they believe.

"The seeds that fall on good soil stand for those who understand the message and let it take root in their lives. They stay faithful to all they have heard, and their lives produce astonishing results."

Dear God, Keep me faithful to you.

241

The kingdom of heaven

*Dear God,
May each
glimpse I have
of your
kingdom build
into a clear
picture.*

Listen," said Jesus. "My message is all about God's kingdom – the kingdom of heaven. I want you to understand what it is like.

"Think of a man who takes a mustard seed and sows it in a field. The seed is tiny – just a speck; almost unseen, it grows and grows. In the end it becomes a huge tree with spreading branches. All kinds of birds come and make their nests in it. The kingdom of heaven is like that.

"Or think of it this way: a woman takes some yeast and mixes it into dough. Just a handful makes the whole batch of bread rise to perfection.

"Here's another parable about the kingdom. A man is digging in a field. Suddenly, he finds buried treasure. If only it were his! He'd be the richest man in the world! So quickly he covers it up, sells everything he has – and goes to buy the field.

"And another: a man is looking for fine pearls. He is offered one that is beautiful: the color, the shape, the size – all utterly perfect. He hurries to sell everything he owns and then he comes back to buy that pearl.

"Now think about fishing. The fishermen cast their nets and haul in the catch. Then they sit down on the shore and sort the fish: the good ones go into buckets, the worthless ones are thrown away. At the end of time, angels will come and sort the evil people from the good."

The storm on the lake

ONE EVENING, JESUS and his disciples went down to the shore of Lake Galilee.

"Let's get into the boat," said Jesus. "Then we can go across to the other shore."

As the little boat sailed out on the lake, Jesus fell asleep. Suddenly a strong wind came down from the hills, roaring and gusting and scattering spray. Up from the lake, great waves began to crest and fall, the white foam tumbling across the dark and swirling water. Then the waves grew larger and more threatening. One crashed into the boat and the water swirled and gurgled around everyone's feet.

"It's made the boat unsteady," shouted Peter. "Bale for all you're worth, men, or we'll drown out here."

"Wake Jesus," called another disciple, urgently. "He's got to help us."

Someone went and shook him hard. "Master! Master! Don't you care that we're about to die?"

Jesus sat up. He looked around, trying to make sense of the scene of turmoil all around. The boat pitched and tossed and yet more spray pelted down on them all.

Jesus gripped the edge of the boat and pulled himself up. Then he spoke.

"Be quiet," he said to the waves; to the wind he said, "Be still."

All at once, the wind trailed away with a whisper that sounded almost like an apology. The waves rolled away from the boat and sank down into the water. The lake was completely calm.

Jesus smiled. "Why were you afraid?" he asked his disciples. "Do you still not have any faith?"

But after what Jesus had done, the disciples were more afraid than ever. "Who is this man?" they asked one another. "What kind of person can tell the wind and waves what to do?"

*Dear God,
Save me from storms that trouble me, and calm my fears.*

Peace on Earth

243

*Dear God,
Please banish
all the evil
things that
torment us.*

The herd of pigs

🐋

JESUS AND HIS disciples sailed on to the far side of Lake Galilee. As they stepped out of the boat, they heard shrieking: a man with wild hair hanging over his bruised and bleeding body came and swore at them.

"Listen to me, evil spirit," said Jesus sternly. "Leave that man alone."

"You"re Jesus, aren't you?" shouted the man as he ran and fell on his knees in front of Jesus. "What do you want with me? Call yourself the Son of the Most High God, do you? Don't try to hurt me!"

Jesus bent down and looked at the man calmly in the face. "What's your name?" he asked.

"My name is 'Mob,'" said the man. "There's a mob of devils in me and they want to stay." He came closer to Jesus and almost spat in his face. "Don't you dare send them into that pit of darkness. They'd rather go and live with the pigs on the hillside."

"Good. Then they can go there," said Jesus.

The man gave a bloodcurdling shriek. Almost at once, the herd of pigs stampeded into the lake.

The men who had been looking after the pigs fled into the nearby town. "Come and see!" they exclaimed. "Jesus is by the lake! He sent a crowd of devils into the pigs and drowned them!"

When the townspeople came to see what happened, they found Jesus talking to the man. Someone had given the man clothes to wear. He was talking calmly to Jesus.

"Please, Jesus," said the townspeople. "We've heard the news. We're scared of you. Just go. Leave us in peace."

Jesus and his disciples sailed away, leaving the man to spread the news of how he had been healed.

The woman in the crowd

❧

WHEN JESUS RETURNED to the other side of the lake, crowds were waiting for him. As soon as he stepped off the boat and onto the quayside, they began to push and to jostle.

"Let me through, please, let me through," begged one man. Some people recognized him and let him past them: he was Jairus, an important man at the synagogue and deserving of respect.

When Jairus reached Jesus, he flung himself down at his feet. "Please come and help me. Come quickly. My daughter is dying. She is only twelve years old."

Jesus agreed to go with him, but they struggled to make their way through the streets together. The crowd seemed to be growing all the time. Peter did his best to keep the group moving; all those years hauling nets full of fish had made him strong, and he could give a good shove when needed.

Suddenly Jesus stopped and looked around. "Who touched me?" he asked. His eyes flashed from one person to the next.

The crowd suddenly shrank back. "Not me, no, must have been someone else. Sorry," came the general murmuring.

"Master," said Peter, "the people here can't help being pushed into you. This crowd is a nightmare."

"Someone touched me," said Jesus. "I felt power go out of me."

A woman with streaks of gray in her hair stepped forward nervously. "I just needed to try for a miracle," she said. "I've had bleeding for twelve years and the doctors couldn't do a thing to help. It was me who touched you, and I already know I'm better."

"Your faith has cured you," said Jesus. "May you be well."

*Dear God,
Please help those who are too nervous to ask for what they need.*

*Dear God,
Bring hope to
those who
mourn.*

Jairus and his daughter

JAIRUS WANTED TO tug on Jesus' arm, to hurry him along to where his daughter lay dying. As he reached out to do so, he felt someone tap him gently on the shoulder. He turned to see who it was.

"I'm sorry," whispered the messenger. "Your daughter has just died. You can tell the teacher not to bother anymore."

Jairus' face crumpled in grief, but Jesus spoke to him calmly.

"Don't be afraid. Trust me: she will be well."

Together they made their way to Jairus' house. Outside, a group of mourners had gathered – their wailing and fluting announcing a death.

"Don't cry," Jesus told them. "The girl is only sleeping."

The mourners replied scornfully, "That's nonsense! We know what a dead body looks like. That girl is dead."

"You're a heartless fool to pretend otherwise," added one, as Jesus and three of his disciples went inside the house with Jairus.

Jesus went to where the girl was lying. He took her hand. "Little girl, get up," he said.

At once, the girl turned her head slightly on the pillow. She opened her eyes and sat up. "I'm really hungry," she said brightly.

"There," said Jesus to her parents. "Time to get a meal ready, I think. Just one thing I ask of you: promise not to talk about this."

Food for five thousand people

*Dear God,
Take the little
that I have
to offer and
use it to do
great things.*

ONE DAY, A HUGE crowd of people gathered to listen to Jesus. He preached to them all through the day. He told them about God's kingdom. He healed those who were sick.

Slowly the sun slipped lower in the sky. The shadows grew long. None of the listeners wanted the day to end.

The twelve disciples came closer to Jesus and waved to get his attention. At last he stopped talking to ask what they wanted.

"Look at the time!" they said. "You've got at least 5,000 people out in the open countryside. Send them away to the farms and villages nearby. Then they can at least find food and a place to stay for the night."

"Why don't you yourselves give them what they need?" asked Jesus.

"I'll tell you why," said the disciple called Andrew, beckoning to a young boy to come forward. "This boy here is the only person who has any food with him. And what have you got, young man?"

"Five loaves and two fish," came the reply.

"Not quite enough for the crowd," said Andrew. "Do you think we should go and buy food for them? It won't be cheap."

"Just tell everyone to sit down in groups – fifty people in each," said Jesus.

When everyone was sitting, Jesus took the loaves and fishes, looked up to heaven, gave thanks for the food, and broke it into pieces for his disciples to share among the crowd.

"How"s it going?" whispered Peter to his brother Andrew as they each walked to yet another group.

"I never seem to have any less food than before," replied Andrew. "I can't quite see how it's happening."

Somehow, there was enough food for everyone. When the disciples gathered up the leftovers, there were enough to fill twelve baskets.

*Dear God,
When I am
sinking into
despair, lift
me up.*

Walking on water

WHEN THE DAY was over, Jesus told the disciples to take the boat to the other side of the lake.

"I'm going to stay here and pray," he told Peter. The disciples set out, rowing the little boat across the rippling water.

It was not until they were some distance out that the weather changed. There came a stiff breeze and white-tipped waves. It was going to be another Galilean storm.

Peter stood in the stern, steering the boat as skilfully as he could. He was keeping a sharp lookout for the safest route when he saw – well – something. At first he thought it was a trick of the shadows; or maybe a plume of spray where a fish had leaped and dived. Then he saw more clearly. It was human!

"It's a ghost!" he shrieked. "Look! Tell me it's not true! What can this mean for us all?" The others dropped their oars to look, then tumbled back down, shrieking with fear. "We're going to die! We're going to die!"

"It's me!" Jesus said. "What's the panic for?"

"Jesus?" shouted Peter. He didn't sound convinced. "If it's you, Jesus, tell me to walk to you."

"Come on then, Peter!" said Jesus.

When he recalled the incident, Peter himself was amazed at what happened next. He simply stepped out onto the water. For the first few steps, all was well. Then a gust of wind made him lose his balance. He panicked and started to sink. "Help!" he screamed.

Jesus reached out and grabbed him by the hand. "What happened to your faith, Peter?" he asked. "Why did you doubt? Come on, let's get back to the boat."

As they both climbed aboard, the wind died down.

The other disciples looked at one another. They looked at Jesus. "You can't deny it, can you?" they said. "You really are the Son of God."

The bread of life

THE CROWDS WHO had shared the loaves and fish were eager to find Jesus. Soon, the word went out that he and his disciples had landed in Capernaum. As many as could hurried there at once and squeezed into the synagogue where he was expected to preach.

Jesus sighed when he saw how many had come.

"I suspect that the only reason that you wanted to find me is because I gave you food to eat," he said. "I don't think you understand my message.

"You're making a mistake to spend your lives working for ordinary bread, which goes stale. Work for the food that brings eternal life."

"All right," they said. "Tell us what God wants us to do."

"Believe in the one God sent," replied Jesus simply.

"Then make it easy for us! Show us another miracle. Come on: God gave our people manna in the time of Moses. 'Bread of heaven,' they called it. We want something like that! Come on! You can do it, can't you?"

"The real bread that God gives is not manna," replied Jesus. "The real bread is the one God sends to give life to the world."

"Then give it to us."

"I am the bread of life," said Jesus. "Those who come to me will never be hungry or thirsty. I will welcome everyone who comes and they can all be sure of eternal life."

"None of this makes sense," they grumbled. "You're just Joseph's son. We know who your parents are. You didn't come from heaven."

Many of them wandered away. They were no longer interested in following Jesus.

*Dear God,
Make me hungry
for the things
that are
worthwhile,
and satisfy my
hunger.*

249

*Dear God,
Help me to
understand
who Jesus
really is.*

Who is Jesus?

ᘒ

ONE DAY WHEN the disciples came looking for Jesus, they found him deep in prayer. He seemed thoughtful, as if something were puzzling him.

"Tell me," he said to them. "The crowds who follow me around: who do they say I am?"

"Oh, they have all sorts of ideas," came the reply. "Probably the most popular idea is that you're John the Baptist, come back to life. King Herod is afraid that might be true – after all, he was the one who executed John.

"Others say you're Elijah – well, he was one of the greatest prophets of our people, wasn't he? There are some who think you might be any one the prophets from long ago whose words are part of our scriptures."

"What about you?" asked Jesus. "Who do you say I am?"

"You're God's messiah," replied Peter. "As they say in Greek, *Christ*."

Jesus turned to Peter. "You're a rock, you know that. On this rock foundation I will build my church. I know I can trust you to lead many people into the kingdom of heaven. You're like the gatekeeper, the one who holds the keys to the kingdom."

Then he looked sternly at the twelve. "Whatever you do, don't go around describing me as the messiah!" said Jesus.

The light on the mountaintop

❧

ABOUT A WEEK LATER, Jesus went up a mountain with Peter, John and James. He went ahead to pray. The three men settled themselves among the rocks and scrubby vegetation.

"This isn't much of a place," they grumbled to themselves. "I wonder how long Jesus is going to make us stay up here."

The hours went by. The distant landscape shimmered in the sunlight. In spite of themselves, they all nodded off.

Then something woke them. There in front of them was a sight so amazing it was almost like a dream… except that they were all awake and they were all seeing it. Just a little way ahead was Jesus himself, dressed in dazzling white; he was talking to two other men who also shone with all the glory of heaven. The disciples knew that these were two of the greatest prophets of old.

"Praise God!" said Peter to Jesus. "Let's make shelters up here – one for you, one for Moses and one for Elijah."

As he was speaking, a cloud came and covered everything. The disciples heard a voice: "This is my Son: listen to him."

Then the scene vanished. Everything was as it had been. Jesus was standing there by himself telling them it was time to head back home.

Dear God, May I listen to the words of Jesus and let them enrich my life.

As they walked back down the mountain together, Jesus had little to say. "Don't tell anyone about what you saw," he said, "until the Son of man has been raised from death."

Streams of life-giving water

*Dear God,
May I set my
heart on the
things that
truly satisfy.*

Oₙₑ ᴅᴀʏ, Jᴇꜱᴜꜱ went to Jerusalem. He wanted to be there for the festival called Shelters, with all its reminders of the years when the people had lived in tents as they traveled from Egypt to Canaan.

Jesus had tried to keep his visit a secret, but people soon recognized him and began to whisper.

"He's such a good man," said some.

"No he's not! He's misleading the people," argued others. "Anyway, the religious leaders don't like him, so it's unwise to show open support."

When the festival was half over, Jesus began preaching in the Temple. The religious leaders gathered around, angry and astonished.

"Listen!" he said. "The things I say are what God wants me to say. You claim to know all about Moses and the Law – but you don't obey the Law. Why are you trying to kill me?"

"You're out of your mind!" they exclaimed. "What makes you think there's some dark conspiracy? Who would do such a thing?"

Even so, tensions in the city continued to rise. It seemed that everyone had a different opinion about Jesus: some were convinced he was the messiah, and were expecting great things of him. Others dismissed him as a country preacher whom no one need take seriously.

On the last day of the festival, Jesus stood up to preach again.

"Listen," he said. "Anyone who is thirsty should come to me. They will be more than satisfied. It will be as if they have a stream of life-giving water pouring from them. God will be with them and bless them."

His words further enraged the religious leaders. "How dare this upstart from Galilee set himself up as a prophet!" they fumed. "It's outrageous!"

The light of the world

THE NEXT DAY, Jesus went back to the Temple courtyard. A crowd soon gathered around him. Jesus sat down and began preaching to them.

Suddenly, a cluster of rabbis appeared. They hustled a woman to the front.

"Look at her," sneered one of the rabbis. "Well may she weep and wail, but she is the cause of her own misfortune."

"I'm sorry," sobbed the woman. "Please let me explain –"

"This wretch has been having an affair," continued the rabbi. "We actually caught her with her lover. Now, according to the Law of Moses, she should be stoned to death. What do you say, Jesus?"

"Unfair question," murmured one of the bystanders. "Everyone knows it's against Roman law for us Jews to pass a death sentence."

Jesus bent over and began writing in the dust with his finger. "Come on, answer," said the rabbis. "Prove your worth as a preacher!" They huffed with impatience as Jesus continued to ignore them.

At last he sat upright again. "Whichever of you has committed no sin can throw the first stone," he said. Then he went back to writing on the ground.

The rabbis glanced at one another. The people were staring. One rabbi glanced up at the sun and then hurried off, as if suddenly remembering an errand that had to be done by a certain time. Another followed him.

One by one, they all slipped away. Jesus and the woman were left alone in the wide, sunlit courtyard.

"Where are they?" asked Jesus, innocently. "Is there no one left to condemn you?"

"No one, sir," she said.

"Well," said Jesus. "I don't condemn you either. Go, but do not sin again."

He went to speak to the Pharisees. "Remember this," he said. "I am the light of the world. Whoever follows me will have the light of life and will never walk in darkness."

*Dear God,
May I not
condemn others.
May I not
continue to do
what I know
to be wrong.*

*Dear God,
May I be
willing to
serve others.*

Who is the greatest?

❧

As Jesus and his disciples were walking back to Capernaum, Jesus strolled on ahead. Behind him came the sound of arguing.

"So, three of you get to go up the mountain with the master," one of the disciples was saying. "Aren't you the important ones! Never mind the work the rest of us have done. We've been just as busy preaching the message. But you're 'special.'"

"Peter thinks he's more than special," said another. "Wasn't he thrilled when Jesus said he was 'the rock he can rely on?' Jesus obviously hasn't seen the side of Peter I've seen."

"I just do my best," said Peter irritably. "It's not something to be ashamed of that Jesus does, well, value me, perhaps, more highly than…"

"More highly than who?" asked his brother, Andrew. "More highly than me? I think you're forgetting that at the beginning I supported Jesus before you did."

"Anyway, John is obviously his favorite," said Peter, hastily.

When they reached Capernaum, a group of children started waving at Jesus. He beckoned to one to come nearer. Then he turned to face his disciples. "I could hear you all the way," he said. "Here's what you need to know. If you welcome a child in my name, you welcome me. If you welcome me, you welcome the one who sent me.

"Whoever wants to be the most important among you must place himself last and be a servant to all."

The way to eternal life

❧

A TEACHER OF THE Law came to speak to Jesus. He was finding it hard to resist a smile. "Jesus has been telling the crowds that God will give eternal life to those who believe in him and his teaching," he said to himself. "So, when I ask my question, he's sure to hint that he's the Son of God. When he does, it will be an open confession of his wrong thinking. Indeed, putting himself alongside God is blasphemy. That's a serious crime… and we'll get him for it!"

He bowed his head and looked respectful as he came up to Jesus. "Teacher," he said, "I would very much value your wisdom. What must I do to have eternal life?"

Jesus looked at him thoughtfully. "I can see you're a teacher," he said. "What do the scriptures say on the matter? How do you think we should understand what we read in them?"

"Ah, that's easy," said the man. "Two commandments sum up the rest of the Law. 'Love the Lord your God with all your heart, with all your soul, with all your strength and with all your mind.' That's the first. The second is, 'Love your neighbor as you love yourself.'"

"You are right," said Jesus. "Do that, and you will live."

The teacher of the Law felt more than a little annoyed. His plan had not worked at all. Jesus had said none of the wild things that he was rumored to say. Indeed, he had tried to give the impression that he supported the ancient Law wholeheartedly. Was it possible that Jesus had guessed that the question was a trick?

"But it's never that simple, is it?" the teacher went on. "Who is my neighbor? That's the hardest thing to get right."

"Then listen to this story," said Jesus.

*Dear God,
May I act in
the way I know
in my heart
to be right.*

The good Samaritan

❧

Dear God,
May I have
the courage to
be a friend to
those in need.

JESUS BEGAN TO tell a story. "There was once a man who was going from Jerusalem to Jericho. It's a long walk, and lonely in places. On the way, robbers leaped down from among the rocks. They attacked the man, beat him up, took what he had and left him for dead on the road.

"Then, by chance, a priest came along. The man looked dead, and a priest isn't supposed touch a dead body just before he leads the Temple worship. He walked by on the other side of the road.

"Then a Levite came along. Of course, a Levite works in the Temple too… but at least he came to have a look at the man. He grimaced at the sight of the blood, and then looked around fearfully. 'Bandits,' he breathed, and then hurried on.

"Then a Samaritan came along. Well, of course, Samaritans wouldn't even think of going to worship at the Temple, would they? They think their own holy mountain is a good enough place, don't they? But here's the difference: when he saw the man, he felt sorry for him. He went and cleaned his wounds, wrapped him in bandages, helped him onto his donkey and led him to an inn. There he took care of him.

"The next day he had to travel on. He gave two coins to the innkeeper. 'Take care of this man for me,' he said. 'If it costs more, I will pay you when I return.'"

Jesus looked at his listener. "So, who do you think was a neighbor to the man attacked by robbers?"

"The one who was kind to him," said the teacher of the Law. "Now go and do the same," said Jesus.

256

Mary and Martha

ONE DAY, JESUS and his disciples arrived in a village called Bethany. A woman named Martha greeted them as friends. "You must come and stay with us," she said. "Nothing would make me happier."

She rushed around to get the house ready. "First I'll get a big batch of bread rising," she said to herself; "then I can easily sweep out the guest room, and find spare bedding."

When this was done, she hurried to the garden to gather extra vegetables. As she bent over the row of onions she tried to remember: how many people needed a meal? Jesus, and twelve disciples, and her brother and her sister and herself… She'd need more water.

"Oh, I'll never have time to fetch water," she exclaimed crossly.

She stood up and put her hands on her hips to ease her aching back. "So, what's my sister doing?" Martha wondered.

She marched back to the house. She could hear Jesus talking. Everyone seemed to be in the same room. Martha hurried to look.

There she was! That idle Mary: she was sitting on the floor in front of Jesus, hanging on his every word.

"Jesus!" interrupted Martha. "Don't you care that my sister has left me to do all the work by myself? Tell her to come and help me."

Jesus looked directly at her. "Martha!" he replied. "Don't be so upset. You worry about so many things, but there's only one thing that's important. Mary has chosen to do the most important thing. It is not going to be taken away from her."

*Dear God,
May I know
what are the
important
things to do.*

257

Dear God,
Please give me
your blessings
and welcome me
as a home-
coming child.

Ask, and you will receive

JESUS' DISCIPLES HAD a question: "Does God always answer prayer?" Jesus replied with a story.

"Imagine," he said, "that a friend turns up on your doorstep late one evening. "You're glad to see him, but then you realize there's a really embarrassing problem: you have no food in the house. What on earth are you going to do? It would look very bad indeed not to provide for him.

"I'll tell you what you do: you hurry round to a neighbor's. It's midnight, but this person is a friend. The place is dark. You rattle the door and start calling. 'Can you hear me? Please help. Can you lend me some food? It's for a guest.'

"You wait for a moment and try again. And again. At last, you hear a thump. Someone's coming to the window. 'Go away!' you hear your neighbor shouting. 'I've locked up for the night and everyone's in bed. I can't help you.'

"You really need that food. You rattle again and shout. 'Come on, please, you're a friend aren't you?' You find a stick and tap on the window shutters. Then you rattle the door again.

"You know exactly how to keep on trying to make your friend give in to you. Even a grumpy neighbor will eventually give in.

"When you pray to God, it is easier. Simply ask, and you will receive. Seek, and you will find. Knock, and the door will be opened.

"Those of you who are fathers always try to give good things to your children. God is your father in heaven, and God will give the Holy Spirit to those who ask for it."

Faithful servants

❧

JESUS WANTED HIS followers to be completely loyal to God all their lives.

"You must be ready for whatever comes," he told them. "You must be like the most faithful household servants: they stay up with the lamps burning until their master comes home, even if they have to wait until midnight and beyond. You must be ready for God all the time."

Peter was astonished that Jesus said this to everyone. "Do you really mean everyone to live like that?" he asked. "Or just us, your disciples?"

"What would a faithful household servant do for his master?" asked Jesus. "He would take charge of running the house and look after the other servants. The master would come home and find everything in perfect order, and give the servant a promotion!

"But what would a lazy servant do? He would say to himself, 'Ah, the boss is out, I can do what I like. So, I'll give the other servants a really hard time to keep them in order, and meanwhile I can help myself to food from the pantry and drink from the cellar.'

"You can imagine what the master would do to a servant who acted insuch a selfish and disloyal way!

"My followers must act as if God might step right into their world at any moment. If you have more talent than someone else, or more opportunities, then God will expect you to do even more.

"Listen: there was once a man who had a fig tree growing in his vineyard. One day, he went looking for figs and there were none. He said to the the gardener, 'Look at this tree! I've had it for three years and it has produced nothing. I want you to cut it down. It's a waste of good soil.'

"'Be patient a little longer,' replied the gardener. 'I'll dig around the tree and put manure on the soil. If that makes it produce figs, so much the better; if not, you can cut it down.'"

7 September

❖

Luke 12–13

*Dear God,
May the things
I believe lead
me to do good
deeds eagerly
and willingly.*

259

*Dear God,
May I be
generous to
those who are
beyond my
circle of family
and friends.*

How to give a party

❧

ONE SABBATH, JESUS was invited to a meal in the home of an important Pharisee. Some of the guests were choosing to sit in the best places.

"If someone invites you to a wedding feast," said Jesus, "don't sit in the best place. It may be that the host has invited someone more important than you. Then you will be told to move to a lower place, and that will be a huge embarrassment. Go and sit in a lowly place. Then, when the host invites you to a better place, you will be honored.

"If you try to make yourself great, you will be humbled; but if you are humble, you will be made great."

Then Jesus turned to his host.

"Here's something for you to remember. When you decide to have a party, don't just invite your relatives or your rich neighbors. They will simply invite you back and you will have been paid for your kindness.

"Instead, when you give a feast, invite poor and disabled people who can't invite you back. Then God will bless you."

The man next to Jesus turned to speak to him. "No one is more blessed than those who will sit down to eat in the kingdom of God," he said.

Jesus nodded. "Listen to this story," he said.

The great feast

❦

"ONCE UPON A TIME," Jesus began, "there was a man who was giving a great feast. He sent out the invitations and, being generous, invited many people. Then he began to get everything ready: food and drink in abundance, and everything of the finest quality.

"Then he sent his servant to tell the guests what time to come.

"'Oh dear,' said the first. 'I've bought some land. I have to go and look at it.'

"'What a shame,' said the second. 'I've bought five teams of oxen. I'm going to try them out. I'm afraid I'm too busy.'

"'I've just got married!' exclaimed the third. 'I would have come, but… no, I'm sorry. I have so many other important things to do right now.'

"The servant went back to his master with bad news. It wasn't just those three guests who couldn't come. All the invited guests had made excuses. The entire community had turned him down.

"The man was furious. 'Such bad manners!' he exclaimed. 'Such disrespect toward me. I'll show them! I'll… I'll…'

"All at once, the man smiled. 'I'll invite other people,' he said to his servant. 'Go and find some other guests. Let me think who would really like to come: the poor, maybe; and the disabled. Just go looking in the streets and the country lanes – I want my party to be full.

"'As for those who wouldn't come: they won't taste any of the feast.'"

Dear God, May I always be ready to come to your call.

261

Dear God,
Open my eyes
to the truth.

The man who was born blind

ᴥ

ONE DAY, AS Jesus was walking along, he saw a man who had been born blind.

"What did the man do to deserve that?" asked the disciples. "Or is he being punished for something his parents did?"

"It wasn't the fault of any of them," replied Jesus. "It happened so that you will see God's power at work through me. I am the light for the world."

He mixed some mud, smeared it gently over the man's eyes, and then told him to go and wash it off in the nearby Pool of Siloam. As the man splashed the water across his face, he knew something was changing. "I can see!" he whispered to himself. Then he shouted the news: "I'm cured! I can see! It's a miracle!"

A crowd quickly gathered to find out what was going on. "Let's take this man to the Pharisees," they agreed. "They can make sense of what's going on."

But the Pharisees were as puzzled as everyone else. "There's just one thing we can be certain of," they said. "Whatever has happened cannot be proof that Jesus has power from God. He did this thing on the sabbath, and that's against God's laws."

"Perhaps this so-called healing is just a fake," said others. "We can ask the man's parents if he was truly blind in the first place."

Their inquiry did not give them the answer they were looking for: the man's parents insisted that their son had been blind from birth.

The Pharisees went to see the man again. "Tell us more about what happened," they demanded. "That healer is a sinner."

"I've told you everything I know already," said the man. "I don't know if Jesus is a sinner or not. One thing I do know: once I was blind, now I can see. Unless Jesus came from God, he wouldn't have been able to make that happen."

The lost sheep

THE PHARISEES WATCHED stony faced as, once again, the crowds gathered eagerly around Jesus to listen to his teaching.

"Look at the kinds of people who admire him," they grumbled. "The tax collectors, who are all cheats, and a whole ragbag of beggars and lowlifes." They shook their heads and frowned. Jesus noticed their disapproval. He told a story.

"Suppose that you are a shepherd, and you have a hundred sheep," he said. "Then, one day, you notice that a sheep is missing. Just one: you have ninety-nine left. Are you going to do anything about it?

"Of course you are! It's one of your precious flock and you're desperate to get it back.

"This is what a good shepherd does: he leaves the flock of ninety-nine safely in the pasture and goes looking. He does not give up, no matter how long or hard he has to search. He just wants to find the lost sheep.

"Then, when he finds it, all his tiredness vanishes. He carries the sheep home as tenderly as when it was a little lamb.

"When the sheep is safely back with the flock, he invites his friends and neighbors round to his house.

"'Let's have a party!' he says. 'This is a happy day. My sheep was lost, but now I have found it.'

"The message of the story is this: there is more joy in heaven when one person comes back to God than over ninety-nine respectable people."

Dear God, May we all be glad when anyone turns from wrong to right.

The good shepherd

JESUS HAD MORE to say about sheep and shepherds.
"Think about sheep that are safe inside a sheepfold," he said. "Anyone who climbs in over the walls to get to them is a robber and a thief. The shepherd leads them in and out through the gate. The sheep know the shepherd's voice and they follow when he calls."

"What are you talking about?" people asked. "Are you preaching, or telling us about farming? Why do you have to say such puzzling things?"

"It's a parable," said Jesus. "I am the gate for my flock. I am the doorway to life – the full and happy life that God wants people to have.

"I am the good shepherd. I don't run away when danger threatens. I am ready to die to save my sheep. My life is safe with God."

The crowd began to murmur. "Sometimes the parables he tells us are good, and sometimes they're just baffling!" they said. "Worse than that, Jesus sometimes rambles on like someone possessed. You have to wonder if he's in his right mind."

"Remember this!" said others. "Whatever Jesus says, whatever he means, he can work miracles. You have to agree that a man possessed wouldn't be able to do the things he does."

The two sons

JESUS WENT ON to tell another story.
"There was once a man who had two sons. The man was quite wealthy, and the younger son began to dream: if only he could get his hands on his old man's money! After all, some of it would be his when his father died.

"'Please, please let me have my share now,' he begged his father. 'I need it while I'm young enough to make the most of it. I don't want to inherit a farm when I'm old.'

"The father gave in. He divided his property, sold half of it, and gave his beloved son the money. The young man went off to a faraway city and spent lavishly and recklessly.

"Then a famine struck. The price of food soared. The price of everything soared. The young man found himself penniless.

"In desperation, he found a job. It was a disgrace for a Jewish boy to end up looking after pigs, but that job was all he could get. In fact, he was so hungry, he even thought about eating the pigs' food – except that he'd probably be thrown out if he did.

"'My dad's servants live better than this,' he thought.

"That was the moment he came to his senses. 'I know: I'll go home to my father. I'll say that I'm sorry – that I've wronged him and I've been disrespectful of God. Then I'll ask him to hire me.'"

Dear God,
May I recognize
when I have
made a wrong
choice, and be
ready to choose
again.

265

Dear God,
May I rejoice
with those
who rejoice.

The homecoming

JESUS WENT ON with his story.

"The young man walked the long road home. At last, he could just see the rooftop of his home. He bowed his head and trudged on.

"On that faraway rooftop, his father saw the figure approaching. Who could it be? He wasn't expecting a visitor.

"Suddenly he knew! It was his son – his precious son – and he was on the homeward road.

"In a whirl of excitement he ran to greet him, laughing and shouting. When he reached the young man, he gave him a huge hug and kissed him. 'My boy,' he said, his voice dissolving into tears of joy.

" 'Father,' began the son, 'I'm sorry. I treated you wrongly and I treated God wrongly. I don't deserve to be counted as your son anymore.'

"The father wasn't listening. He wiped his eyes and waved back at the house. 'Hurry, hurry,' he called to the servants. 'Clean clothes – the best. And shoes. And get a meal ready – no, a feast. Let's have a feast. A whole roast calf. We have never had so much to celebrate.'

"Meanwhile, the older son was out working on the farm. As he came back to the house, he heard the sound of music and dancing. 'What's all this for?' he asked a servant.

" 'It's for your brother. He's come home. Your father is thrilled.'

" 'That little money-grubber? That lazy, good-for-nothing spendthrift? I don't want him back. I'm not joining in any welcome-home party.'

"His father came out to plead with him, but the elder son was furious. 'You have to be glad,' said the father. 'He was lost. Now he is found. That is the best possible news.' "

One out of ten

JESUS AND HIS disciples set out for Jerusalem. The road they took passed along the border between Samaria and Galilee. When they reached the outskirts of one village, they were greeted by ten men.

"Jesus! Master! Have pity on us," they cried.

Jesus noticed their ragged clothes and unkempt hair. Then, as he went closer, he saw their skin: they all had the same dreadful disease! It was both catching and incurable. No one dared go near anyone who had it. The men were condemned to living as outcasts.

Jesus did not seem concerned. "Go and let the priests examine you," he told the men. "They can say if you are well enough to be part of your communities again."

The men hurried off. "I don't know what the priests will say," said one. "When I pull back my sleeve they'll see my diseased arm. Just look at it!"

The man pulled back his sleeve and gasped. "When did that get better?" he cried. The other men began checking their own skin. Suddenly, the truth sank in. "We're healed!" they gasped. "WE'RE HEALED!"

They began to sing and cheer. "Let's get the proper approval from the priests, and then we'll begin partying!" they said. "Come on! There's no time to lose."

They raced off… and then one stopped in his tracks. "Wait!" he said. "The healer…"

Suddenly he turned and ran back the other way. "Praise the Lord! Praise the Lord," he shouted. He threw himself to the ground at Jesus' feet. "Thank you," he said. "Thank you very, very much."

"I healed ten men," said Jesus, "yet only one has come back to thank God – and he is a Samaritan."

He smiled at the man. "Your faith has made you well," he said.

Dear God, May I remember to give thanks for the blessings I receive.

*Dear God,
Have mercy on
me, even though
I often fail to do
what is right.*

The two men in the Temple

Some people thought that Jesus had nothing to teach them. "We already know how to live as God wants," they said. "We know the Law and we obey it."

Jesus told them this story.

"There were once two men who went to the Temple to pray," he said. "One was a Pharisee and the other was a tax collector.

"The Pharisee went and stood apart from everyone else. He lifted his face to heaven and raised his hands. 'I thank you, O Lord, that I am not a sinner like other people,' he intoned piously. 'I am not greedy or dishonest; I have never committed adultery, even though it seems everyone is having an affair these days. Thank you, O Lord, that I am not like that tax collector over there.' He cast a glance scornfully over his shoulder.

"'Remember, O Lord,' he continued, 'how hard I try to serve you. I fast two days a week and I give you a tenth of my income.' On and on he prayed, listing the many examples of his wonderful deeds.

"While all this was going on, the tax collector hung around at the back of the crowds who had come to pray. He bowed his head in shame. 'O God, I have done the most awful things,' he wept, wincing at the memory of them. 'Have pity on me.'"

Jesus looked at his listeners. They looked slightly offended at the twist in the story. "I can tell you," said Jesus, "that it was the tax collector who went home with God's blessing, and not the Pharisee. People who think of themselves as great will be humbled; people who humble themselves will be made great."

Jesus and the children

THE DISCIPLES WATCHED as a group of mothers and children came hurrying toward them.

"Come on! Hurry! There's no need for wailing!" the mothers were saying.

Some of the children were very young. It was hard for them to keep up on their little legs. "Is it far? Will we have to wait? Does he know we're coming?"

"Listen to all that din!" exclaimed one of the disciples. "Children crying, children shrieking. It reminds me of days when all the relatives come over for a meal. I feel worn out just listening."

The mothers came right up to the disciples. One of them stepped forward, carrying a baby. She beamed with happiness. "We've come to see Jesus," she said. "We want him to bless our little ones."

The men stared at her, looking slightly shocked. "You must be joking!" they said. "Jesus has serious work to do. He doesn't want… brats."

For a moment there was silence. Smiles vanished. Then a young child spoke in a loud wail. "I've come MILES for NOTHING. It's all HORRIBLE!"

Jesus must have heard. He was a little way off, talking to some grown-ups. "Come over here," he called cheerily. "I want to see you all!"

One of the disciples spoke to him through clenched teeth. "We told them to go away," he said. "Don't encourage time-wasters."

"Let the children come to me, and don't try to stop them," said Jesus. "The kingdom of God belongs to such as these."

Dear God, May I be kind and respectful toward little children.

*Dear God,
May I hold
on only to
the things that
are of eternal
value.*

The rich man

❧

As Jesus was starting out on his way again, a man came running to speak to him. "Good Teacher," he said, "please tell me: what must I do to have eternal life?"

"You shouldn't call me good," said Jesus. "Only God is good. You know the commandments: do not murder; be faithful in marriage; do not steal; do not tell lies about people to get them into trouble; do not cheat; respect your father and your mother."

"Oh, I do. I've tried to be faithful to the commandments ever since I learned them as a boy," came the reply.

Jesus looked at the man: it was clear he was honest and eager. "There's just one more thing that you should do," said Jesus slowly. "I can see you are wealthy. Sell what you have, give the money to the poor, and come and follow me."

The man's face fell. "Oh!" he said, rather faintly. "I don't think I can do that. Well… It would be a big decision… and quite complicated…"

His voice trailed away as Jesus continued to look him in the eye. He bit his lip and then turned and walked away looking sad and dispirited.

Jesus looked at his disciples. "It's going to be hard for rich people to enter the kingdom of God. It would be easier for a camel to go through the eye of a needle."

"You mean it can't happen," they laughed.

"Well, God can make anything happen," replied Jesus.

"We gave up what we had in order to follow you," said Peter.

"You did," agreed Jesus, "and whatever people give up to follow me they will receive back a hundred times and more. In the time that is to come, those who are privileged now will find themselves with nothing; those who are nobodies now will be the most important."

Not long after, Jesus took his disciples aside. "We are going to go to Jerusalem," he said. "Everything the prophets wrote about the Son of man will come true. He will be handed over to the authorities and put to death. Three days later, he will rise to life again."

The disciples listened wearily. Jesus had made such gloomy predictions before.

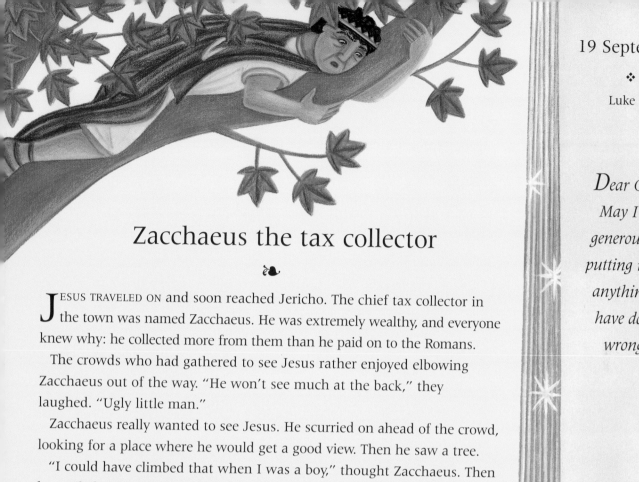

Zacchaeus the tax collector

❧

JESUS TRAVELED ON and soon reached Jericho. The chief tax collector in the town was named Zacchaeus. He was extremely wealthy, and everyone knew why: he collected more from them than he paid on to the Romans.

The crowds who had gathered to see Jesus rather enjoyed elbowing Zacchaeus out of the way. "He won't see much at the back," they laughed. "Ugly little man."

Zacchaeus really wanted to see Jesus. He scurried on ahead of the crowd, looking for a place where he would get a good view. Then he saw a tree.

"I could have climbed that when I was a boy," thought Zacchaeus. Then he smiled. "Maybe I still can!"

He scrambled up the bark, snagging his tunic as he did so. He ripped it free and crawled along a branch among the leaves. He felt rather smug as he saw Jesus coming right underneath. Why, the man was even stopping to look around. Zacchaeus had an excellent view.

Then Jesus looked up. "You up there! Zacchaeus! Come on down! I want to stay in your house today," he called.

Zacchaeus didn't know whether to be embarrassed or delighted. He could hardly get down fast enough. As he led the way to his house, he tried not to hear the grumbling behind him. "Whatever is going on? Jesus can't know much about Zacchaeus! Chief tax collector and chief sinner."

That day, everything changed. Zacchaeus listened to what Jesus had to say. Then he stood up and made an announcement. "Beginning today, I am going to give half my belongings to the poor. If I have cheated anyone, I will repay them four times what I took."

Jesus was delighted. "This is what I came for," he said, "to bring people back to God."

Dear God, May I be generous in putting right anything I have done wrong.

271

*Dear God,
May I use my
time and my
money to do
what is right.*

The gold coins

ᔰ

JESUS HAD ALMOST reached Jerusalem. Many people were expecting that the kingdom of God was about to become reality – that Jesus was actually going to take over the government. Jesus told this story to caution them.

"There was once a man who was going to a country far away to be made king," he said. "Before he left, he called his servants. 'I am going to give you each a gold coin,' he told them. 'See what you can earn with it while I am away.'

"When he had gone, his own people turned against him. They sent messages warning him never to come back. However, he did return and called his servants to find out what had happened to his money.

"'I have run a small business,' said the first, 'and look – from investing one coin I have made ten.'

"'Well done!' said the man. 'You have done well in small things. Now I will put you in charge of ten cities.'

"The second spoke. 'Sir, I too have made a profit. I now have five coins.'

"'Well done!' said the man. 'I will put you in charge of five cities.'

"Another servant came. 'Sir, I was afraid of losing your money, so...' He began rummaging in a pocket. He pulled out a handkerchief and unwrapped the coin. 'There, safe and sound,' he said.

"'That's useless!' said the man. 'You could at least have put it in a savings account. Then I'd have got the interest.'

"He spoke to the people around him. 'Take his coin, and give it to the servant who has ten.'

"'That's very harsh!' they replied.

"'Those who have a lot will be given more,' replied the man. 'Those who have nothing will lose the little they have.'

"Then he spoke even more severely. 'Now, those of my people who didn't want me back,' he said. 'Bring them to me to be punished.'"

The death of Lazarus

❧

A MESSENGER CAME HURRYING up to Jesus. His face was solemn. "I bring bad news from Mary and Martha," he said. "Their brother Lazarus is ill. It's very serious. They want you to go and see them."

It was something of a risk for Jesus to make the journey. Lazarus lived in Judea, and Jesus had received death threats from the people there. The disciples were even more nervous and tried to dissuade him from going.

When at last Jesus arrived in the village, he found that Lazarus had died. In fact, he had been buried for four days. Martha hurried to greet him. "If only you had been here," she wept. "Then my brother wouldn't have died. But I know even now that God will give you whatever you ask him for."

"Your brother will rise to life," said Jesus.

"I know that," she replied. "I believe he will be resurrected on the last day."

Jesus replied. "I am the resurrection and the life. Those who believe in me will live, even though they die. Do you believe that, Martha?"

"Yes," she replied. "I believe you are the messiah, the Son of God."

Then Martha went to get Mary and they all went to the grave. Many people had come to mourn Lazarus. The sisters were weeping. Jesus was overcome at the thought of his friends' suffering and his own loss, and wept alongside them.

Then he spoke. "Roll the stone away from the entrance," he said.

"No!" warned Martha. "The body is rotting – it will smell dreadful!"

Jesus insisted, and in the end some of her neighbors agreed to do as Jesus wanted.

"Lazarus, come out!" called Jesus.

To everyone's amazement, Lazarus came walking from the tomb.

Dear God, Give hope to those who are bereaved.

Riding to Jerusalem

*Dear God,
May everyone
rejoice at the
coming of the
king of peace.*

J ESUS AND HIS disciples journeyed on toward Jerusalem. As he came near to the Mount of Olives, he sent two of them ahead.

"I want you to go on to the next village. You will see a young donkey tethered there. Untie it and bring it here to me. If anyone asks you what you're up to, just say, 'The Master needs it.'"

The two set off, and everything went as planned. "That was all set up," said one. "Did you see the owner wink when we said, 'The Master needs it?'"

"I hope the Master wants it when he sees it," said the other. "You can tell that this colt has never been ridden." He prodded the donkey along.

When they reached Jesus, the disciples loaded their cloaks onto the donkey's back. Then they helped Jesus get on.

The little animal skittered this way and that, suddenly unsure of its footing on the steep hill and uncertain of how to deal with its heavy load.

"Easy there," murmured Jesus. "Take your time. We're in no hurry."

Soon the creature settled to a steady plod. Jesus rode along among crowds of pilgrims who were going to Jerusalem to celebrate Passover. When they saw Jesus, they began to chant.

"God bless the king! God bless the king." Some threw their cloaks on the road for the donkey to walk on. Others cut huge palm leaves and threw them down.

Grown men cheered and shouted, women clapped their hands and children danced in glee at all the excitement. "Alleluia! Alleluia!"

Some Pharisees in the crowd were shocked. They marched up to Jesus.

"Stop this disgraceful parade at once!" they said. "Tell this rabble to behave themselves."

"Even if they kept quiet, the stones would shout out what is happening," replied Jesus.

The market in the Temple

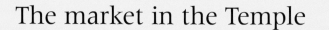

23 September

❖

Luke 19, John 2

JESUS RODE UP the hill to a hero's welcome. Then he walked up the steps into the Temple courtyard.

It was crowded with traders. There were people selling animals to be used as offerings for the festival that was about to begin… the festival of Passover. Calves mooed, sheep bleated, the pigeons fluttered in their cages. Money changers had set up their tables. They were selling the special Temple coins pilgrims needed and haggling noisily.

Jesus picked up some lengths of cord that had been left untidily on the ground. He knotted them together to make a whip. Then with a sudden flick, he sent some calves stampeding.

"Hey! Stop!" shouted a man. A woman screamed.

"Baa! Baa!" A group of sheep began bleating all at once. One made a dash for the gate and the rest of the flock came jostling and jumping.

Panic spread. In a few seconds, the courtyard was in uproar. Jesus ran past the money changers' tables, tipping each one over. Then he grabbed one of the people who were selling pigeons and pointed to the way out. "Take all your cages and go. Yes, and you, all of you. Out."

He jumped up on a stool and began to call out to the crowd. "This Temple is meant to be a house of prayer. You're turning it into a marketplace and a den of thieves."

The Temple authorities rushed to challenge him. "How dare you?" they asked.

"I don't need to answer that!" replied Jesus.

Dear God,
May I value
times of silence.
May I learn
to reflect and
to pray.

275

Dear God,
May I live
in agreement
with you.

The owner of the vineyard

❧

JESUS KNEW THAT the religious leaders were plotting to get rid of him. He told the people this story.

"There was once a man who planted a vineyard. Then he found he had to travel far away. He found some tenants to take care of the vineyard in his absence.

"The time came to gather the grapes. The owner of the vineyard sent a servant to collect his share of the harvest.

"'Not likely,' the tenants whispered among themselves. 'We don't have to stick to what we agreed. We can declare our own terms now!' They beat the man up and sent him away without a thing.

"'This is ridiculous behavior!' declared the owner when he found out what had happened. 'I shall send a second messenger with a serious warning.'

"The second messenger duly arrived, but he too was beaten up and sent away.

"Astonishingly, the same thing happened a third time.

"The man called for his son, whom he loved dearly. 'I want you to go this time,' he said. 'I'm sure the tenants will respect you.'

"When the tenants saw the son coming, they laughed. 'This is our chance!' they exclaimed. 'The property will soon be ours!'

"They seized him, hustled him out of the vineyard and killed him."

Jesus looked at his listeners. "What do you think the owner will do now?" he asked. "I'll tell you: he will come and kill those men and hand the vineyard over to others."

"This is a very grim story!" said the people in the crowd. "Surely you don't mean all this?"

"Think about this line from the psalms," said Jesus. "'The stone which the builders rejected has turned out to be the most important.'"

The tax question

HE CHIEF PRIESTS and some teachers of the Law knew exactly what the story about the vineyard meant. One of the chief priests beckoned to the others and they gathered more closely around him.

"Shall I get a couple of the Temple guards to arrest him now?" he asked.

"No, no," whispered the others. "The crowds adore him. There'll be a riot!"

"But we've not made any progress with arresting him when he's alone. No one is giving us information."

"Well… What can we do? Any ideas?"

"I know! Let's get some people to ask him questions that will make him look like a rebel to the Romans. Then we can turn him over to the governor."

They duly bribed some men to act as spies, and sent them to Jesus.

"Teacher," they said. "We know you are willing to speak quite plainly about what is right in God's eyes. Is it against our own Law to pay taxes to the Roman emperor?"

Jesus laughed. "Oh, a tricky question about religion and politics, I see! The sort to get people into trouble. Well, let's have a look at a silver coin!"

They handed him one and he held it out to them. "Whose name and face are on it?" he asked.

"The emperor's," they replied.

"Exactly," said Jesus. "So pay the emperor what belongs to the emperor, and pay God what belongs to God."

25 September

❖

Matthew 22,
Mark 12, Luke 20

*Dear God,
I will obey
the law of the
land out of
obedience to
you.*

❖

Dear God,
May those who
are rich and
powerful work
for justice.

The Temple collecting box

NOT LONG AFTER, when Jesus and his disciples were at the Temple, he gave them a warning. "Be on your guard against the teachers of the Law," he said. "Look at them! They love to walk about in their long robes. They love it when people bow and speak to them respectfully and call them Rabbi. And have you noticed how they always get themselves reserved seats in the synagogues? How they are always sitting at the head table at wedding feasts and the like?

"Have you noticed how they get poor women to give to their little causes and then end up evicting them from their homes? They will pay for all that at the end of time."

He looked around. Beyond were the Temple offering boxes with their trumpet-shaped openings. Wealthy people were strolling by and emptying handfuls of silver coins into them. The coins glittered and jingled as they fell.

Then he saw a poor woman – clearly a widow. She waited for a quiet moment. Then she dropped two small copper coins in the trumpet-shaped opening and walked away.

"Look!" he exclaimed to his disciples. "The other people could afford to give without hardship. They have riches to spare. She is poor, and she gave all she had to live on."

Judas Iscariot

❧

THAT NIGHT, AS ON previous nights, Jesus and his disciples left the city and walked across the valley to the Mount of Olives. It was easy enough to find a place to hide among the closely planted trees, and easier to sleep knowing that enemies would have a hard time finding them.

But one of the disciples lay awake for hours. His name was Judas Iscariot, and he had been worrying for some time. Weeks, certainly, maybe even months. The things he had dreamed of when he first agreed to follow Jesus had not come true. He wanted everything to be different. He couldn't shake off the idea that he ought to be doing something. But what? He sat up and watched the first patches of light appear in the sky.

Another of the group of friends nudged him. "What are you sitting up for? You're looking worried. Do you think the priests have got wind of where we hide out at night?"

"I'm just… thinking," said Judas.

The thought wouldn't go away. It just wouldn't. The next day, when Jesus was back in the Temple courtyard again, preaching to the crowds, Judas sat at the back.

"Curse the man," he heard a priest mutter to one of the Temple guards. "If only we could get him!"

Judas turned to look at him. He got up and went over. "I could help you," he said. "I could arrange for you to get Jesus on his own. Where… to whom… should I go… to find out if you're really interested?"

The priest looked at him sharply. "Go and sit down again," he said. "I'll have someone who isn't wearing priestly robes come and have a little word with you."

27 September

❖

Luke 21–22

Dear God, Keep me safe from the wild imaginings of a sleepless night.

*Dear God,
Make me ready
to serve others
in humble
ways.*

The Passover meal

Soon came the day for the Passover feast. Jesus sent Peter and John off with instructions:

"As you go into the city, a man who is carrying a water jar will meet you. Simply follow him to a house. Then go in and say, 'The Teacher is asking, "Where is the room where my disciples and I can eat the Passover meal?"' He will show you an upstairs room. You can get everything ready."

In the evening, they all met there. Just as they were about to eat together, Jesus got up and tied a towel around his waist. He poured some water into a basin and began to wash his disciples' feet.

"You're not going to wash my feet," said Peter. "I'm not going to treat you as some kind of household servant."

"You must let me," replied Jesus, "or you won't be my disciple anymore."

Peter laughed. "In that case, wash all of me! It's all of me that wants to be your most faithful disciple."

"It will be enough to wash your feet," said Jesus. "You're all clean enough to be my followers… all except one, that is."

The disciples looked at one another uneasily. They all shrugged. Jesus often said things that puzzled them, but nothing had gone wrong yet.

When Jesus had washed the feet of all of them, he calmly returned to his place at the table. "Do you understand what I have done?" he asked. "You call me Teacher and Lord, because that is what I am to you. But I have washed your feet, as a servant. You must wash one another's feet, and be ready to serve one another."

Bread and wine

JESUS AND HIS disciples began the celebration meal. "I really wanted to share this Passover meal with you before my sufferings begin," he said.

The disciples looked at him quizzically: they all knew that the Passover was meant to be a celebration of God's rescuing the people and putting an end to their suffering. What was Jesus thinking of now?

"But I can't enjoy it," continued Jesus. "Not until it is given its full meaning in the kingdom of God."

Then he took a cup of wine and said a prayer of thanks. "Take this and share it among yourselves," he said. "I tell you that from now on I will not drink this wine until the kingdom of God comes."

Then he took a piece of bread and said a prayer of thanks. He broke it into pieces and gave it to his disciples. "This is my body, which is given for you," he said. "Do this in memory of me."

After supper he gave them the cup of wine. "This cup is God's new covenant," he said. "It is sealed with my blood, which is poured out for you.

"But look! Here at the meal with me is the one who will betray me."

29 September

❖

Matthew 26,
Mark 14, Luke 22

*Dear God,
You welcome us
at your table.*

❖

*Dear God,
Help me to
learn from
Jesus how to
love others.*

Peter's boast

🐋

JUDAS ISCARIOT STOOD up from the table. Jesus watched him walk to the door. "Be quick, now, won't you!" he said.

"Where's he off to, I wonder?" one of the disciples asked his neighbor. "Oh, it must be because he's in charge of the money. Perhaps there's something we've still got to buy for the festival."

"I think Jesus wanted him to give money to help the poor as part of our festival celebrations," came the reply. "That's more likely to be it."

"What did Judas do to deserve that job?" chipped in another.

A fourth disciple joined in. "I've been wondering that. Judas has been acting as if he's somehow superior for a couple of days now…"

"He's not the only one," said the first, angrily. "I'm getting more and more annoyed at the way Peter swaggers around and hands out orders as as if he were second in command. Why do we have to put up with it?"

His complaint sparked a major argument. Jesus shook his head in disbelief. "I've told you this before," he said. "Whether you're the greatest in the group or the youngest in the group, you must serve one another. You will all eat and drink at my table in God's kingdom.

"As for now, I'm not going to be with you much longer, and you can't go where I am going. I am giving you a new commandment: love one another as I have loved you. If you do this, then everyone will know that you are truly my disciples."

Simon Peter looked defiantly at Jesus. "Wherever you go, I go," he said to Jesus.

"You can"t," replied Jesus. "Not now."

"Why not?" asked Peter. "I"m ready to die for you."

"Are you?" asked Jesus. "Before the rooster crows in the morning, you will deny three times that you know me."

Love one another

ONCE JUDAS HAD gone on his secret assignment, Jesus knew that he had little time left to speak to his remaining disciples. "Whatever happens," he said to them, "you must not be worried or upset. Believe in God and believe in me. There are many rooms in my Father's house, and I am going to prepare a place for you. You know I wouldn't say that if it weren't true. And after I've gone and got everything ready, I'll come and take you there. You know the way."

Thomas frowned a little. "We don't even know where you're going, so how do we know how to get there?"

Jesus replied, "I am the way, the truth and the life. No one goes to the Father except by me."

"Show us the Father, then," said Philip.

Jesus replied, "You have seen me and that means you have seen the Father. I and the Father are one.

"If you love me, obey my commandments. I will ask the Father to give you the Holy Spirit to help you and stay with you forever.

"Anyway, it's time for us to be getting out of the city. But remember all that I am saying. I am the vine, my Father is the gardener. If you are like a branch that bears no fruit, you will be broken off. If you are like a branch that does bear fruit, you can expect to be pruned. In other words, there will be hard things for you to face, but as a result you will do even greater things.

"Always remember this: love one another, just as I love you."

Dear God,
Help me to
love as
Jesus loved.

283

*Dear God,
Never let
hard times
defeat me.*

The garden of Gethsemane

JESUS AND THE disciples left the city and went, as they usually did, to the Mount of Olives. There they hid themselves in the olive grove known as the garden of Gethsemane.

"You should pray for yourselves," warned Jesus. "Pray that the testing times ahead will not defeat you."

Then he went a little way ahead of them. Deep among the shadows of the olive trees, he prayed.

"Father," he said. "I don't want to taste the bitter drink of suffering. However, if that is your will, I accept."

Jesus looked up. He saw one of heaven's angels, and he knew what God's answer was.

Jesus prayed more desperately. Dark beads of sweat poured down his face and fell to the ground. After hours of anguish, he went back to the disciples. They were fast asleep.

"Get up!" he warned urgently. "Pray for yourselves, just as I told you."

His words were interrupted: armed men burst from the shadows. Judas Iscariot stepped forward and greeted Jesus with a kiss.

"Is this how you betray me?" asked Jesus.

"We can fight!" shouted someone. Peter drew a sword and struck a blow. His victim fell to his knees.

"Stop!" said Jesus sternly. Peter had severed the man's ear. Jesus touched the wound and healed him. Then he turned to the other armed men. "Why come with all this force, as if I were an outlaw? I was in the Temple every day. You could have arrested me then.

"But no: this is what you must do. The power of darkness rules."

284

A dark night for Peter

THE ARMED MEN led Jesus away. Peter followed, always staying just far enough behind not to be noticed. When Jesus was led inside the house of the high priest, Peter managed to slip into the outer courtyard.

The servants had gathered around the fire there, for the night was cold.

"That Jesus – he's in big trouble now!" said one. Some of the servants who had gathered belonged to the high priest's household, others to various of his guests. There was only one topic of conversation.

"I don't know what charge they'll pin on him," argued another. "He's a clever preacher – he hasn't really said anything they can get him for."

"But I know who's here to say that he has," added a third. "I saw how much money changed hands."

"Ah."

As the servants exchanged nervous glances, a woman noticed Peter. "You!" she said. "You were with Jesus."

"No I wasn't!" Peter growled his answer, hiding his anxiety. "I don't even know him."

The woman shrugged; but soon a man came along and noticed Peter. "Hey!" he called. "You're one of the Jesus followers, aren't you?"

"No I'm not!" retorted Peter. "I must look like someone else you've seen."

The man sidled away, looking back at Peter with suspicious eyes.

About an hour later, another man came striding out from where a group of servants had been gossiping together. "Hey! You! We know from your accent you're from Galilee. We've found you out, haven't we: you're one of Jesus' disciples."

"I absolutely AM NOT!" shouted Peter, and raised his fist.

At that moment, a rooster crowed. All at once Peter remembered what Jesus had said.

Peter had done exactly what he had insisted he would never do: he had denied knowing the man he said he would die for. He went outside and wept.

*Dear God,
Forgive me
my failings.*

Jesus is accused

❧

WHEN MORNING CAME, the elders, the chief priests and the teachers of the Law all met together. Jesus was brought to them. He looked tousled and unkempt: the guards always enjoyed bullying their prisoners, and they had roughed Jesus up a bit while he was in their charge.

The religious leaders looked haughty and pious as they began their questioning. "Tell us," they said sharply. "Are you the messiah?"

"If I tell you, you won't believe me," said Jesus. "If I ask you a question, you won't answer. But from now on the Son of man will be seated at the right hand of God."

"Son of man! That means nothing. Are you the Son of God?"

"You say I am," replied Jesus.

"Well, that's all the evidence we need!" exclaimed the religious leaders. "We don't even need the witnesses we've assembled. I think we are all agreed that we should now take him to the Roman governor. We need him properly punished."

At the back of the council, a man named Joseph who had come from the town of Arimathea stood up. "I simply can't agree with any of this!" he called out. "There is no reason in law to accuse this man."

The high priest glared back. "We have decided by a huge majority to take this man to the governor," he announced. Then he swept away.

Pilate and Herod

THE RELIGIOUS LEADERS brought Jesus to the Roman governor in Jerusalem. His name was Pontius Pilate and he watched anxiously as he saw the crowds gathering outside his palace. They could so easily turn into a troublesome mob. What was it all about?

The priests announced the charge against Jesus. "We found this man involved in criminal behavior," they said. "He has been leading the people astray and telling them not to pay taxes to the emperor. He claims that he is a king himself. The word we use for king is messiah. It means 'anointed by God'. The Greek word for that is *Christ*."

Pilate sighed to himself and then leaned toward their prisoner. "Tell me the truth," he said grimly; "are you the king of the Jews?"

"So you say," answered Jesus.

Pilate gazed back at him. The man was clearly resolute in his beliefs, but Pilate didn't think he looked like a violent fanatic. Nor did he like to think the priests could tell him what to do. He turned back to them. "I don't think there's a case here for me to condemn him to die," he said.

"Then you can't have understood," argued the priests. "His teaching is going to lead to riots. It began in Galilee and now he's stirring things up here in Jerusalem."

"Oh, Galilee!" said Pilate. "That's King Herod's territory. He's in Jerusalem right now. Take him to Herod. That's much more suitable."

Herod was delighted to have the chance to meet Jesus. He had heard a good deal about him and wanted to see a miracle, right in front of his very eyes. "Come on!" he said. "Show me what you can do!"

Jesus remained unmoved. "Don't upset me," taunted Herod. "My influence could be useful to you right now."

Still Jesus said nothing. In the end, Herod tired of an interrogation that was going nowhere.

"Send him back to Pilate!" he ordered.

Dear God, May I know when it is wise to stay silent.

The death of Judas Iscariot

❧

JUDAS ISCARIOT SAT outside the high priest's house looking out over the city. The sun was climbing higher in the sky. The buildings of Jerusalem seemed to shake in the heat haze. It was if the world that he had known was dissolving in front of him.

Judas felt strangely numb, as if his mind was disconnected from his body. Why had he agreed to take Jesus' enemies to arrest him? Now they were planning to have him put to death. Why had he not seen the risk? Why was everything spinning out of control?

A purse containing thirty silver coins lay at his feet. This was what he had been paid. Suddenly he snatched it up.

He hurried off to find the chief priests. "I must see them… I must see them now," he said, arguing his way past the guards. At last he came within shouting distance. "I tried to help you," he shouted, "and you have used what I did for your own evil purposes! Now I find that I've betrayed an innocent man."

The priests looked up to see who was causing the noise. They turned away. "That's your business," they said.

"You can have your money back!" raged Judas. "It's got blood on it."

He turned and fled. Then he went away and hanged himself.

Pilate and Jesus

☙

J ESUS WAS HUSTLED into the room where Pilate sat waiting to deal with him. Pilate motioned to the guards to stand a little further away so he could speak to Jesus more privately.

"Now," said the governor. "You are here on a serious charge and I need some serious answers. The priests in charge of your religion are waiting outside my palace for me to give my judgment. I would rather leave matters of religious law to them, but they say the matter is political as well. It's quite clear they want me to pass the death sentence. So there is one thing I need to know: are you the king of the Jews?"

Jesus looked at him. "Is this your question or is this something other people have said?"

Pilate slumped back in his chair and frowned. "Do you think I'm a Jew?" he asked. "It was your people and your chief priests who handed you over to me. I just want to know what you have done so I can judge whether or not it is something that I, as governor on behalf of the Roman authorities, need to deal with."

Jesus replied, "My kingdom does not belong to this world. If it did, my followers would fight for me. They wouldn't let me be arrested like this."

"So you are a king?" said Pilate.

"That's what you say," answered Jesus. "I came into this world to speak about the truth. People who love the truth listen to me."

"And what is truth?" asked Pilate. He sat and tapped his fingers on the arm of his chair. As far as he could tell, Jesus had done nothing for which Roman law demanded the death penalty. The whole affair had to do with the local religion and didn't seem to be any kind of threat to the overall running of the empire. The best way forward would be to smooth the whole thing over. But how?

Dear God,
May I love
the truth.

289

Crucify him!

🐌

As Pilate sat wondering what to do about Jesus, the roar of the crowd in the street below grew louder. An official came hurrying in. "It's about the Passover custom," he reminded Pilate. "The people are expecting you to release one prisoner as a favor. Jesus Barabbas has already been mentioned as the popular choice."

Pilate nodded slowly, pondering the matter. Then he smiled. The custom could provide the way to solve the problem of the preacher he had just been questioning. He stepped out onto a balcony to face the crowds. "Which prisoner do you want?" he cried. "Jesus Barabbas or Jesus called the messiah?"

He sensed someone behind him. A slave handed him a message. He scanned it quickly. "Have nothing to do with that Jesus," it read. "He is innocent. I had a warning dream last night." The note came from his wife. Pilate crumpled it thoughtfully. Then he turned to the crowd.

"Which prisoner do you want to free?" he asked.

The crowd was shouting and chanting. "Barabbas! Barabbas!" they cried. Barabbas was in prison for riot and for murder.

"What shall I do with Jesus called the messiah?" he asked.

Then the noise of shouting grew louder. "Crucify him! Crucify him!"

Pilate felt anxious: the people seemed to be on the brink of rioting. He beckoned to a slave. "Bring me a bowl of water," he said.

He waited until the slave was ready, then raised his hand to ask for quiet. Very slowly and deliberately, he washed his hands. "My hands are clean of guilt," he said. "I take no responsibility for the death of this man. It's what you chose."

The crowd seemed not to care. "We want Barabbas! We want Barabbas!" they chorused. The guard brought out the prisoner and set him free.

Pilate gave a captain his orders. "Have that so-called messiah whipped and then crucified," he said.

The crown of thorns

THE ROMAN SOLDIERS hustled Jesus down into the barracks. The whole company gathered around him. They began to jeer.

"So, this is the preacher who was causing all the fuss, is it? Well, King Jesus, welcome to your coronation."

Someone draped a crimson cloak around his shoulders. Another twisted a few thorn twigs into a circlet and crammed it on his head.

"A scepter, your majesty," said a third, thrusting a stick into Jesus' hand.

Then they knelt before him. "Long live the king of the Jews," they laughed. "Long life and health and… oh, sorry, change of plan. We have a note here that brings bad news. 'Crucify by noon at the latest,' it says. That'll be the end of your reign!"

With that they snatched the stick and began to hit him. Jesus stood firm, flinching only slightly as the blows rained down on him. Then the soldiers took off the robe, gave him back his own clothes and prodded him along into the courtyard.

"There's the wood for your cross," said a soldier. "Nice bit of timber it is too. Pick it up and carry it… and take care not to drop it or I'll kill you."

His companions laughed riotously.

"Off we go!" they said. "There'll be three of you on execution hill today. Won't that look pretty as the sun goes down? Red sky, three crosses. What a picture for your friends to remember you by."

Dear God, May I oppose torture in every way I can.

291

The road to the cross

આ

JESUS WALKED ALONG the cobbled street, his shoulders bent under the weight of the beam. He could not keep from wincing as the rough wood rubbed against his shoulders. The whipping and the beating had left his flesh bruised and bleeding.

"Faster! You can't get out of it; might as well get on with it!" snapped a soldier. Jesus stumbled. The guard on the other side yanked him up. Again Jesus tripped.

"Stop messing around," hissed the first soldier, and kicked his ankle. Jesus tumbled to the ground.

"Useless!" sneered the Roman. "We'll never get where we're going at this rate. Hey, you over there! You look strong. Get a move on!"

A man named Simon was coming to Jerusalem from the country. He looked baffled as the soldiers grabbed him. What had he got caught up in? Everything looked very ugly.

"Piece of wood for you to carry," said the soldier. "It's for the king of your people. What a nice thing to do for him. Stay BEHIND him."

As they walked, a noisy crowd milled around the little procession – now pressing in, now cowering back as the guards brandished their swords. Among the most persistent were some of the women of Jerusalem who were weeping and wailing and screaming against Jesus' tormentors for their cruelty and injustice. Jesus turned to look at them. "Don't cry for me," he said. "Weep for yourselves and your children. You can't imagine the troubles that are coming."

"MOVE!" shouted a soldier. "Clear the city gate. Everyone, stand back. We've got prisoners coming through. I SAID, OUT OF THE WAY!"

The crowds shrank back as he led the way further along the route and beyond the city walls. There in front of them was the place of execution.

Jesus breathed out, a slow, trembling breath. Then he said a prayer: "Forgive them, Father! They don't know what they are doing."

*Dear God,
May I show
solidarity
with those
who are
unjustly
treated.*

Jesus and the two criminals

❧

JESUS AND THE two criminals were nailed to their crosses and hung up to die. Above each of them was a notice that named his crime. Pilate himself had written the one for Jesus:

"Jesus of Nazareth, the king of the Jews."

The words made the chief priests anxious. "I told him to change it," whispered one to his companion. "I told him it should say, 'This man said, I am the king of the Jews,' but he wouldn't change it once it was done.

"So, there it is, for the whole world to see: in Hebrew, Latin and Greek. Not much chance of anyone not understanding the words. Oh well, he'll soon be dead and buried and – we can only hope – forgotten."

His companion merely shook his fist at Jesus and jeered. "Come on! Save yourself if you're God's Son! Get yourself down from that cross!"

Some teachers of the Law who were standing close by took up the cry. "Aren't you the king of Israel? Come on! Prove it! We'll believe in you if you can do that."

One of the criminals who was hanging next to Jesus joined in. "Aren't you the messiah? Save yourself and us too!"

The other criminal opened his eyes dully and turned his head. "Leave that Jesus alone," he growled. "You're going to have to answer to God soon. We've both got plenty to confess. That's why we're here. That Jesus, he's done nothing wrong. Absolutely nothing."

He looked at Jesus. "Remember me when you come as king," he said.

Jesus nodded. "I promise you that today you will be in Paradise with me," he said.

*Dear God,
May I be part
of your
everlasting
kingdom.*

*Dear God,
May the
younger
generation
take care
of the old.*

Jesus sees his mother

FROM HIGH ON the cross, Jesus looked out across the crowd. He could see a group of women gazing toward him, weeping. There was Mary Magdalene, Mary the mother of James and Joseph, and Salome. There were others, too – doubtless the ones who had come with him all the way from Galilee. They had all been so loyal. Now they were in despair.

He watched as some of them crept through the crowds, trying to get nearer to him. Mary Magdalene got as close as the soldiers would allow. She looked up at Jesus: she was trying to look brave and determined. Tears were flooding down her cheeks.

A soldier turned around and let another woman come even closer. Jesus saw his own mother. On one side stood her sister; on the other, his disciple John. John: the disciple he had always liked and trusted.

He caught his mother's gaze and nodded toward John. "He is your son," he said; to John he added, "She is your mother." He could die more easily now, knowing that John would take care of his mother in her old age.

The death of Jesus

❧

A<small>T THE FOOT</small> of the cross, the soldiers were arguing noisily. "Don't rip it!" one was saying. "It's got quality! Woven in one piece. A coat for a messiah – or, should I say, FROM a messiah!"

He looked up at Jesus. "Hey, Messiah," he jeered. "Are you going to get God to rescue you? Or can we have this?" He cackled with glee, and his companions cheered and jeered.

"Let's roll for it so one of us gets it whole," said another. "I've got dice."

The soldiers bent over their game. "Hey, you're in my light," said one, pushing a comrade out of the way. "Look – it's getting really dark."

"That's odd," said another. "The sun was overhead: where's it gone?"

They finished their game and stood glowering at the crowds. "It's like nighttime," muttered one of the soldiers. "How long do you think we're going to have to wait here?"

They shifted about uneasily in the eerie half-light, guarding the place of execution. At three o'clock, Jesus gave a loud cry. "My God, my God, why have you abandoned me?" he said. He paused a moment, panting for breath as his body sank under its own weight. "I'm thirsty," he gasped.

Someone ran up with a wine-soaked sponge on a stick. "Here, drink this," he offered.

Jesus tried to moisten his lips, but he was now very weak. "Father, into your hands I place my spirit," he said. "It is finished." Then he died.

At once the earth shook. In the Temple, the curtain that screened the innermost room was ripped in two.

The officer in charge gripped his spear. "That Jesus really was the Son of God," he declared.

*Dear God,
May the world
recognize Jesus
for who he is.*

295

*Dear God,
May I be
respectful in
the face
of death.*

Jesus is buried

THE JEWISH LEADERS went to Pilate with a request. "Tomorrow is the sabbath," they said. "We must get corpses down before our holy day. Have your soldiers break the criminals' legs, so they die before sunset."

The command was given and soldiers were dispatched. "This Jesus, he's dead already," said one soldier.

"Just checking," said another, as he plunged a spear into his side. "Well, we'll soon be able to dump the bodies and finish our day's work. Hey, what are those old men doing? You two, out of the way."

The last remark was to a couple of Jewish men who had come bustling near. "No, no, I'm here with Pilate's permission," said one. "See – I'm Joseph, from Arimathea. I have come to get Jesus' body."

The soldiers checked his authorization. "Oh, take it," they grunted.

Gently and respectfully, Joseph took the body. Together with Nicodemus and some servants who had come with them, he wrapped it in a linen sheet and loaded it onto a funeral stretcher. Then he led the way as it was carried to a rock-cut tomb – the one he had had made for his own burial.

A group of women followed them. They watched tearfully as the broken body was placed in the tomb. "We can come back after the sabbath and wrap it according to the proper customs then," they whispered.

The stone door rolled shut. The sun was setting and the sabbath day of rest beginning. It was time for everyone to go home for the night.

The stone is rolled away

THE DAY AFTER Jesus' death and burial was the sabbath. In spite of all the rules about the day of rest, the chief priests and the Pharisees met with Pilate.

"Sir," they said. "That liar Jesus talked a lot of nonsense before he died. He knew what was going to happen to him, and he used to say he would be raised to life on the third day after he was executed. There's no telling what his friends might do in these circumstances. They could conspire to steal the body and claim their beloved leader was alive again. That would be more trouble than ever."

Pilate was irritated by the whole affair. "Oh, take a guard," he said. "I want an end to all this. Do all you need to satisfy yourselves that the tomb is safe from meddlers."

The religious leaders went at once. They put a seal on the stone and instructed soldiers to keep a careful watch.

The sabbath ended and night fell. As Sunday dawned, some of the women who had been followers of Jesus came to the tomb. Among them was Mary Magdalene. They brought the spices they needed to prepare the body properly for its final burial.

"I don't know how we're going to move the stone from the door," said one. "It was very heavy."

As they drew nearer, they heard a strange rumbling – low, ominous… then silence again. "Was that an earthquake?" whispered one. "Did you feel the ground shake?"

"No!" breathed another, her voice full of awe. "It must be a storm – look – there's the lightning."

They all felt unnerved as they crept forward to the tomb. They saw soldiers lying on the ground, as if unconscious.

"And the stone door has been rolled open," whispered Mary Magdalene.

*Dear God,
Open my eyes
to see your
miracles.*

The empty tomb

*Dear God,
Help me to see
that life and
goodness can
flourish in
the darkest
places.*

THE ENTRANCE TO the tomb was a low doorway. The women looked around, suddenly afraid that they were not alone.

Then they crept inside. "Where's the body? I'm sure it was on this ledge here," whispered one.

"It was," said another. "I made a point of remembering." She looked up in horror. "It's gone! Someone's taken Jesus' body! Who did that? And where is Jesus' body now?" Tears flooded her eyes.

"Let's see what else is in this tomb! How many chambers are there? Perhaps Joseph moved it farther in… I don't know!"

The women began to explore. The slightest sound echoed against the rock. Suddenly they froze – the dim light of the tomb had suddenly changed to dazzling brightness.

Fearfully they turned to see what had happened. Behind them were two figures dressed in shining clothes. Their eyes were twinkling as if they had just been laughing. "You'll only find dead bodies in a tomb," said one, "not someone who is alive. He isn't here; he has been raised to life."

"But… that can't be!" began one of the women.

"Remember what he said to you when you were in Galilee: 'The Son of man must be handed over to sinners, be crucified and three days later rise to life.'"

"Oh yes!" they agreed, "he did. But Jesus said lots of puzzling things… We never really paid much attention."

The women looked at one another. When they looked back at the speakers, they had gone.

"Hurry! Let's tell the others!" they said. They ran to find the disciples.

The disciples hear the news

PETER SIMPLY SHOOK his head when he first heard the news. "Jesus! His body's gone! He's alive again!" The women were shrieking the news, laughing and crying all at once. Peter looked round at the other disciples. They looked baffled and annoyed by the noisy awakening.

"Come and see!" insisted Mary Magdalene. "Find out for yourselves if I'm telling the truth or not. Please hurry – this is so important!"

John heaved a sigh. "Oh, all right, I'll come," he said.

Peter got up at once. "I'll come too," he said.

Once they were on their way, they each wanted to be first. John ran ahead. He glanced inside the tomb. "I can only see the linen wrappings," he said.

"Let me go in!" Peter walked straight inside. His companion was right.

"I don't know what to make of it," he whispered to John. "This isn't what I was expecting. Come on, let's go back."

On the way, they saw soldiers hurrying away from the high priest's house. They were laughing and fingering heavy purses. "Those priests must be desperate!" they said. "All this money, just to say we fell asleep and woke to find the body gone."

"Let's hope they keep their word though," said another, "and persuade the governor that we weren't really falling down on the job."

"Though seeing an angel would make anyone fall down," joked another. And they strode away chortling.

Dear God, May I not be bribed into saying what is not true.

299

Dear God,
May I recognize
the face of Jesus.

Mary Magdalene

ﹶ

MARY MAGDALENE HAD thought she was leading Peter and John to the tomb. In their impatience, they had run ahead, and now they were already hurrying away. She found herself alone outside the open tomb, feeling completely abandoned.

Once again, she wanted to cry. Whatever had happened, the body of Jesus was gone. Or was it? Maybe, if she looked again, she would find it right where it should have been.

She bent over to look through the low entrance and gasped.

The tomb was not empty: there were two people dressed in bright shining clothes sitting where the body had been. A single thought flashed into her mind: angels! Of course!

They smiled at Mary. "Why are you crying?" they asked.

"They've taken the body of Jesus and I don't know where they've put it," she said, and the tears ran freely down her cheeks.

Then she turned. A man was standing behind her. He asked the same question: "Why are you crying?"

"Are you the person in charge of this olive grove?" she said. "Did you come and take the body? If you did, please tell me where you put it and I will go and get it."

The man stepped closer and looked into her eyes.

"Mary?" he said.

At once she recognized his face. "Teacher!" she said joyfully. She reached out to hug him.

"Don't hold on to me," said Jesus. "Go and tell my disciples that I am going back to God: my Father and their Father."

On the way to Emmaus

⤫

LATER ON THAT same Sunday, two of Jesus' followers left Jerusalem. As they walked the few miles to Emmaus, another man who was going the same way came along. They nodded to him and continued their conversation.

After a few minutes, it seemed that the man could not contain his curiosity. "What are you talking about?" he asked them. "It all sounds astonishing."

They stopped and looked at him, openmouthed. "Haven't you heard about the things that are going on in Jerusalem?" said the one named Cleopas. "I can't believe you've been to Jerusalem and not been given a dozen different stories about what's happened."

"About what?" said the man.

"About Jesus of Nazareth," they replied. "Many people thought he was a prophet, but the religious leaders conspired to get rid of him. He was crucified on Friday. Stone cold dead he was, and buried before sunset. Now some women are saying his body isn't in the tomb. They say that angels told them Jesus is alive. But… no one from our group has seen Jesus, so we don't know what to think."

The man shrugged, as if the news was only what might be expected. "I'm surprised you don't understand," he said. "Remember what the scriptures say about the messiah." He went on to explain the whole story of the Bible, starting with the books of Moses.

As they came to Emmaus, the two travelers still wanted to hear more.

"Come and stay with us!" they said. "The day is almost over and you'll need lodging."

The three went into their house and sat down to a meal. Then the man took the bread, said the blessing and shared the bread with them.

As they looked at him, they suddenly knew. "It's you!" they cried.

Suddenly, Jesus was no longer there. The two hurried back to the disciples in Jerusalem to tell them what had happened.

Dear God,
May I recognize
your presence
in unexpected
places.

Thomas

*Dear God,
May I have
faith to believe
what is true.*

LATE ON SUNDAY evening, the disciples were together in one room. They had locked the doors, afraid that the religious leaders would be out looking for them.

Suddenly, Jesus was there in the room with them. There was no doubt it was really Jesus: his body still bore the wounds of crucifixion. But there he really, truly was: alive and well and eager to talk! He began to explain all that had happened and what he wanted them to do next.

However, it so happened that one of the disciples was not there at the time. When he came back, he found the other disciples talking excitedly. "We have seen Jesus!" they exclaimed.

"Nonsense," said Thomas. "I'm not falling for that, and I won't change my mind unless I see Jesus and touch the scars in his hands."

For a week, Thomas had to endure their endless chattering about Jesus. He simply shook his head in disbelief.

Then, while they were indoors together, Jesus came and stood among them. "Hello, Thomas," said Jesus. "Please touch my hands. You can see the nail marks clearly. There's a spear wound in my side, too. When you see and touch, you won't be in doubt anymore. You'll have to believe."

Thomas looked at Jesus. "My Lord and my God," he said.

"I'm glad you believe, now that you've seen the evidence," said Jesus. "But God will truly bless those who believe without seeing me."

Peter goes fishing

AFTER ALL THE turmoil of Jesus' crucifixion, the disciples were eager to leave Jerusalem. They went back to Galilee. As the day came to an end, Simon Peter found himself looking glumly at the lake. Until Jesus had come along, his whole life had been centered on making a living from its waters. He'd worried about boats and nets and storms and the price he could get for his catch. Everything used to be so simple. Could life ever be that simple again?

"I'm going fishing!" he said suddenly, and six of his companions agreed at once to go with him.

They worked hard all night, but they didn't catch anything. As they returned to shore at sunrise, they saw someone on the beach watching them.

"Haven't you caught anything?" called the man.

"No!" they answered.

"Throw the net out on your right," he shouted.

Peter shrugged and then nodded to the others to do so. All at once, the net was full of fish – so full they could not pull it back in.

John glanced at the man and understood. "It's Jesus!" he shouted. Peter jumped into the water. Fishing was no longer important. He splashed his way to shore to greet his friend while the others brought in the boat.

"Look," said Jesus. "I've got a fire going, fish cooking and some bread. Bring some of the fresh fish too."

Together they shared a meal. Jesus went and spoke quietly to Peter. Only he used his old name, not the nickname that meant "rock".

"Simon," he said instead, "do you still love me as you once said?"

"Yes, of course!" said Simon Peter. "You know I do."

"Take care of my lambs," said Jesus. Jesus asked the question a second time and got the same answer. Then he asked a third time.

"Look after my flock of followers," said Jesus. "Whatever happens through the years, follow me."

Dear God, May I be faithful in the work I am called to do.

The Lord is my shepherd.

Dear God,
Show me the
right time
to act.

Jesus ascends to heaven

THE RISEN JESUS appeared to his disciples many times. The wounds on his hands and feet proved to them that he was indeed their master. Even so, they struggled to understand what was happening.

"I foretold all of this," Jesus reminded them. "Everything is just as the scriptures say: look in the books of Moses, the writings of the prophets, the words of the psalms – you will find out that all this is part of God's promise to bless the world.

"However, you must wait until the time is right. Stay in Jerusalem until then. But for now, let us walk the few miles to Bethany."

They had gone as far as the Mount of Olives when Jesus stopped. "I know you want something dramatic to happen," he said, "but you must wait for the right time, which God will choose. At that moment, the Holy Spirit will give you the strength you need. Then you will bear witness to me in Jerusalem, in Judea, in Samaria – and to the ends of the earth."

As Jesus said this, he was taken up to heaven, and a cloud hid him from their sight.

The disciples were still looking at the sky when two people dressed in white appeared beside them. "You're from Galilee, aren't you?" they said. "The Jesus whom you followed has gone to heaven. One day, he will return in just the same way."

The twelfth apostle

꿈

23 October

❖

Acts 1

THE DISCIPLES KNEW for sure that Jesus had gone. Everything that Jesus had worked for now depended on them. They hurried back to Jerusalem to rally the group of people who had remained loyal. Among them was Jesus' own mother, Mary, and several of his relatives. They often met to pray together.

One day, there were about 120 people at a meeting when Peter stood up to make a special announcement.

"We need to be ready for action when the time comes," he told them. "Judas Iscariot is dead. Scripture itself teaches us that we should choose someone to take his place. That person must be someone who has been part of the group for the whole time that Jesus went about preaching, and also someone who is a witness to Jesus' resurrection."

The people who had assembled gave the matter serious thought. In the end, they came up with two names: Joseph Barsabbas and Matthias were both considered excellent candidates.

Only God could decide which of them was more suitable for the task that lay ahead.

As a group, they prayed: "Lord, you know the thoughts of everyone, so show us which of these two you have chosen to serve as an apostle."

Then they drew lots, and the one chosen was Matthias.

Dear God,
When I cannot
make a final
choice, show
me your will.

305

Dear God,
May your
Holy Spirit
give me
strength and
confidence to
live my life
for you.

The day of Pentecost

ɞ

FIFTY DAYS AFTER Passover came the Jewish festival called Pentecost. Once again, all the believers were in a room together. Suddenly they heard a noise from the sky.

"Is that the wind?" said one.

Everything began to rustle as the wind danced across the room, and then it was as if the wind turned to gold. Around everyone's head danced something that looked like a flame of fire. It made them want to laugh and to sing.

As they did so, they began to laugh even more. Out of nowhere, they were speaking in different languages, and they were suddenly eager to go out and use those languages to tell the world about Jesus.

In their hearts, they knew: God's Holy Spirit had come among them as a friend, and was giving them power and strength beyond anything they had ever dreamed.

The believers danced out into the streets of Jerusalem, singing and laughing. The city was crowded with pilgrims who had come from every part of the empire for the festival, and soon a large crowd gathered.

"Those people are from Galilee," they said to one another, "but listen – some of them are speaking our language."

"That group over there are talking in our dialect: I didn't think anyone outside our home region knew it!"

"Those people over there are talking in very good Latin: they wouldn't be out of place in Rome itself!"

"We can understand the words, but what are they talking about? Their God has raised a man to life? That just doesn't happen!"

"I think they're drunk."

"Look – that group of men at the top of the steps. One of them is waving for silence."

"Let's see if if he's sober enough to stay upright and speak."

"Shh. It could be something interesting."

Peter's message

PETER'S VOICE WAS was strong enough to carry a long way. "Listen," he said. "Fellow Jews and everyone in Jerusalem. First of all, we're not drunk."

"No, it only looks like it," heckled a group of young men.

"After all," said Peter earnestly, "it's only nine o'clock in the morning." This caused more laughter and Peter had to wait for calm again.

"What you are seeing is what the prophet Joel talked about:

"'In the last days, says God, I will pour out my spirit on everyone.

"'Your sons and daughters will proclaim my message.

"'You will see miracles and all kinds of wonders.

"'And whoever calls to God for help will be saved.'"

The crowds were intrigued. They fell silent as Peter told them about Jesus: that he was God's messiah; that he had been crucified; that God had raised him to life.

"If this is true," they said to each other, "then maybe we should pay more attention to God. But how would we actually do that?"

Peter gave them the answer.

"You must turn away from wrongdoing. Be baptized in the name of Jesus – the messiah, the Christ. Then your sins will be forgiven and the Holy Spirit will come and live as a friend with you."

On that day, 3,000 people were baptized.

*Dear God,
Show me what
I must do to
live at peace
with the
world and
with you.*

*Dear God,
Thank you for
your blessings,
which are
more valuable
than riches.*

A miracle by the Temple

THE COMING OF the Holy Spirit changed everything. After the crucifixion, Jesus' followers had been unsure of what to believe and scared of what might happen to them. Now they were joyful and confident, and everyone in Jerusalem was talking about them.

"Those people who believe in Jesus – they're living like one big family," they said. "Whatever it is they believe in, it's certainly making a difference in what they do. And you have to admit, they genuinely seem to care for one another."

And indeed they did. The believers were selling what they owned and sharing the money among themselves so that everyone had what they needed. Each day they met in the Temple to worship God. Afterward, they gathered in each other's homes to share meals together. It was little wonder that more and more people wanted to join them.

One day, Peter and John went to the Temple to pray. At the entrance called the Beautiful Gate was a man who had never been able to walk. He simply sat by the gate begging for money. When he saw Peter and John, he began his usual plea.

"Look at me," said Peter.

The man looked up, expecting a large gift.

"I have no money at all," said Peter. "No gold coins, and no silver coins either. But there is something I can give you: in the name of Jesus Christ of Nazareth, I order you to get up and walk."

Peter pulled the man to his feet. The beggar gasped with astonishment. Then he began to dance. "I can walk! I can jump! Praise God!" he shouted.

It was a miracle no one could deny.

In prison

❧

THE MAN WHO had been healed clung to Peter and John, and news of the miracle spread through the Temple. Soon a crowd gathered around the men.

"Why are you staring at us like that?" asked Peter. "We didn't cure the man because of our own power or holiness. We worked the miracle in the name of Jesus. You didn't believe in him – you had him crucified; now God has given him all the glory.

"So now is the time to learn from that dreadful mistake. Turn away from wrongdoing. Ask God for forgiveness. God wants to bless you all."

At this point some priests came striding by, along with the officer in charge of the Temple guards and other religious leaders. "Just listen to them! Those troublemaking believers will be telling the people that their precious Jesus rose from the dead. Now that is wrong teaching. It simply can't be allowed – especially not here in the Temple."

One of the priests gave the nod and the guards arrested John and Peter.

"It's too late in the day for us to deal with these men now," said the priest. "Take them off to the jail. Tomorrow we can have a proper meeting to listen to what they have to say and decide on the appropriate course of action."

Yet the sight of Peter and John being marched off to prison did nothing to deter people from believing in Jesus.

From 3,000 on the day of Pentecost, the group of believers had grown to 5,000.

Dear God, May I be confident of what I believe.

A firm warning

*Dear God,
When there is
something I
should tell,
may I not be
silenced.*

THE NEXT DAY, the religious leaders gathered in council to deal with Peter and John.

The chief questioner turned to fix them with a steely gaze. "By what power did you work that miracle?"

Peter smiled. "We did it in the name of Jesus Christ of Nazareth whom you crucified and whom God raised from death. Jesus is the one who was sent by God to bring salvation. There is no one else who can save us."

The whole room of religious leaders exchanged glances. A low murmuring of disagreement began.

"Take them away," ordered the priest in charge. "We have things to discuss by ourselves."

When the accused had left, the low murmuring turned to uproar.

"Those men are uneducated fishermen. How dare they tell us about God? What do they know about how to interpret scripture? It's nonsense!"

"They worked a miracle. There's no denying it – there were crowds who saw it happen."

"Well, that clearly has been a damaging report. But we can contain it. We shall order them to stop speaking about Jesus anymore."

When the council had settled on the verdict, Peter and John were ushered back.

"This is our decision," said the speaker. "We are not going to do anything about what has happened so far. But we do insist that you stop preaching about Jesus. If you don't, there will be consequences."

"What do you expect us to do?" replied Peter. "Are we to obey you or obey God? We can't stop speaking about the things we have seen and heard."

"You must stop. We agree you have not done any wrong, or we would keep you in jail. However, this is a clear warning: stop preaching about Jesus. Do you understand?"

The two apostles did not make any promise.

Miracles – and an angel

❧

PETER AND JOHN went back to the group of believers. "We must listen to what the religious leaders had to say to us," they announced. They're not at all happy. There are going to be problems."

The believers agreed with them. "We shall pray to God to help us," they said. "We shall ask God to make us all bold in spreading the news about Jesus, and to give us power to work miracles in the name of Jesus."

As they prayed, it seemed as if the place where they were meeting shook, and that God's Holy Spirit was all around them.

Soon they saw their prayers being answered in amazing ways. They worked so many miracles in Jerusalem that news quickly spread. People from the towns around Jerusalem began making trips to the city in the hope of a cure. Sick people were carried out onto the streets hoping that at least Peter's shadow might fall on them as he passed by.

All this only made the priests and the religious leaders angrier. "We'll arrest them and give them a harsher trial," they agreed.

The apostles were flung into the public jail; but in the night, an angel came and let them out. When the priests ordered the men to be brought to them, they discovered they were at large again; and not only at large – but in the Temple, preaching.

Dear God, May I see my prayers answered.

311

*Dear God,
May those who
are wise have
the confidence
to speak out.*

Gamaliel's wise words

❧

THE PRIESTS WERE utterly dismayed to find that their prisoners had escaped. They ordered the guard to go and arrest the prisoners without delay, and once again Peter found himself standing in front of the council. He was as confident as ever.

"We must obey God, not people," he said. "You had Jesus killed and God raised him to life, to be our people's savior. We are witnesses to that. Now you have the chance to turn away from wrongdoing and God will forgive you."

The priests were furious and argued among themselves about what to do. "This kind of talk is completely dishonoring to God," agreed the majority. "Surely these troublemakers deserve the death penalty."

In the midst of the uproar, a Pharisee named Gamaliel stood up. "I think we should be cautious," he said. "We've had popular movements like this before. Whenever the leader has died, the whole thing has fizzled out. I say we should leave them alone. If they are talking nonsense then their group will soon fall apart and the whole affair will be forgotten. On the other hand, if there is a shred of truth in what they are saying… Well, we'd better pay attention, or we could find we are fighting against God."

Everyone listened to Gamaliel's advice. The religious leaders had the apostles whipped, told them to stop preaching and let them go.

For a while the believers were left alone. As if to prove the truth of Gamaliel's words, more and more people joined the community in Jerusalem. Everyone shared their wealth as well as their faith.

This success brought complications. The job of distributing the money began to take a lot of time – even more so when there were quarrels.

The twelve apostles called a meeting with all the believers. "We want to spend all our time praying to God and preaching," they said. "We want you to choose seven helpers whom the Holy Spirit has blessed with wisdom. They will look after practical matters."

One of the seven was a man named Stephen.

Stephen

❦

EVERYONE AGREED THAT Stephen was exceptional. However, one particular group of Jews was angry that he could argue so convincingly for his faith. They conspired to get him into trouble. All too soon, Stephen found himself on trial at the religious council.

His enemies were ready with their accusations. "We heard him say that Jesus of Nazareth will tear down the Temple and change all the customs that have come to us from Moses," they shouted.

The high priest eyed the young man sternly. "Is this true?" he asked. It was an accusation for which he could condemn the young upstart.

In answer, Stephen gave an inspired speech. He explained the scriptures that they all knew so well, beginning with the time of Abraham. "These stories remind us," he said, "that over and again our ancestors failed to understand what God was saying to them. They rejected those who foretold the coming of God's righteous servant. Now you are the ones who have the responsibility of preserving God's Law, but you do not obey it."

Stephen's listeners were furious at the accusation, but the young preacher continued. "Look!" he said. "I see heaven opened and the Son of man standing at the right-hand side of God."

With a howl of rage, the religious leaders hustled Stephen out of the city. They flung their coats at the feet of a young religious teacher named Saul for him to look after and began to hurl stones at Stephen.

"Lord Jesus," he cried. "Do not condemn them for what they are doing."

Saul smiled grimly as Stephen collapsed and died.

Dear God, Bless those who are bold enough to defend the truth.

The blinding light

Dear God,
May I not
let fear and
prejudice blind
me to what
is good and
right.

FROM THAT DAY forward, Saul did his best to silence the news about Jesus. First he hunted down believers in Jerusalem and threw them into jail. He was dismayed to discover that some had escaped and had begun preaching in Samaria and beyond. He soon realized he would have to pursue his campaign elsewhere. He went to the high priest.

"You know how eager I am to stamp out this Jesus nonsense," he said. "I hear that these so-called Followers of the Way of the Lord are active in Damascus. Can you write to the leaders of the synagogues there and explain that I have your authority to arrest them?"

"An excellent plan," agreed the high priest. "And you must bring any suspects back here to Jerusalem."

Not long after, Saul set out for Damascus. As he was coming near the city, a light from the sky flashed around him. He fell to the ground. Then he heard a voice speaking: "Saul, Saul, why are you persecuting me?"

Saul sat up, dazed and confused. "Who are you?" he cried out wildly.

"I am Jesus," said the voice. "Now get up and go to the city. There you will be told what to do."

Saul tried to stand, but then fell back, trembling with fear. "Is there anyone there?" he shouted. "I can't see. The light has dazzled me. Help."

The men who were traveling with him helped him to his feet. "Come on," they said. "We'll lead you to the city."

Saul in Damascus

*S*AUL BLINKED AND blinked again. Even with his eyes wide open he could not see anything. Meekly he allowed himself to be taken to Damascus. There he stayed on Straight Street with a man named Judas.

He spent his time fasting and praying, for he knew that only God could help him. As he prayed, he had a vision: that a man named Ananias came to the house to heal him.

It so happened that there really was a believer in Damascus named Ananias. God spoke to him too: in a vision, God told him where to go to find Saul.

"Lord!" said Ananias. "That man has done terrible things to your people in Jerusalem. He has only come here to arrest more believers."

"Go to him," replied God. "I have chosen Saul to preach about me to the Gentiles and to all the people of Israel. He will face many hardships, but he will do so because of his great devotion."

Ananias trusted God. Even so, he took a deep breath as he stood in front of the man whose cruel deeds had made him feared. Then he spoke God's message. "Brother Saul," he said. "The Lord Jesus who appeared to you on the road sent me here. I have come to heal your eyes, and to pray that you will know God's Holy Spirit."

At once, something like fish scales fell from Saul's eyes. He could see again! In no time, he was baptized as one of the believers.

Dear God, May we be surrounded by friends who help us to see more clearly.

315

*Dear God,
Help us to be wise
and inventive in
doing good.*

Saul in danger

❧

SAUL WAS A CHANGED man! He spent a few days learning all he could from the believers in Damascus. Then he went straight to the synagogues and began to preach.

He didn't need the carefully worded letters of introduction from the high priest. He was no longer on a secret mission to arrest people. The Holy Spirit had made him bold enough to tell the world about Jesus – to tell everyone that Jesus was the Son of God.

"What a surprise to hear him say those things," said the listeners in one synagogue. "We thought he was here on behalf of the authorities in Jerusalem."

"He's turned rebel," agreed others. "And a rather fiery rebel at that."

Everyone who heard him found their own beliefs turned upside down. "The trouble is," they said, "that Saul from Tarsus does argue his case well. He had a very fine religious education in Jerusalem, didn't he? Now he's using all his learning for the sake of Jesus – a self-taught preacher from Galilee. It's an astonishing situation."

The more Saul preached, the more the Jews in Damascus felt uneasy about his message. It didn't take long before they had turned against him. In the end they met with the city governor to discuss the best way to get rid of him.

"No problem!" said the governor. "I'll have the guards on the city gate arrest him. As soon as he tries to leave, we'll silence him for good."

Somehow, the plan was leaked to the believers. "The city guards have orders to kill Saul!" they whispered. "What can we do to protect him?"

They made a plan: one night, Saul and a handful of others crept to an opening in the city walls. There, Saul climbed into a huge wicker basket. His companions let him down on ropes to the outside. He was free! He had escaped unharmed!

Saul and Barnabas

SAUL HURRIED BACK to Jerusalem. He was eager to make friends with the believers who were still there.

At the same time, he knew exactly why they were afraid of him.

"You watched Stephen being stoned," they reminded him accusingly. "You hunted down every one of us you could. Then you went off to Damascus to continue your dirty work there. Now you want to be one of us! And we're supposed to believe you."

"But I have truly changed!" pleaded Saul. "Jesus himself appeared to me. I am utterly convinced that he is the Son of God, the one promised in our scriptures. I want to tell the world the good news."

At last someone stepped forward to help him. The crowd of believers looked at the man warily. "Remember why we call him Barnabas," muttered one. "Son of Encouragement: that's what the name means. Trust him to have something to say."

"Let me take Saul to the apostles," said Barnabas. "Let me tell them what I know about his preaching in Damascus. If they are convinced of his conversion, then I think we should all accept him."

Barnabas spoke cheerfully on behalf of Saul, and the apostles agreed to accept him as a believer. At once, Saul began preaching all over Jerusalem. His zeal in the task soon made him enemies: a group of Greek-speaking Jews had hatched a plot to kill him.

The believers were dismayed. Hastily, they arranged for Saul to go to the port of Caesarea and to sail from there to his hometown, Tarsus.

After that, there was a time of peace, and the young churches thrived in Judea, Galilee and Samaria.

Peter and Tabitha

IN ALL THE REGIONS around Jerusalem, the number of believers went on growing. Peter journeyed to many places to encourage each new group.

His travels took him to a place called Lydda. There, he was introduced to a man named Aeneas. "This poor man hasn't been able to get out of bed for eight years," his hosts told him. "Can you help him?"

Peter spoke directly to the man in bed. "Aeneas," he said. "Jesus Christ makes you well. Get up."

At once, the man did so. News of the miracle spread like wildfire as far as the believers in the nearby seaport of Joppa. "We must go find Peter at once!" they agreed. "The death of our dear friend Tabitha has been a real blow. Maybe he can help us."

When Peter arrived, they took him to the upstairs room where she lay lifeless. The widows who had been Tabitha's friends crowded around. "She was such a good woman," they wept, "and so generous."

"Look at these things," said one, opening a wicker chest. "All these shirts and coats that she made – see the tiny stitches! Hours of work she put in, just to make sure she'd always have something to give to anyone in need."

Peter nodded, and then asked them to leave him in the room. He knelt down and prayed. Then he turned to the body and said, "Tabitha, get up."

The woman opened her eyes. "Come," said Peter. "Your friends will be so pleased to see you."

Peter's dream

ETER STAYED IN Joppa for a long time. A man named Simon, who was a leather tanner, welcomed him into his house.

One day, around noon, Peter went up onto the roof terrace to pray. While he was praying, he began to feel hungry. When would a meal be ready? he wondered. Peter looked down into the courtyard. Someone was kneading bread. That meant the meal was at least an hour away. He sighed, and decided to rest for a while.

As he dozed, he had a dream. There, above him, was the entrance to heaven. A sheet that was held by all four corners was being lowered to earth. In the sheet were all kinds of animals and reptiles and wild birds. A voice spoke: "Kill something and eat it."

"No, I won't," answered Peter. "Those creatures are all the ones our Law says are unclean and unfit to eat. In all my life I have never broken the food laws and I'm not about to start."

"Nothing that God made should be treated as unclean," snapped the voice. At once the sheet was whisked back to heaven.

The same thing happened three times. Peter tried to shake himself awake… He couldn't make sense of his dream at all. Then he heard footsteps outside the house. "Is there anyone here called Simon Peter?" he heard someone calling.

Suddenly Peter knew that God was directing everything that had happened. He must go and talk to whoever was calling at the door. This was an important mission.

Dear God,
Help me to
understand
the new and
unexpected
things you want
to teach me.

*Dear God,
Help me truly
to understand
your love for all
people – those
we consider
insiders and
those we
consider
outsiders.*

Peter and Cornelius

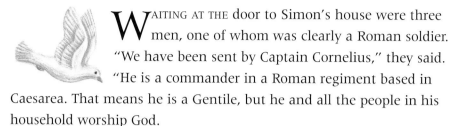

WAITING AT THE door to Simon's house were three men, one of whom was clearly a Roman soldier. "We have been sent by Captain Cornelius," they said. "He is a commander in a Roman regiment based in Caesarea. That means he is a Gentile, but he and all the people in his household worship God.

"Captain Cornelius is also a very charitable man. The Jews in Caesarea speak highly of him. He is deeply religious and has expressed a sincere wish to hear more about the message you are preaching."

Peter was intrigued and agreed to return with the messengers the very next day. When they reached Caesarea, Captain Cornelius came to greet him. He fell to his knees at Peter's feet and bowed low.

"Please stand up," said Peter. "I know you are thinking that a Jew such as I am will not go to the home of a Gentile. However, God has told me not to think of anyone as unclean or unworthy. Tell me what you want."

"About this time three days ago, I was praying," replied Cornelius. "Suddenly an angel appeared and told me to send for you. We are eager to hear your message."

Peter told them all about Jesus. "The events of the last few days have shown me that God wants you Gentiles to believe in Jesus and be saved," he said.

As the people in Cornelius's household listened, the Holy Spirit swept down and enabled them to praise God in strange and lovely languages. Peter ordered that they all be baptized in the name of Jesus Christ.

When he returned and told the believers in Jerusalem, they were amazed. None of them had imagined how much God wanted to bless Gentiles as well as Jews.

Cruel King Herod

❧

THE KING IN Jerusalem at this time was a man named Herod Agrippa. "I'm suspicious of some of these Jesus believers," he said to himself. "I think it might be a good idea to silence them."

Right away he began to treat them as outlaws. James, the brother of John, was executed.

The Jewish leaders were delighted. "Your Majesty," they told the king, "thank you for all your efforts to get rid of these troublemakers."

Herod Agrippa smiled. His plan to win support was working. "I haven't finished yet," he said, and motioned to an officer. "Go and arrest the man called Peter. I know it's Passover time, so keep him in jail until the festival is over and I can put him on trial. Watch him very, very carefully."

Peter was flung into jail. He sat uncomfortably in heavy chains, while the guards on either side of him grumbled at having to sit in a gloomy cell. The hours trickled by. Peter hoped that his fellow believers were praying for him. There wasn't much else they could do. He sighed and lay down to sleep.

Suddenly he was awake. Someone was shaking him by the shoulder.

"Hurry! Get up!" came the whisper. "Now!"

Peter sat up. The chains fell off his hands. "Here's your belt… and your sandals… and your cloak… come."

The shadowy figure danced ahead, holding a tiny light. They edged past the first guard, and the second. Sometimes darting, sometimes hiding, they came to the city gate. It swung gently open.

"Down this street," said Peter's rescuer. "You'll be all right on your own now."

Suddenly, the mystery rescuer was gone.

"Oh," breathed Peter. "One of God's angels!"

Dear God,
Give us
laughter even
when we face
difficult times.

The midnight caller

ALL AT ONCE, Peter found himself chuckling. "Herod's not going to be happy when he finds out I've gone," he said to himself. "Nor will all those solemn old men on the council."

Then he remembered he was still not entirely safe. He slipped through the maze of streets until he came to the house of Mary, the mother of John Mark, where the believers often met to pray.

Peter knocked quietly but firmly on the door. A servant girl named Rhoda came hurrying to answer it.

"Who's there?" she demanded before unlocking.

"It's your favorite escaped prisoner," replied Peter.

Rhoda's hand flew to her mouth as she tried not to scream with delight. She raced back to the main room. "It's Peter! Peter's outside! Our prayers have been answered!" she squealed.

"Calm down, Rhoda," said an older woman. "I know it's what we want, but we keep praying that the trial will go well for Peter tomorrow."

"It is Peter, I heard his voice, come and see," she insisted.

A couple of strong men ambled slowly to the door. "Well, she's right – there's someone outside," said one. The rapping on the door was now quick and urgent.

"It could be a trick," said the other man. "Let's go and get a few more of us who could help out if it's a soldier out there."

Finally, with a group of believers at the ready to fend off armed men, they slid back the bolts.

Peter stood there, hands on his hips. "I hope I'm not dragging you away from anything important," he said, beaming all over. "Now listen: I have the most amazing story to tell. You're going to love it… unlike the prison guards, who are going to wake up to a very bad morning."

The Christians of Antioch

THE BELIEVERS IN Jerusalem had been wary of all officials since the death of Stephen. Many believers had fled, and one of the places where they had gathered was a town called Antioch, many miles to the north.

The church flourished in the city. The believers preached to everyone that Jesus was truly the Christ, God's chosen one. As a result, the people called them "Christians". It was the first place that the word was used.

The church in Jerusalem heard about how rapidly the church was growing in Antioch and they decided to send Barnabas there to help with the work. From Antioch, it was not far to Tarsus, and Barnabas soon made time to go to look for Saul there. The two returned and worked side by side in preaching and teaching. They seemed to have more wisdom and understanding than anyone else.

One day, when some of the Christians in Antioch were praying, they felt that God was telling them the same thing: Saul and Barnabas should be allowed to go and preach about Jesus in other places.

Everyone agreed. With the blessing of all the church, Saul and Barnabas set out. A young man named John Mark was chosen to go with them. They went to the nearby seaport of Seleucia and sailed away to Cyprus.

Dear God,
May all who
call themselves
Christians be
worthy of
the name.

Saul and the magician

🐋

THE COMPANIONS LANDED in Cyprus and traveled across the island to Paphos. News of their mission had gone ahead of them, and the governor himself was eager to meet them. He invited them to give their message.

One of the governor's close friends was more suspicious. He was a Jew, known on the island as Elymas, and he claimed to be a magician. As Saul finished speaking, Elymas turned to whisper to the governor. "These men talk nonsense," he said. "They sound as if they understand the Jewish scriptures, but they are twisting their meaning. As for Jesus of Nazareth, he was executed as a criminal and they have no proof he was raised to life. His followers are just an odd little sect of beggars and outcasts. A man with public responsibilities such as you should ignore them."

"Hmm," said the governor. "When you put it like that, I'm inclined to agree."

Elymas turned around and faced Saul with a look of triumph.

Saul knew at once what God wanted him to say. "Elymas," he said. "You belong to the devil! You hate everything that is good and rely on evil tricks. God wants to make it plain that you are wrong, and for this reason you will lose your sight – not forever, but long enough for you to learn a lesson."

Elymas cried out: already a dark mist seemed to be gathering around him.

"Help!" he cried. "I need someone to lead me home. Help."

"Someone take him," said the governor. "Now, you over there. Come and tell me more about your message."

It was not long before the governor was utterly convinced that Saul's preaching was true.

Saul becomes Paul

❧

W HEN SAUL BEGAN to travel round the empire, he began to use the Roman form of his name: Paul. He and his companions sailed from Paphos, on Cyprus, to the mainland. When they reached Perga, John Mark left them to go back to Jerusalem. His departure left Paul and Barnabas feeling very let down, but they decided to continue their mission with just the two of them and went to another city in the region. Like the city from which their journey had begun, it was called Antioch.

On the sabbath they went into the synagogue and sat down. "It's not just Jewish people who worship God, is it?" whispered Barnabas. "Look how many Gentiles have come."

Paul nodded his agreement. "Some of the people are quite wealthy," he commented. "Look at those Gentile women over there! I expect they wield quite a bit of power locally."

Then they settled down to listen to the service. However, because they were visitors, they were also invited to speak.

Paul spoke confidently. "Fellow Israelites and all Gentiles here who worship God: hear me!" he began. "I am going to explain to you the scriptures that we cherish. I will show you how they point to Jesus, a descendant of our great king David. He is the one God has sent to rescue our people from their sins. He is also the true light for the Gentiles – the one who enables them to see God."

The people listened in amazement. "You must come back next week and explain all of this more fully," they insisted.

Soon, the news about Jesus had spread through all the region. Many believed all that Paul said.

Not all the Jews were pleased. "These beliefs are new, untested – and possibly quite wrong!" they said. "We must speak to all the influential people who worship with us to put an end to such nonsense."

Within a short time, their plan had succeeded. Paul and Barnabas were made fully aware that they were no longer welcome.

Dear God, Give me the wisdom to know when the right thing to do is to travel on.

Mistaken for gods

Paul and Barnabas traveled on. In Iconium, the same things happened as in Antioch: first they were welcomed and made many converts; then some of the leading people turned against them. In the end, they were forced to flee under a hail of stones thrown by an angry crowd.

"Next stop, Lystra," said Barnabas cheerfully. "Being chased out of town certainly reminds us to keep on spreading our message further."

Among the crowd in Lystra was a man who had never been able to walk. Paul noticed him and knew at once that he could be healed.

"Stand up!" he called out.

The man looked at them, feeling slightly puzzled. Then he tried to pull himself upright. As he did so, his eyes opened wide with wonder. "Praise God!" he cried. "I can walk! I can run! I can jump!"

The crowd began to whisper among themselves. "What do you make of that! These men have healed a crippled man. They must be gods."

"Indeed they must. Look – that one must be Zeus, and the one who is speaking is the messenger god Hermes."

"Quick! Go and tell the priest at the temple of Zeus to get ready! We must bring bulls to sacrifice and flowers for garlands."

Too late, Barnabas and Paul realized they were being made part of a pagan ceremony. "NO! Stop!" they cried. "We're only human. Turn away from your old and worthless beliefs! Trust in God, who made heaven and earth and sea and everything that is in them."

Even though they pleaded, they found it hard to stop the crowd from treating them as gods.

An angry mob

IN THE MIDST of all the excitement, a crowd of Jews suddenly called for attention.

"Everyone settle down. Settle down!" they cried. The crowd drew back in astonishment.

"You think these men are gods, do you? Well, listen to this. They've already caused an uproar in Antioch and elsewhere. In spite of many warnings, they won't stop preaching their own strange tale of nonsense. It's all a lie, and utterly disrespectful of our ancient faith."

"Stone them!" called someone from the back of the crowd.

"We can understand why people would want to stone them," continued the speaker. "Now, we all know that a public lynching is strictly not allowed under the rules of the Roman empire although…"

"Ah, this has nothing to do with the Romans," called a gang of youths. "Let's sort this out among ourselves."

"Yes, stone them," called some others. "Come on, everyone!"

In no time, the crowd had changed from marveling to murderous. Paul was hit so hard that he fell to the ground and passed out. The mob dragged him out of town and left him for dead.

Barnabas was rescued and hustled to safety by a crowd of believers. "We must go and find Paul! We can't just abandon him," shrieked Barnabas. "Don't give up on him. Come on."

When it was quiet enough, a group of believers went to find Paul's body. To their amazement he sat up. "Ouch," he said, touching a wound on his head. "That was scary. Help me up, please."

He spent the day recovering. The next day, Paul and Barnabas went on to Derbe.

Dear God, May I never be lured into wrongdoing by an angry crowd.

Dear God,
May I pass
through troubles
undefeated.

The return to Antioch

❧

DERBE WAS THE furthest point of Paul's first big trip to spread the news about Jesus.

"The best thing we can do now is return by the way we came and visit the new believers," said Barnabas. "That will encourage them to stay faithful – even though they may pass through many troubles before they reach the kingdom of God."

Wherever they went, they chose elders who could provide wisdom and leadership for the young churches. They felt joyful as they made their way back to their home church.

Their old friends in Antioch were eager to hear their news of how God was blessing both Jews and Gentiles. They were delighted that the mission they had supported had been so successful.

While they were there, some believers arrived from Jerusalem. "This news about the Gentiles believing is good," they agreed, "but there is a problem. The message we preach has its heart in the Jewish faith, and Gentiles haven't been brought up to obey all its laws. If they want to be part of God's kingdom, they must do so."

"Surely that's not needed," argued Paul. "I am myself a scholar of the Law, and I think that, because of Jesus, God is doing something entirely new for the world."

"Besides," added Barnabas, "having to keep some of the old laws of the faith would only discourage them."

This sparked a fierce argument. In the end, Paul and Barnabas knew they would have to go to Jerusalem to sort things out.

At a great meeting of church elders, Peter agreed with Paul and Barnabas that the Gentiles were welcome in God's kingdom. Everyone agreed on a plan to help the Gentiles be respectful of the Jewish laws without having to follow all the rituals.

A letter of guidance

❧

THE CHURCH IN Jerusalem knew that it was important to mend the quarrel. They decided to send two of their number to explain the plan that had been agreed upon. They chose two men who were both highly respected: Judas, also called Barsabbas, and Silas. These two men were entrusted with a letter. Its message was clear:

"We, the apostles and elders of the church in Jerusalem, were sorry to hear of the upset that was caused when believers from here came and told you that even Gentile Christians should keep the Jewish laws. We had not asked them to teach any such thing.

"Now, with the help of your friends Paul and Barnabas, we have thought seriously about the matter. The Holy Spirit and we do not want to burden you with lots of rules. Out of respect for our traditions, however, we would like you to do the following: don't eat food that has been offered to idols; eat no blood; and eat no animal that has been strangled. Also, keep your sexual conduct pure. That will help you to live as believers should."

When Judas and Silas arrived in Antioch and read the message from the church in Jerusalem, everyone felt encouraged. The two messengers were also wise teachers, and they stayed for a while, helping people understand more about their new faith.

In this way, an incident that had threatened to cause a rift became the opportunity for two groups of believers to grow closer in friendship and understanding.

Dear God, May I be worthy of the respect of those around me.

The quarrel

PAUL AND BARNABAS had put a lot of effort into their mission and they were glad to be able to spend some time in their home church in Antioch. Then, one day, Paul had an idea.

"Let's go back to the places we visited and see how everyone's getting along."

"Good idea," agreed Barnabas. "It would be a good chance for John Mark, too. I think he's sorry he gave up on the trip last time."

Paul stood up very straight and looked at Barnabas severely. "Your willingness to give everyone a second chance can go too far," he said. "I don't trust John Mark not to give up again. I don't want him upsetting our plans."

Barnabas looked puzzled. "I'm sure he'll be fine. He was very young to come on the first trip with us and he's grown up a lot as a result of his experiences. I'd like to make the case that he should come."

"Really!" said Paul. "You're too soft. I've had a lot of experience over the years and I've learned that some people can't be trusted."

Suddenly, Barnabas' cheerful face clouded with anger. "Let me remind you of the biggest risk I ever took with giving people a second chance," he said. "I pleaded for the believers to accept a narrow-minded young man with a proven history of causing trouble. His name was Saul – you know, the one who watched Stephen being stoned to death. Maybe I shouldn't have been so kind to him."

Paul almost spat at him. "Why drag that in?"

"Because it shows that it's important to give people more than one chance. I believe I was right to let you join the church. I want you to be more encouraging. If you can't work with John Mark, then I can't work with you."

"Then don't," said Paul. "You sail with John Mark to Cyprus. I'll find other companions."

Dear God,
Forgive our
quarrels and
bring
something
good out
of them.

Silas and Timothy

❧

*Dear God,
Help me to
grow in
righteousness,
godliness, faith,
love, endurance
and gentleness.*

Paul chose Silas to travel with him, for he had already proved his wisdom and trustworthiness. They went north overland and in this way reached Derbe and Lystra again.

In Lystra, Paul met a young believer named Timothy, who was part Jewish and part Greek. Everyone spoke well of him.

"His grandmother Lois and his mother Eunice are believers," they explained. "Their deep faith has inspired him, and their wise upbringing has made him mature and sensible. With the right guidance from you, he could be an excellent leader in the church."

Paul was impressed with the young man. "I would like him to come with me on my travels," he told the believers. "He will be able to learn more about the faith and in this way prepare himself for greater responsibilities later on."

"You will face hard times," Paul warned Timothy, "and you can forget about ever being wealthy. Not that that should be a problem: being too fond of money leaves a person always wanting more and more things but never being satisfied. By contrast, a strong faith is wealth indeed, and will bring the inner contentment that people really long for. You will grow in righteousness, godliness, faith, love, endurance and gentleness – and so be ready for when Jesus Christ appears."

So it was agreed. Paul, Silas and Timothy were in good spirits as they set out from Lystra. As they went through the various towns, they explained the teaching of the elders in Jerusalem about which traditional rules to keep. In this way, they helped strengthen people's faith and the little churches continued to grow.

Paul's dream

Dear God,
May I recognize
your voice
in unexpected
places.

Once Paul and his friends reached the Roman provinces of Asia, however, the disappointments began. No one wanted to listen to their preaching. They journeyed on until they reached the coast. There they found a place to stay for the night, and to think about which direction to take next.

The following morning, Paul was exuberant. "I had a dream," he said. "I saw a man from Macedonia – which is just over the water from here – begging us to go and help the people there. I'm sure God must be calling us to go there."

Paul's companions were convinced. They left by ship, landed in Macedonia and went inland to Philippi.

The city was impressive with many fine homes.

"It's popular with retired Roman officers," explained Paul. "Even so, there's bound to be a Jewish community. We must try to find out where they meet."

It was more difficult than they had imagined. The people they asked said they had never heard of a synagogue in the city.

"The Jewish community must be too small to have its own building," said Paul. "But they may still meet for prayer on the sabbath. We should try to find them and begin our preaching there."

Their inquiries finally led them to go looking along the riverbank. There, in the shade of a willow tree, they found a small group of Jewish people praying – most of them women. They sat down and began to explain about Jesus.

In Philippi

AMONG THE WOMEN who had met together for prayer was someone called Lydia. She listened earnestly to all that Paul and his companions had to say about Jesus.

"I want to be baptized as a believer at once!" she exclaimed. "Then, if you think I am a true believer, please honor me by coming to my house. I am a successful businesswoman – I deal in the finest purple cloth that only the very wealthy can afford – and my house is big enough to accommodate you as my guests."

"We would be delighted to do so," agreed Paul. "We would like to spend more time in this city preaching and teaching our message."

"Then make my house your base here," she said. "It can be a meeting place for all the new believers."

Paul was delighted at the warm welcome he received. As the days went by, he marveled more and more at the kindness and generosity of the new believers in Philippi.

"I hope your faith will always make you joyful," he told them. "Don't worry about anything, but in your prayers ask God for what you need, and be thankful.

"Fill your minds with those things that are good and that deserve praise: things that are true, noble, right, pure, lovely and honorable.

"Then your lives will shine out in a wicked world as brightly as the stars in the sky."

The Philippian Christians took his words to heart, and were to remember Paul as a true friend even when his travels took him far away and the only way he could stay in touch and remind them of these things was by letter.

*Dear God,
May I fill my mind with the things that are good and that deserve praise: things that are true, noble, right, pure, lovely and honorable.*

The fortune-teller

Dear God,
Heal those
whose minds
are troubled.

O NE DAY, AS Paul and his friends were walking through the streets of Philippi, a young woman sprang out screeching. "Look at these people!" she cried. "They are the servants of the Most High God. They can tell you how to be saved."

People in the street shook their heads and tried not to notice. Then a man came and grabbed the woman by the hand. "Come on! We've got customers who want you to tell their fortune. They pay us well for it."

Paul watched as she was led away. "Poor woman," he said. "Some evil force has got control of her."

The next day, the woman spied Paul again. She began ranting on in the same way as before. The same thing happened for many days.

In the end, Paul could not stand it anymore. When he heard the familiar screech, he turned around sharply and spoke to the evil thing that controlled her. "In the name of Jesus Christ, come out of her," he said.

The woman fell silent. She and Paul eyed one another. "Sorry to bother you," she mumbled. "Sorry if I said anything foolish."

As she backed away, the man who took care her came hurrying up. He glared at Paul. "You leave her alone, she works for me," he said.

Arrested

THE FOLLOWING DAY, Paul and his friends were out as usual. They didn't see the young woman, but her guardian ambled out in front of them.

"So, it seems you played a little trick on us," he said. "That young woman doesn't screech anymore, does she?" He walked even closer and grabbed Paul by the shoulder. "She doesn't tell fortunes anymore, either. And we don't like that, do we, boys?"

At that moment, a gang of men sprang out from behind Paul. They grabbed him and Silas and dragged them in front of the Roman authorities in the town square. "These men are Jews and they're causing trouble," they complained. "They are teaching things that are against the law. We're Roman citizens: we can't let that happen."

Their noisy accusations drew a crowd. Soon everyone around Paul and Silas was shouting angrily. "Punish them! Whip them! Fling them in jail!"

The officials in charge nodded their agreement. They tore the clothes off Paul and Silas and gave orders for them to be whipped severely. Then Paul and Silas were hustled down the street and thrown into jail.

The jailer took them to an inner cell. He clamped their feet between heavy blocks of wood. "Those are the orders," he grunted.

*Dear God,
Keep me calm
even when
things are
going wrong.*

335

Dear God,
Help me to
sing for joy in
trying times.

In the Philippian jail

❧

FOR A WHILE, both Paul and Silas felt too battered to speak. Finally Silas lifted his head. "Paul," he said. "I think we were on our way to a prayer meeting. As we may have missed it, shall we say a few prayers here?"

Paul nodded. They thanked God they were still alive. They prayed for the Christians in Philippi. They said the prayer Jesus had taught his disciples.

"Let's sing a few hymns," said Paul. "I like the one we sang yesterday – the one where every verse ends with 'Jesus Christ is Lord.'"

They sang noisily. In the cells nearby, the other prisoners opened their eyes. "It's midnight," muttered one. "What are those madmen going on about?"

"Some religious nonsense," said another. "Still, it cheers my heart to hear people putting up a bit of resistance to being in here. Whoa! What was that?"

Suddenly, the whole building tilted and swayed. The doors rattled and shook – and then swung open. The chains that bound the prisoners clattered to the ground.

The jailer had been dozing in a chair. He was jolted awake and then began trembling with fear as he saw that the cell doors were open.

"Oh no," he whispered. "OH NO!" he cried. "They've all escaped! Why did it have to happen on my watch?" His mind was racing. He was bound to be executed for his slack behavior. "Well, I'm not going to have my commanding officer gloat," he muttered. He grabbed his sword and shouted, "Yes, it was my fault and I pay the price! I die with honor!"

"Stop!" The voice was clear and forceful. "Don't hurt yourself! We're all here!"

The jailer

Tᴴᴇ ᴊᴀɪʟᴇʀ ᴄᴀʟʟᴇᴅ for a servant to bring a light. He rushed to Paul's cell and fell trembling at the feet of Paul and Silas.

"What can I do to be saved?" he pleaded.

"Believe in Jesus," they replied. "You, and all your family."

The jailer was eager to find out more. He took Paul and Silas to his own house and gave them a meal. In return, they told him about Jesus. That very night, he and all his family were baptized as believers.

In the morning, the Roman authorities sent police over with the order to let Paul and Silas go.

They could not have been expecting what happened next. Instead of cheering, Paul turned to the police officers with an icy stare. "We are innocent men who didn't even have a trial to prove it," he said. "The authorities had us whipped in public and now they want to cover up their illegal actions. I would like to point out that we're both Roman citizens. Our rights have been seriously abused. The authorities must come and apologize to us here… unless they want us to take the matter further."

The police took the message back to the authorities.

"You're telling us we whipped Roman citizens?" they exclaimed. "Oh dear, oh dear. What very bad news."

City officials hurried over to Paul and Silas. "I gather there's been a bit of a mix-up with your case," began one.

"I gather there's been a gross injustice," replied Paul.

"Um… that may be," said the official, his face turning red with embarrassment. "So… on behalf of the city… we're very sorry. Very very sorry. And now, maybe, we can help you on your way… You will be leaving soon, won't you?"

Paul and Silas smiled and waved them farewell. They stopped only to visit Lydia and to tell the believers all that had happened.

Dear God, May I use the opportunities I have to stand up to injustice.

Dear God,
May I know
when the best
thing to do is
to live as quietly
and peaceably
as I can.

In Thessalonica

THE NEXT STOP for Paul, Silas and Timothy was a place called Thessalonica. For three sabbaths in a row, Paul went to the synagogue there. He talked about Jesus and explained how the news about Jesus fitted with the old Jewish scriptures. Many people were convinced, both Jews and Greeks.

However, some of the Jews were jealous of his success. "We'll need more support if we want to get rid of these believers," they said to each other. "Let's go and talk to some of the people who spend their time hanging out on the street: we could surely get a crowd together."

Soon they had a noisy mob that put the whole town in an uproar. "I bet those preachers are at Jason's house," shouted someone. "He's a believer."

"To Jason's house!" came the roar.

The mob swarmed into Jason's house, kicking over furniture and overturning everything. They grabbed Jason by the throat: "So? Where have you hidden them? Hand that Paul and Silas over or you'll be sorry!"

"Just look around you! You can tell they're not here," spluttered Jason. "Leave us alone!"

The men paid no attention to his words. Instead, they hauled Jason and some other believers in front of the city authorities.

"These troublemakers are breaking the laws of the emperor. They're saying there is another king – Jesus. There's a whole movement to overturn law and order. You must punish them – or things will get worse."

The city authorities were worried. "These accusations are serious," they told the believers. "You can pay a fine to secure your release, or we can take it further."

The believers hurried to pay the money. Jason and the others went back home well shaken up by the whole event.

Paul and the citizens of Athens

THE BELIEVERS IN Thessalonica sent Paul and his companions on to Berea. The people there welcomed them and were interested in listening to their message. It wasn't long, however, before some Jews arrived from Thessalonica with the usual rumors. Once again, Paul, as leader, was in danger. His new friends sent him on to a safer place. He went as far as Athens and there waited for Silas and Timothy.

Paul had plenty of time to explore the ancient city and he was dismayed at what he saw. "There are so many idols to worthless gods here," he said to himself. "I must tell the people about Jesus and the resurrection."

The Athenians were puzzled at his teaching. "It's not very rational, is it?" they said to one another. "That new preacher is full of confidence, but what he says hardly appeals to the intellect. Resurrection indeed!"

"Mind you," said others, "anything new is always fascinating. I think we should ask him to address the city council at a public gathering. Then he can try to explain his message."

It was all arranged. When the day came for Paul to speak, he stood up boldly. "I can tell from the many places of worship in this city that you Athenians care about religion," he said. "However, you are not sure what to believe: I saw one altar dedicated to 'The Unknown God.' Now I am going to tell you about God who made heaven and earth, who is not very far from any one of us, and whose plan for humankind has been revealed through someone who rose from the dead."

Paul explained to them about Jesus. Everyone was intrigued. A few were convinced of the truth of all he said.

Dear God, May I worship you as you truly are.

*Dear God,
May I not be
afraid to talk
about my faith;
may I not grow
discouraged in
my beliefs.*

In Corinth

FROM ATHENS, PAUL went on to the elegant city of Corinth. There he met up with a Jewish couple, Priscilla and Aquila. They had their own tent-making business. Paul himself was a tentmaker by trade, and the three worked together to make a living. On the sabbath he always went to the synagogue: there, he tried to convince both Jewish and Greek worshipers about Jesus and the resurrection.

At last Silas and Timothy were able to join Paul in Corinth. Now Paul was able to spend all his time preaching. As had happened so many times before, the Jews turned against him.

"I am quite sure that God wants me to go on doing what I am doing," he told his friends. "However, I think it is best for me to work with Gentiles. There is a Gentile named Titius Justus who has invited me to stay with him."

It so happened that his new lodgings were next door to the synagogue, and the leader of the synagogue, Crispus, became a believer. Then one night, in a dream, Paul heard God speaking to him: "Do not be afraid, but keep on speaking and do not give up."

With this encouragement, Paul stayed for a year and a half in Corinth and was able to preach to many people. Then a new governor was appointed. The Jews saw a new chance to get rid of Paul. They hurried to arrest him and dragged him before the governor.

"This scoundrel is trying to get people to worship God in a way that is against the law," they said. "We've brought him so you can deal with him."

The governor turned on them angrily. "You Jews!" he said. "You always seem to be arguing about words and names and hundreds of laws about goodness knows what in your religion. It has nothing to do with Roman law; I'm not getting dragged into your petty squabbles. Out, all of you."

Paul the letter writer

❧

A<small>FTER A LONG STAY</small> in Corinth, Paul felt it was time to return home. He sailed with Priscilla and Aquila as far as Ephesus, and then he continued on his way alone. He went first to Jerusalem, to meet with the church there; at long last he reached Antioch.

All the time, he was eager for any news about the new churches he had helped to set up. Some were thriving. In others, people were beginning to argue with one another about what to believe. There were disagreements about how to live as a follower of Jesus.

Paul was very concerned that the good work he had begun should continue. He resolved to stay in touch in touch with the young churches by writing letters.

"I shall hire a scribe in order to get the job done properly," he said to himself. "My handwriting is really not much good, but I can tell a scribe what to write. After that, I'm sure I will be able to find people in the community of believers who will act as messengers. That way, I will be able to correct wrong beliefs and to encourage everyone."

Indeed, the church in Corinth was soon in need of more than one letter. It was hardly surprising. It was a wealthy city where people from all over the empire could indulge themselves. No wonder the new believers found it difficult to pursue holiness and righteousness.

"Be careful how you conduct yourselves," Paul wrote. "Your body is not something you can treat recklessly. Think of it as a temple in which God's Holy Spirit has made its dwelling. You should avoid the immorality that is so common in Corinth and instead use your bodies for God's glory."

He had many things he wanted to instruct them about. The time had come to speak clearly about what it meant to live the Christian life.

*Dear God,
May I treat
my body as a
holy temple.*

*Dear God,
May I pay
attention to
wise teachers.*

About the Lord's Supper

❧

PAUL HAD HEARD unsettling news about the way the church meetings in Corinth were being conducted.

"It was I who taught you about the ceremony of sharing a meal," he wrote, "the one that I called the Lord's Supper. The Lord Jesus, on the night he was betrayed, took a piece of bread, gave thanks to God, broke it, and said, 'This is my body, which is for you. Do this in memory of me.' In the same way, after the supper he took the cup and said, 'This cup is God's new covenant, sealed with my blood. Whenever you drink it, do so in memory of me.'"

"This means that every time you eat the bread and drink from the cup, you proclaim the Lord's death until he comes. For this reason, it is very serious if you take part in the ceremony in a disrespectful way. It should never be a scramble for food and drink, with some indulging while others are left hungry.

"You must learn to recognize the real meaning of the ceremony. You must learn to treat Jesus with respect as you take part in it. You must learn to treat one another with respect."

The church and the body of Christ

❧

PAUL WANTED TO make his message clear and simple. "Listen," he wrote. "Those of us who believe in Jesus have a duty to represent him on earth. We are his body now. Just as a body has many different parts to do different things, so all of you have different jobs to do.

"It doesn't matter what your background is: Jew or Gentile, slave or free – we have all been baptized by the same Holy Spirit.

"Every one of you is important, and you all belong together like members of one body. Just as a body has different parts, so you, the community of believers, have people with different gifts and talents. A foot is useful to the body because it's a foot. It isn't more or less important than a hand. An ear is useful to the body because it's an ear. It isn't more or less important than an eye.

"In the church, some people are apostles; others are prophets; others are teachers. Some have the power to heal people. Others speak in strange languages and praise God in a special way. Yet others explain what they are saying. All of these things matter. But there's one thing that is even more important."

Dear God,
May I value my
own talents
and gifts
and also those
of other
people.

Dear God,
Give me faith;
give me hope;
teach me
to love.

Faith, hope, love

❧

PAUL PAUSED FOR a moment to collect his thoughts. What he was about to say was central to being a Christian. He wanted to make sure that what he wrote would be complete and accurate and persuasive.

"Love is the most important thing of all," he wrote. "It is more important than being a great preacher. It is more important than being a wise teacher. It is more important than deep faith. It is more important than being ready to die for what you believe in.

"Love is patient and kind; it is not jealous or conceited or proud; love is not ill-mannered or selfish or irritable; love does not keep a record of wrongs; love is not happy with evil, but is happy with the truth. Love never gives up; and its faith, hope and patience never fail.

"Love is forever. Everything else will pass away, but love will last for all eternity.

"When I was a child, I thought childish things were important. Now that I've grown up, I see things differently.

"In a way, we're all like children here on earth. We think some things are hugely important, but they will come to nothing in the end. When we see God face to face, then we will know what is important.

"Three things will matter: faith, hope and love. The greatest of these is love."

Paul in Ephesus

PAUL WAS GLAD to visit old friends in Jerusalem and Antioch, but after a while he was eager to go on more travels. He set off through Galatia and other parts of Asia, encouraging the young churches wherever he could. His journey brought him back to Ephesus, where he met up with a group of about twelve new Christians.

"Did you receive the Holy Spirit when you became believers?" he asked them.

"We have never heard that there is a Holy Spirit," they replied.

"Then what kind of baptism did you have to mark your conversion?" he asked.

"The one that John the Baptist preached," they said.

"Oh," said Paul. "That baptism was all about turning away from wrongdoing and getting ready to believe in Jesus. You should now be baptized in the name of Jesus."

When the ceremony was performed, Paul placed his hands on the twelve and asked God to bless them. At once the men felt the power of God's Holy Spirit within them. They spoke in strange and beautiful languages and began to speak boldly about their faith.

Paul was encouraged by the way his work in Ephesus had begun, and he went on to preach at the synagogue in the hope of persuading more people about Jesus and the new faith – the Way of the Lord. However, not everyone was convinced, and after a few months he was asked to take his preaching elsewhere. He rented a separate hall in which to preach and teach, and once again attracted a good deal of interest from near and far. After two years of this work, everyone in the province of Asia had had the chance to hear the news about Jesus, and this included both Jews and Gentiles.

Dear God,
Transform me
by your spirit.

*Dear God,
Help me to see
the difference
between
faith and
superstition.*

Miracles and magic

❧

THE PEOPLE OF EPHESUS were intrigued at what they heard Paul say. However, it was the news of what he was doing that really captured everyone's interest.

"Paul can work miracles," people said. "More than that, even the things he touches seem to be able to make people well."

Soon, Paul had a steady stream of visitors who came to ask for towels and other things he had touched that they could take to sick relatives. Whatever they took seemed to bring the healing that was so desperately needed.

It so happened that there was a group of wandering healers in the region. They were brothers, and they claimed to have the power to cast out evil spirits. When they heard about Paul, they decided to use the same words as Paul used when he said a prayer for healing.

A man was brought to them who had been driven mad by whatever controlled him. "Evil spirit," they said, "I command you in the name of Jesus, whom Paul preaches, to come out!"

The reply from the spirit was sharp and angry. "I know Jesus, and I know about Paul – but who are you?"

Then the man who was controlled by the evil spirit attacked them violently and drove them away bleeding and disheveled. The news shocked everyone, but it served a useful purpose. Many people – including believers – revealed that they too had tried to use magic for all kinds of purposes. Now they realized that such practices were dangerous, so they brought out their books of spells and incantations and burned them in public. As a result, more and more people came to respect Paul and the message about Jesus.

The believers in Rome

*Dear God,
Reach out
to me as
a friend.*

AFTER THE EPISODE with magic, Paul decided it was time to leave Ephesus. He wanted to tour the churches in and around Macedonia before going back to Jerusalem and then setting out for a place he had not yet visited: Rome, the heart of the empire.

He knew that there was already a thriving group of believers in the city: several years had passed since the day of Pentecost when Peter had first preached about Jesus to the pilgrims in Jerusalem, and in that time believers had taken their new faith to places throughout the Roman world. He decided to prepare the way for his visit by writing a letter:

"This is a letter from Paul – a servant of Christ Jesus and an apostle chosen and called by God to preach his Good News.

"It is written to all of you in Rome whom God loves and has called to be his own people.

"May God our Father and the Lord Jesus Christ give you grace and peace.

"I am so looking forward to coming to see you. My hope is that we will be able to help each other – you by my faith, and I by yours.

"I want to tell you about my confidence in the gospel: it is God's power to save all those who believe, both Jews and Gentiles. The gospel reveals how God restores our friendship with him: it is by faith from beginning to end.

"Even though we had all fallen short of God's standards, Jesus Christ came to die for us – and our old and wicked selves died with him.

"God raised Jesus to life, and by faith, we share in that same life.

"Now you have been set free from sin and all its worthless deeds which lead only to death.

"You have become slaves of God. Your gain is a life fully dedicated to him, and the result is eternal life."

*Dear God,
May I not
give in to
wickedness;
may your
spirit of
holiness
direct me.*

An appeal to the Romans

❧

NOW THAT WE have been raised to new life," wrote Paul, "we do not have to live as our human nature tells us. Instead, we can live as God's Holy Spirit wants.

'If you live as your human nature tells you, it will lead to death; if you live a life controlled by the Spirit, you will enjoy life and peace.

'In fact, you should not think of yourselves as slaves to a master who makes you afraid. Rather, God's Spirit makes you God's own children, and you can truly call God your Father and expect many blessings.

"And so I appeal to you: live a life worthy of a servant of God. That alone is true worship. Don't let yourself be shaped by the standards of this world, but let God transform you inwardly by changing your beliefs and your values.

"Each of you should use the special gifts God has given you to help and encourage one another.

"Hate what is evil, hold on to what is good.

"Love one another warmly as Christian brothers and sisters, and be eager to show respect for one another.

"Work hard and do not be lazy.

"Let your hope keep you joyful, be patient in your troubles and pray at all times.

"Share your belongings with your needy fellow Christians, and open your homes to strangers.

"Pray for those who treat you badly. If someone has done you wrong, do not hit back. Instead, try to do what everyone can agree is good and kind. Do all you can to live in peace with everyone.

"Do not let evil defeat you; instead, conquer evil with good.

"May God keep you firm in your faith."

The riot in Ephesus

EVEN WHILE PAUL was making plans for his next round of travels, trouble erupted in Ephesus.

It so happened that the city was a center for worshiping the goddess Diana, and many pilgrims came to the temple that was dedicated in her name. Several silversmiths had grown wealthy by making and selling little models for the pilgrims to buy. One of them, named Demetrius, realized that Paul and his message threatened to undermine their trade. He called a meeting of the silversmiths.

"We have to do something to stop all that enthusiastic preaching by those 'Way of the Lord' people. They're trying to convince everyone that gods made by human hands are not gods at all. Well, no one will buy our wares if Diana is discredited in this way. We will be ruined."

His angry words sparked a riot. "Great is Diana of Ephesus!" shouted someone, and the uproar spread through the city. Two of Paul's companions were dragged to the open-air theatre where the shouting and chanting continued for two hours.

In the end, the town clerk managed to call for order. "Fellow Ephesians," he said. "We all know that our city contains the holy shrine of Diana. However, your zeal for the goddess is not a reason to act illegally. The men you accuse should be brought to a proper court. For now, go home."

*Dear God,
May I value
the laws of the
government as
a way to order
and peace.*

349

Dear God,
May I know my
mission and
give my life to
completing it.

The long journey to Jerusalem

PAUL AND HIS supporters were now more than anxious to get out of Ephesus safely. They journeyed to places in Macedonia and Achaia and planned to sail from there to Syria. However, Paul discovered that the Syrian Jews were plotting against his life, so he retraced his steps. Eventually, he and his companions all met in Troas.

On the Saturday evening, the believers there gathered for the fellowship meal. Paul took the opportunity to preach one last time. The hours wore on until midnight, and the lamplit room grew warm. A young man named Eutychus was sitting in the window, but the heat made him so sleepy that he fell from the third story to the ground. Those that rushed to help him were dismayed to find that the fall had killed him.

Paul hurried down and hugged the body. "Don't worry," he said, "the boy is still alive!"

To everyone's delight, Eutychus revived, and everyone went back upstairs, where they ate a meal and then continued listening to Paul until sunrise.

Then the companions went on their way again down the Asian coast. There was no time to stop in Ephesus, but Paul sent a message to the elders of the church there so they could meet him at the port town nearby. "I have worked hard to help you understand all about Jesus," he said, "and now I must go to other places. I know that prison and troubles lie in wait for me, but I firmly believe that I must complete my mission and finish the work that the Lord Jesus gave me to do, which is to declare the Good News about the grace of God.

"So keep watch over yourselves and over all the flock that the Holy Spirit has placed in your care."

After many fond farewells, Paul and his companions made the journey from one port to another until finally they reached Caesarea. From there it was overland to Jerusalem.

Paul at the Temple

P AUL WAS WELCOMED by the believers in Jerusalem but found himself in the middle of an argument. It had to do with the fears among Jewish Christians that Paul was not teaching Gentile believers to keep the laws as agreed.

"We know you were part of our agreement as to which customs the Gentiles should respect," said the church elders, "but many remain suspicious of you. However, we think we have a way forward. There are four people here who have taken a vow. If you pay their expenses for the ceremonies involved, then it will be a clear sign to everyone that you are faithful to our laws. That will settle it."

The plan should have worked. However, on one of the occasions when Paul went to the Temple, some Jews from Asia saw him. All their fear about what he was doing turned to rage. "There's the man who goes about preaching against our people and saying that our ancient laws don't matter," they cried.

"And now he's at the Temple with his Gentile friends. That is strictly forbidden. Look! There's the sign saying where Gentiles must stop. This is an outrage!"

What they said was not true. Paul had indeed been seen with a Gentile from Ephesus, but he had not taken him to the exclusively Jewish part of the Temple. However, these were nervous times, and the rumors sparked a riot.

Dear God, May I never trample over the traditions that others hold dear.

The riot in Jerusalem

🐌

I N THE FORTRESS in Jerusalem, the Roman commander heard about the rioting. Quickly he assembled a band of guards and himself led the way to the center of the trouble.

The mob drew back, allowing the commander to go and arrest Paul.

"So," he demanded, "who is this man and what has he done?"

His only answer was a cacophony of angry shouting. "I can't make sense of this," he said. "Take the prisoner to the fort."

The mob grew even angrier. "Kill him! Kill him!" they began to chant. They crowded in on the soldiers, and tried to tear Paul out of their grasp.

As Paul was just about to be taken inside the Roman fort, he coolly asked permission to address the crowd. "Oh, you speak Greek!" replied the commander. "I thought you must be that Egyptian terrorist. Go ahead."

Paul surveyed the crowd. His accusers were Jews like him and he wanted them to see that Jesus was the long-promised messiah.

"Listen," he said. Now he spoke in Hebrew and that made people quiet down a bit. "I am a Jew myself," he said. "I was born in Tarsus but came as a student to Jerusalem. I learned what I know about our scriptures from a highly respected teacher. In the beginning, I thought that people who followed the way of Jesus were completely wrong, so I was determined to get rid of them.

"I was one of the people who helped scare the believers out of Jerusalem. I set off to hunt them down in Damascus. On the way, I was blinded by a light from heaven. I heard Jesus speaking to me. He told me to go to the believers in Damascus and listen to what they had to say. I didn't just get my sight back: for the first time, I understood Jesus' message. Not long after, I realized it was my job to spread the message to the Gentiles."

These last words made the crowd wild with rage. "Kill him! He doesn't deserve to live!" they shouted. They began to stamp and wave, sending clouds of choking dust into the air.

Paul and the Jewish Council

❧

T HE ROMAN COMMANDER growled an order to his officers. "Take that man and whip him. Find out what it is he's saying that makes these Jews so angry."

Paul realized what was happening as his captors tied him up and brought the metal-tipped lash.

"Is it legal to whip a Roman citizen who hasn't been given a proper trial?" he asked.

"I'll check my orders," grumbled the officer in charge.

Then the commander came and prowled around his prisoner. "So, a Roman citizen, eh?" he said. "I paid a lot of money to be made a citizen. "

"Did you?" said Paul. "I was born a Roman citizen."

The commander eyed him uneasily. "Well, I'll call a meeting with the Jewish Council," he said. "They're the ones with the specialized knowledge to deal with a matter of this nature."

So the very next day, Paul stood in front of the Jewish Council. He was full of indignation at what was happening, and the high priest in charge was in a sour mood. The atmosphere was tense and angry.

Paul looked around, wondering how to begin. He noticed that the members of the council belonged to one of two groups: the Sadducees, who didn't believe in life after death, and the Pharisees, who did. He decided to take advantage of their long-standing hostility.

"I'm a Pharisee," he said. "I'm here because I have the hope that the dead will rise to life."

The plan worked. In no time, the two sides were arguing among themselves about the whole issue of resurrection. The Pharisees began to shout that Paul wasn't entirely wrong. The Sadducees shouted back.

At the back of the hall, the commander slumped a little. His plan was not going well. He motioned to his soldiers. "Just take Paul back to the fort," he said. It had been a bad day.

Dear God, May I know what isn't worth arguing about.

*Dear God,
May I be
confident of
myself in spite
of what any
accusers say.*

On trial in Caesarea

৯

THE ROMAN COMMANDER was eager to be rid of the whole business concerning Paul. Then he heard of a plot against the preacher's life to which even the chief priests and religious elders had agreed. He called two of his officers and told them to take Paul to the governor in Caesarea.

"That will get the whole affair out of Jerusalem and my jurisdiction," he explained. "Governor Felix is married to a Jewish woman anyway. He'll have a better understanding of the religious arguments. I'll write a letter to give him the background to the case."

The high priest was most upset when he found out what had happened. Now he too would have to make the journey to Caesarea. He set out with the best lawyer he could hire to pursue the case against Paul.

Within a week, the trial was under way. The high priest's lawyer began by flattering the governor, and then launched into his attack on Paul. He said he was a dangerous nuisance, a threat to public order and disrespectful of the religious laws.

Then it was Paul's turn. "I've been trained in the Law of our people," began Paul, "so I'm happy to defend myself. I have not been stirring up trouble; my accusers have no proof of the things they say. I am a follower of the Way, but I also believe in the Law of Moses and the books of the prophets. I have the same hope in God that they have, and I try to live in the way that is good and right."

Felix nodded. He had already heard about Jesus and the followers of the Way; now he could find out more. His wife, Drusilla, always loved to talk about religion.

After that, he thought, Paul might want to be free to get on with his preaching. Perhaps he would pay for the privilege. A nice fat bribe was always welcome.

Paul appeals to the emperor

PAUL FOUND HIMSELF stuck in Caesarea for two years. The governor, Felix, amused himself by arranging discussions with him from time to time. However, he began to realize that Paul was unlikely to offer a bribe in return for his release, and there were advantages in keeping the Jewish population happy. He decided to leave him in prison.

Then a new governor was appointed in place of Felix. His name was Festus, and he soon realized that the Jews were eager to pursue their case against Paul. He decided to hear for himself what the prisoner had to say and was quite taken aback by Paul's confidence.

"I have done nothing wrong against the Law of the Jews or against the Temple or against the Roman emperor," declared Paul.

Festus was still eager to see Paul dealt with in a way that would win favor with the Jewish people he now ruled. So he asked Paul if he would be willing to go to Jerusalem for a proper trial.

"No," replied Paul. "I am standing before the emperor's own court of judgment, where I should be tried. I have done no wrong to the Jews, as you yourself well know. If I have broken the law and done something for which I deserve the death penalty, I do not ask to escape it. But if there is no truth in the charges they bring against me, no one can hand me over to them. I appeal to the emperor."

Festus nodded slowly. "It's the right of a Roman citizen," he said. "You have appealed to the emperor, so to the emperor you will go."

Dear God, May I recognize when I have done wrong and when I have not.

Dear God,
May I be patient
for the right
path to open
before me.

King Agrippa's visit

PAUL'S CASE WAS not very important to Festus, and nothing happened for a while. Then the local Jewish king, Agrippa, came to visit the governor. With him came his sister, Bernice.

"I'd like your help with an unusual legal case," explained Festus. "It's about your religion, and I don't understand it at all – some nonsense involving a preacher named Paul. Anyway, he has asked to have his case tried in Rome and I've no idea what to put in the documents to send to the emperor."

"Oh, I'd love to hear that man," said Agrippa, "and so would Bernice!"

The next day, the visiting royals were ushered into a great hall with Festus and the military chiefs and the important people in Caesarea. Paul was invited to explain his case yet again.

He carefully explained the Jewish scriptures and the words of the prophets who had foretold the coming of a messiah; he told of his meeting with Jesus on the road to Damascus; he told of how he had preached about Jesus to Jews and Gentiles.

Suddenly Festus lost patience. "You're mad," he shouted. "Your learning has driven you over the edge!"

"No I'm not!" retorted Paul. "King Agrippa! You are Jewish. You believe the words of the prophets, don't you?"

"What kind of question is that!" exclaimed Agrippa. "Do you think you can make me a Christian in the short time I've been listening to you?"

"My prayer is that everyone become a Christian," replied Paul, "however long it takes."

The king looked at Festus. Then they and the other officials swept out of the hall. Outside they laughed about Paul. "Who knows what he's going on about," they said. "Whatever it is, it doesn't deserve the death penalty."

"If he hadn't appealed to the emperor, I'd let him go," said Agrippa. "But he has."

On course for Rome

❧

AT LAST IT was all arranged for Paul to be sent to Italy, where the great capital city, Rome, stood magnificent and proud. An officer of the emperor's regiment was put in charge of him. He and his companions boarded a ship and sailed northward round Cyprus to Myra, on the southern coast of Asia. Then they were put on another boat bound farther west than Paul had been before: to Italy.

It was slow going: the wind was not favorable, and the sailors chose to make their way along the more sheltered coast of Crete. At last they took the boat into a place called Safe Harbours. By now the weather had made the change from summer to autumn. "We should not sail farther this year," Paul warned the officer in charge. "We risk losing the cargo and the people on board."

The officer was not convinced. "The captain is happy to sail on, and so is the owner of the boat," he replied. "This particular harbor is a grim place to spend the winter. There's a better place called Phoenix that is only a short distance farther along the coast. Everyone else is in favor of going there."

A soft wind from the south began to blow, and the sailors felt sure they could make the trip to the chosen harbor. They pulled anchor and set the ship on a course as close to shore as they dared.

Suddenly the sail began to flap noisily. "The wind's changing direction," shouted one of them. "It's a northeaster. To the sail, men, let's see how close we can go."

For a while, the sailors struggled to stay on course. They soon realized that the wind was too strong. "Take down the sails. Let the ship go!" shouted the captain. "We're better going with the wind than fighting it."

The passengers and crew huddled together. Where would the wind take them all?

Dear God,
Bring me calm
in the center of
any storm.

The storm

❧

FOR MANY DAYS the ship plunged through the stormy waters. Dark clouds hung low: there was not even a glimmer of sunshine by day; neither moon nor stars could be seen at night. The wind blew relentlessly.

It didn't take long before the food on board was running low. Even Paul and his companions began to fear the worst.

As the crew and passengers sank into gloom, Paul stood up and called out to the captain. "You should have listened to me!" he said. "If you had, we'd still be safe in Crete. Still, that chance has gone and we need something else to hope for now.

"Last night an angel spoke to me and told me not to be afraid. God is going to keep me and all of you who are with me safe. We are going to be driven ashore on some island."

The sailors were unconvinced, but on the fourteenth night of the storm they sensed that they were near land. They checked the depth of the sea and found they were indeed moving into shallower waters.

"Drop the anchors! We don't want to be driven onto rocks!" they cried. The sailors were anxious to escape in their landing craft, but Paul warned the soldiers not to let them go.

"We should all stay on board and wait for dawn," he said.

The shipwreck

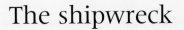

WHEN EVERYONE HAD eaten, the captain ordered the crew to throw the ship's cargo of wheat into the sea. "That'll lighten the boat so it rides higher," he said. "It could make or break the landing."

As the sky paled, the sailors scanned the coastline. They looked at one another and shook their heads.

"We don't recognize it; and we haven't been able to keep track of how far we've come. Still, there's a bay up ahead with a beach. We could try to run the boat aground there, but there's no telling what's underwater as we go."

A plan was agreed. The sailors cut the anchors, untied the steering oars and raised the sail at the front of the ship so the wind would blow the boat forward. It lurched its way through the swell.

"We may be lucky – we"re right on course," cried the captain. Then, "Drop the sail… I SAID, DROP THE SAIL!"

The boat shuddered to a stop. The captain shouted orders, the sailors worked frantically to obey; but the front of the boat was wedged in a sandbank and the end was being tossed from side to side by the waves that raced to shore.

Paul watched everything carefully. He saw the soldiers arguing with their officer. They had drawn their swords. They were pointing at the prisoners. He could guess what they were planning: to kill the prisoners rather than give them a chance of escaping.

Paul's very survival hung in the balance.

Dear God,
Keep me safe
from any
who plot
against me.

359

*D*ear God,
Give me
something
to cling to.

Swim for your lives!

❧

THE OFFICER IN charge had a strong sense of duty. He marched over to Paul, his soldiers milling sullenly around behind him.

"This prisoner is a Roman citizen," he declared crisply. "It's my job to get him to Rome for his court hearing. So our main task right now is to get him to shore alive. In fact, our main task is to get everyone we can to shore alive."

He grabbed the railing on the side of the boat to steady himself as the boat heaved dangerously.

"Can anyone here swim?" he barked. "All swimmers, I want you here, right now."

A few people stepped forward, looking at one another anxiously. "Come over here and jump in. Swim for your lives. It's not far. Just keep moving your arms and legs. Don't give up."

The non-swimmers were wide-eyed with fear as they watched the others jumping into the water. The officer whispered to his men and they set to work, hacking bits of the boat apart and assembling a pile of planks.

"Non-swimmers!" shouted the captain. "I'm giving you all a piece of wood as a float. DON'T LET GO OF IT. Kick your legs, take good calm breaths and say your prayers before you set out."

A welcome on Malta

❧

Everyone agreed it was a miracle: the crew and passengers all reached the shore safely. Some of the islanders had spotted the shipwreck and had come down to shore to welcome the survivors.

"You've landed on Malta," they explained, "in dismal weather."

Already it was beginning to rain again. The islanders gathered wood and lit a fire to help warm people up.

Paul himself gathered a bundle of sticks. Just as he was putting them on the fire, a snake slithered out from underneath it and latched on to his hand.

"Aargh!" cried the islanders. "What has that man done? Is he a murderer whom Fate does not want to live?"

"No, I'm not," said Paul, shaking the snake onto the fire. "I'm fine."

The islanders looked at him, expecting him to swell up and die. Nothing happened. "Perhaps he is a god," they began to whisper.

Soon after, the chief official of the island came to welcome the survivors. When he found out that the official's father was sick with fever, Paul went to him and prayed for his recovery. As soon as he placed his hands on him, the old man was healed.

Now the islanders were truly awestruck. "Can you heal others?" they asked. "Can we bring you our sick people?"

"Of course," replied Paul.

Because of his faith in God, he was able to heal many people on Malta. The islanders were overcome with gratitude.

Dear God, May I welcome those who need my help, however unexpected their arrival.

Dear God,
Show me how
to make the
best use of the
time I have.

Under house arrest in Rome

FOR THREE MONTHS, all those who had been shipwrecked enjoyed a warm welcome in Malta. When spring came, the islanders gave them gifts and helped them find a new boat on which to sail.

The winds were favorable now. The ship sailed to port in Sicily and then on up the western coast of Italy. At last they landed in the port of Puteoli. From there it was a road journey to Rome.

The believers in the empire's capital were thrilled to hear of Paul's safe arrival on the mainland. An enthusiastic group set out to welcome him even before he reached the city and Paul felt most encouraged.

However, he soon found himself with little to do. He was allowed to live by himself with just one soldier on duty all the time to guard him… and then wait for his case to be called.

"It might take a couple of years," an official explained.

Paul decided he might as well continue his missionary work, and so he called the local Jewish leaders to a meeting.

"I'm a teacher and preacher," he explained. "I believe in the news about Jesus. The religious leaders in Jerusalem had me arrested because they thought I had offended against our laws and customs. I can assure you I haven't: I am here to convince the emperor of my innocence. Meanwhile, I want to reassure you that I have nothing against any of my fellow Jews."

His listeners looked surprised. "No one has sent any letters or messages condemning you," they replied. "Tell us what you preach."

To Paul's delight, it was agreed that a day should be set aside for him to explain to them about Jesus. Paul preached with fervor and enthusiasm, but as always only some were convinced.

Paul sighed. "The prophets themselves warned that the Jews wouldn't believe in God's salvation," he said.

The letter to Ephesus

PAUL BELIEVED MORE firmly than ever that God wanted him to take the news about Jesus to the Gentiles. In some ways the situation was not promising. He was under house arrest, and soldiers took turns guarding him. However, apart from being restricted in where he could go and being constantly watched, he could choose how to spend his time.

"Even though I am now a prisoner in Rome, I can go on writing letters of encouragement to all the churches," he said to himself. One of the places that he remembered fondly was Ephesus. He called a scribe to come and do the writing, while he spoke aloud.

"To God's people in Ephesus," he said. "May God our Father and the Lord Jesus Christ give you grace and peace.

"Let us thank God for the many blessings we have been given through Jesus Christ. We have become God's sons and daughters… We have been created for a life of good deeds.

"You are Gentiles by birth. In the past, you had no right to call yourself God's people. Now that barrier has gone. We are all God's people together. We fit together like the stones of a temple, and Jesus himself is its cornerstone.

"So let us live by the standards God wants. Be humble, gentle and patient. Show your love by being tolerant with one another. Be ready to forgive one another, as God has forgiven you through Christ.

"Husbands must love their wives, and wives must respect their husbands. Children must obey their parents, and parents should be wise enough not to make that too difficult a task. Slaves should do their work cheerfully, and their masters should remember to treat their slaves as God's own children."

Dear God, May I take my place among those who believe in the truth.

363

21 December

❖

Ephesians 6

*Dear God,
Make me
strong enough
to resist the
forces of evil.*

The armor of God

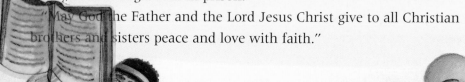

PAUL PAUSED FOR a moment. The guard who was chained to him sighed and went on polishing his helmet. There wasn't much work to do, simply guarding a preacher. By the time his turn of duty was over, his gear would be gleaming.

"Finally," continued Paul, "make yourselves strong. Put on the armor of God so that you will be able to resist all the hardships the devil can throw at you. Our struggle is not really with the authorities who rule this world: it is with the spiritual forces in the heavenly world.

"Be ready for whatever comes, with truth as a belt around your waist, and righteousness as your breastplate.

"For shoes, simply be ready to go and announce the Good News of peace.

"Carry faith as your shield against the burning arrows of doubt and discouragement. Accept salvation as your helmet.

"For a sword, use the word of God and speak as the Spirit leads you.

"Pray at all times, and never give up. Pray for me too – that I may speak boldly, even though I am in prison.

"May God the Father and the Lord Jesus Christ give to all Christian brothers and sisters peace and love with faith."

The church in Colossae

THE CHRISTIANS IN Ephesus had always been eager to follow Paul's instructions. One of those instructions was to continue to spread the news about Jesus, and it was they who had helped establish a growing church in the city of Colossae.

Paul was delighted that the church there was thriving, but he was alarmed at some of the reports he had heard. It seemed that some of the people who came to teach the young Christians were misleading them about what to believe. They were telling them to follow all kinds of rules instead of simply trusting in God's forgiveness through Jesus. He wrote a long letter to help and encourage them.

"You have been raised to life in Christ," he wrote, "so set your hearts on the things that are in heaven, not on things here on earth.

"Get rid of all the unholy and impure desires within you – anger, passion, hateful feelings. Do not use insults or obscene words and do not lie to one another. You must say good-bye to your bad old self and become your new self – one that reflects the goodness of God.

"Accept one another, no matter what background you come from, because you all belong to Christ.

"You are the people of God; he loved you and chose you for his own. So you must clothe yourselves with compassion, kindness, humility, gentleness and patience. Be tolerant with one another and forgive one another whenever any of you has a complaint against someone else. You must forgive one another just as the Lord has forgiven you. And to all these qualities add love, which binds all things together in perfect unity.

"The peace that Christ gives is to guide you in the decisions you make, for it is to this peace that God has called you together in the one body; and be thankful.

"Everything you do or say should be done in the name of the Lord Jesus, as you give thanks through him to God the Father."

22 December

❖

Colossians 3

Dear God, Give me peace in my heart when I make wise choices.

Dear God,
May my whole
life be useful.

Philemon and Onesimus

PAUL CONTINUED DICTATING his letter to the church at Colossae.

"I am sending Tychicus to you with this letter," he wrote. "He will cheer you up with all the news of the Christians here. With him comes Onesimus, whom you know.

"Several people have asked to be remembered to you in person, including Luke, who is the doctor among us and a very great friend.

"When you have read this letter to all the Christians, please send it on to other churches in the area."

Paul reached over and asked the scribe to let him have the pen. "Greetings from Paul," he added as a final flourish.

Then he asked the scribe to start a fresh piece of writing. "This is for one particular person in Colossae," he explained.

"Dear Philemon," he began, "I am so happy to hear of your love for all God's people and for your faith in Jesus.

"I know I can trust you to do something special to please me even more. You remember your slave, Onesimus – the one who ran away from your service? He's here in Rome and he has been very helpful to me. More than that, he has become a Christian.

"I am returning him to you now and I want you to welcome him as a brother in Christ. If he robbed you in any way in his past life, I will pay whatever he owes."

Paul reached forward and asked to take the pen again. "I, Paul, will pay you back," he scribbled in his own hand.

"I hope to be free and able to visit you sometime soon – so make sure you have a room ready and waiting!

"Greetings from all of us here. May the grace of the Lord Jesus Christ be with you all."

A letter of Peter

*Dear God,
Make me
obedient to
the truth.*

ALL OVER THE Roman world, the church went on growing. Even though Paul was under arrest, there were other apostles and preachers traveling from place to place spreading the news about Jesus. They, like Paul, sent letters to the new churches.

In Galatia, one of the church leaders smiled at the believers who had gathered for worship.

"Listen, everyone. I have a letter to read to you all and it begins like this: 'From Peter, apostle of Jesus Christ.'"

There was a murmur of excitement. A letter from a great teacher who truly understood the faith was something very important.

And indeed, Peter's letter was full of encouragement. It reminded the believers to live good and holy lives. It told them to be respectful of the Roman authorities, even though they seemed to be getting more hostile toward the believers. It warned them that there would be hard times ahead.

"My dear friends, do not be surprised at the painful test you are suffering. Rather be glad that you are suffering as Christ did. Accept whatever God sends you in life. God will lift you up in good time. Leave all your worries with God, because God cares for you.

"Be alert to danger, too. The devil is prowling around like a roaring lion. Here in the wicked city, who knows what will happen. All the believers send you their greetings.

"May peace be with all of you who belong to Christ."

The church leader looked up again. He leaned toward his listeners.

"The news I hear about Rome gets worse and worse," he said.

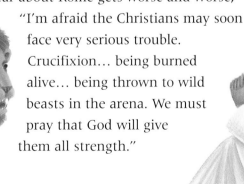

"I'm afraid the Christians may soon face very serious trouble. Crucifixion… being burned alive… being thrown to wild beasts in the arena. We must pray that God will give them all strength."

Dear God,
May I love
others,
remembering
that you are
love itself.

A letter of John

JOHN WAS REMEMBERING. Years had gone by since the day of Jesus' crucifixion – when Jesus had told him to look after his mother Mary.

On that day, he had thought his world was coming to an end: but then Jesus had risen from the grave. He, John, had seen him with his own eyes. He had been part of the great adventure to spread the news to all the world.

He was getting old now. He wanted to write a clear statement of all he believed in… something to encourage the believers everywhere.

"Dear friends,

"I want you to remember the Word of life, which has existed from the very beginning. We have heard it, we have seen it with our own eyes, we have touched it. We want you to know this Good News so that you will join with us in the fellowship we have with God the Father and with his son Jesus Christ.

"If we obey God's commands, then we are sure that we know him. Those who say that they know him, but do not obey his commands, are liars and there is no truth in them. All those who obey his word are people whose love for God has really been made perfect.

"Those who love their brothers and sisters live in the light, and there is nothing in them that will cause someone else to sin.

"Dear friends, let us love one another, because love comes from God. Whoever loves is a child of God and knows God. Whoever does not love does not know God, for God is love. And God showed his love for us by sending his only Son into the world, so that we might have life through him. This is what love is: it is not that we have loved God, but that God loved us and sent his Son to be the means by which our sins are forgiven.

"We know we are one with God because we have God's Spirit in us. That Spirit enables us to live as God's children should, obeying God's commands.

"We know that none of God's children keeps on sinning, for the Son of God keeps them safe, and the Evil One cannot harm them.

"We live in union with God – and this is eternal life."

The letter to the Hebrews

❦

IN THE EARLIEST days of the faith, all the believers had been full of enthusiasm. But later, when trouble and persecution grew in strength, some were discouraged.

A devoted Christian wrote them this letter:

"In the past, God spoke to our people, Israel, in many ways. But in these last days, God has spoken to us through his Son, who reflects the brightness of God's glory and is the exact likeness of God's own being.

"This son – Jesus – is greater than the angels and greater even than Moses. Moses was a wise prophet, faithful and obedient, but he was just a servant in God's house. Jesus is in charge of God's house, and we need to be faithful to him.

"Jesus is our high priest. Long ago, our people made a tent of worship, the tabernacle. At its heart was the most holy place where only the high priest could enter. There, the priest offered a sacrifice to obtain God's forgiveness for the sins of the people. But now Jesus Christ has offered himself as a sacrifice. The rituals of days gone by are no longer needed. We are forgiven by his death; if we have faith in that, we are free to serve the living God.

"To have faith is to be sure of the things we hope for, to be certain of the things we cannot see. Think of the great faith of the holy men of days gone by: Abel, Noah, Abraham, Isaac, Jacob, Joseph, Moses, Joshua. You know their stories. And the rest – Gideon, Barak, Samson, David, Samuel and the prophets. They achieved great victories because of their faith and worked miracles. They endured many hardships and still trusted God, even in the midst of disaster.

"It was God's will that they and we together should come close to God through Jesus. We will inherit a kingdom that cannot be shaken. Live holy lives, as is fitting, and love one another."

*Dear God,
May I hold on
firmly to the
faith I profess.*

*Dear God,
May I show
my faith by
my good deeds.*

The letter of James

AT A TIME WHEN there were Christian communities all over the empire, a believer who had close family ties to Jesus sat down to write a letter to them all. James wanted to remind them all of what faithful Christians should do to demonstrate their faith.

"Be cheerful, whatever troubles come your way, and do what is right. It is not enough to claim that you have faith and are very religious. You must let that show in all you do. Faith without actions is dead.

"Don't treat one another differently, respecting the wealthy and ignoring the needs of the poor. Everyone is worthy of the same respect.

"Control the things you say. Anger and cursing cause more damage than a raging fire. In fact, if you can control your tongue, you are truly in control of your whole being.

"Don't fret about having more things. This yearning for more and more only leads to quarreling and fighting.

"Don't criticize one another. You have no right to judge – only God can do that.

"Don't boast about the grand things you are going to do – God alone is in charge of the future.

"Beware of riches. Do not pile up wealth for yourselves while the poor suffer every kind of injustice.

"Instead, be patient and prayerful as we wait for God to come and make the whole world new."

A revelation of the future

❧

*Dear God,
May I listen
to what the
Holy Spirit
has to say
to me.*

THERE WAS NO escaping the fact: all over the Roman empire, the ruling authorities were turning against the Christians. It had become a crime to preach the message about Jesus. The believers in the new churches felt isolated. Different teachers told them different things… it was hard to know what to believe.

One day, a messenger arrived in Ephesus. He had important news for the church there.

"You all know what happened to John after he was arrested for preaching, don't you? If you haven't heard the news, he was sent off to the work camps on the island of Patmos. There, he says, God gave him the most amazing revelation of all that's going to happen. He wrote it down; I have a copy here. There are messages for seven churches, too, and the first one is for everyone at Ephesus. Listen."

The message for the church at Ephesus had good news and bad news. The good news was that God had noticed that the believers were faithful and patient. The bad news was that they no longer loved God as much as before. "Listen to the warning: turn away from wrongdoing," said the letter.

The messages to other churches were equally stern. In each place, there had been difficulties. Some had been led astray by unwise teachers. Others had begun to quarrel among themselves. Yet others had simply lost their enthusiasm for the faith with the result that it made little difference to their lives. The message to all of them was that they must hurry to put things right. They needed to be faithful to the truth. They needed to be sincere in living good and righteous lives.

The reader looked up from what the messenger had delivered for him to read. "The rest of what John has written is amazing," he said. "It is like a glimpse into the final struggle to bring about God's kingdom."

*O God,
To you belong
praise and
honor, glory
and might.*

The heavenly throne

❧

THE LISTENERS WERE moved by John's words, even though they were puzzling and mysterious. He described his vision of God sitting on a mighty throne amid terrifying flashes of lightning and deep rumbles of thunder. Four winged creatures stood around – one had the form of a lion, the second the form of a bull, the third had a face like a human, and the fourth had the form of an eagle in flight. They were singing praises:

*Holy, holy, holy is the Lord God almighty,
who was, who is, and who is to come.*

Around the throne were twenty-four elders all wearing white robes and golden crowns. As the creatures sang, these elders threw down their golden crowns and joined in the praises:

*Our Lord and God! You are worthy to receive glory,
honor and power.
For you created all things,
and by your will they were given existence and life.*

Then John saw that God was holding a scroll that was sealed in seven places.

"Who can break these seals?" cried an angel… but there was no one who was worthy enough.

One of the elders spoke gently to John: "Don't worry… from David's royal family has come the one who will open it."

Then John saw a Lamb at the center of the throne. Once again, the twenty-four elders bowed low in worship. Now they sang a new song, and then thousands and millions of angels all joined in a great hymn of praise.

The seven seals are broken

❧

THE LAMB BROKE the first of the seven seals, and the winged lion cried, "Come!"

At once a white horse galloped into view. Its rider was an archer who bowed low enough to receive a crown. Then he rode on as a Conqueror.

The Lamb broke the second seal and the winged bull cried, "Come!"

A red horse reared upward in the dazzling light. Its rider snatched the sword that was offered and shrieked, "War!"

The Lamb broke the third seal and the winged human cried, "Come!"

The black horse was thin and weary. Its rider held a pair of scales aloft as a mysterious voice announced Famine: "A liter of wheat for a day's wages, and three liters of barley; but do not destroy the olives or the vineyards."

As the Lamb broke the fourth seal and the winged eagle uttered its cry, a pale horse appeared through the mist. Its rider was Death, and behind followed the world of the dead. With great solemnity, they were given authority to kill a quarter of all living things.

When the fifth seal was broken, the souls of Christian martyrs appeared and cried to God for justice.

The sixth brought an earthquake. The sun fled into darkness, the moon turned blood red and the stars fell from the sky.

Then appeared angels, and after that a great crowd of people who were dressed in white and waving palm branches. "Salvation comes from God, and from the Lamb," they proclaimed.

Then the seventh seal was broken. All manner of disasters unfolded upon earth and in heaven itself. In the midst of the turmoil and thunder, the archangel Michael led all heaven's angels against the devil. The wicked serpent who had deceived humankind in the very beginning was cast down, and all his angels with him.

A loud voice called out: "Now God's salvation has come."

*Dear God,
Bring forward
the time when
evil is defeated.*

373

A new heaven and a new earth

*Dear God,
Bring me safely
to heaven.*

AT LONG LAST the chaos and bloodshed began to subside. All the people who had ever lived were gathered together and led before the one who sits on the throne. The great and humble – all were judged for what they had done.

Then the old heaven and the old earth vanished into darkness, and, as the light dawned anew, there emerged a new heaven and a new earth. A voice spoke:

"Now God's home is with human beings. God will live with them and they will be God's people. God will wipe away their tears. There will be no more death, no more grief or crying or pain. The old things have disappeared."

The one who sat on the throne spoke: "Look! I am making everything new. I have done all that is required. I am the beginning and the end."

A city appeared out of heaven itself. It was perfectly square and enclosed within high walls. There were twelve gates in the walls, each made from a single pearl. The city itself was made from the purest gold, and yet it was as clear as glass.

Everywhere was light… not from any sun and moon, but because of the glory of God that shone from the throne itself. A sparkling river flowed from the throne and ran glittering through the city. On each side of the river, the tree of life flourished – the leaves green, the fruit ripening to perfection.

The word of Jesus was heard, clear and compelling: "Come, whoever is thirsty: accept the water of life as a gift."

The reader looked up at his listeners. "Finally, John writes a few farewell words," he said. His book ends like this:

Come, Lord Jesus!
May the grace of the Lord Jesus
be with everyone.

375

About the Bible

IN THE BIBLE are reminders of the importance of reading the scriptures. Here are some of them.

Love the Lord your God and always obey all his laws…
Remember these commands and cherish them…
Teach them to your children. Talk about them when you
are at home and when you are away, when you are
resting and when you are working.

Deuteronomy 11

Happy are those who reject the advice of evil people,
who do not follow the example of sinners
or join those who have no use for God.
Instead, they find joy in obeying the Law of the Lord,
and they study it day and night.
They are like trees that grow beside a stream,
that bear fruit at the right time,
and whose leaves do not dry up.
They succeed in everything they do.

Psalm 1

Homes are built on the foundation of wisdom and
understanding. Where there is knowledge, the rooms are
furnished with valuable, beautiful things.

Proverbs 24

Teach me, Lord, the meaning of your laws,
and I will obey them at all times.
Explain your law to me, and I will obey it;
I will keep it with all my heart.
Keep me obedient to your commandments,
because in them I find happiness.
Give me the desire to obey your laws rather than to get rich.
Keep me from paying attention to what is worthless;
be good to me, as you have promised.

Psalm 119

All scripture is inspired by God and is useful for teaching the truth,
rebuking error, correcting faults, and giving instruction for right living,
so that the person who serves God may be fully qualified and equipped
to do every kind of good deed.

2 Timothy 3

Story finder

࿎

THIS BIBLE HAS been retold so that you can read a story on every day of the year. It follows the whole story of the Bible from the beginning.

Sometimes you will want to find stories for different seasons and special reasons. This section will help you find some that are particularly suitable.

Stories for festivals

࿎

Advent
The coming king   1 June
The good shepherd   17 June
Zechariah   16 July
John the Baptist   26 July

Christmas
Joseph   19 July
The baby in the manger   20 July
The shepherds on the hillside   21 July

Epiphany
The star in the east   23 July
The three gifts   24 July

Presentation
In the Temple   22 July

Lent
Temptation in the wilderness   28 July
The warnings of the prophet Amos   24 May

Annunciation and Mary
Mary and the angel   17 July
Mary and Elizabeth   18 July
Jesus sees his mother   12 October
Disciples, followers and family   8 August

Stories for special occasions

੨৯

Baptism

Wedding

Family life

Funeral

Stories for special themes

Caring for the world
Creation   1 January – 3 January
Noah and the flood   7 January – 10 January

Community
The book of the Law   9 June
Jeremiah and the well   13 June
Esther   6 July – 11 July
Rebuilding Jerusalem   12 July – 15 July
The woman by the well   6 August
The tax question   25 September
A letter of guidance   16 November
The church and the body of Christ   30 November
The letter to Ephesus   20 December
The church in Colossae   22 December

Justice
David and Saul   8 April
Solomon the judge   22 April
Naboth's vineyard   5 May
Belshazzar's feast   24 June
Dreaming of home   2 July
Jesus begins to preach   29 July
The Temple offering box   26 September

Peace
Who is truly blessed?   9 August
Who is the greatest?   2 September
The Passover meal   28 September

Stories about values

ꙮ

Believing

God calls Abram   13 January
Sarah laughs   16 January
The holy mountain   12 February
Thomas   20 October

Caring

Jesus sees his mother   12 October
Peter and Tabitha   5 November

Choosing wisely

About money   13 August – 14 August
The sower   19 August – 20 August
The kingdom of heaven   21 August
Mary and Martha   5 September
The prodigal son   13 September – 14 September
The two men in the Temple   16 September
The rich man   18 September
Silas and Timothy   18 November
The letter of James   27 December

Encouraging

The lost sheep   11 September
Saul and Barnabas   4 November

Forgiving

Jacob and Esau   22 January – 28 January
Joseph and his brothers   29 January – 7 February
Jonah   25 May – 29 May
The prayer Jesus taught   12 August
The road to the cross   10 October

Healing

Naaman's cure   12 May – 13 May
The valley of bones   18 June
Jesus in Peter's house   30 July
Jairus and his daughter   25 August

382

Welcoming

Worshiping